W9-CDW-377

IMPROVING OUR COURTS

Collected Studies on Judicial Administration

by

SHELDEN D. ELLIOTT

Director, Institute of Judicial Administration

Published for

THE INSTITUTE OF JUDICIAL ADMINISTRATION, INC.

by

OCEANA PUBLICATIONS, INC.

New York

CONTENTS

Acknowledgments

It is with some misgivings that I venture to offer in a single volume this collection of my articles that have appeared from time to time on the subject of judicial administration. Prepared as some of them were for different groups and from varying points of approach, there is a certain amount of inevitable unevenness, overlap and duplication. For this, I ask the reader's indulgence and his sympathetic concurrence in the fundamental precept that improvements in judicial administration are usually achieved only by repetitive and unrelenting emphasis.

Modernization of our courts, long overdue in many states, does not happen by accident. It requires the cooperative effort of representative citizens in all walks of life. To the end that interest and cooperation may be encouraged, I offer this modest collection of studies. In their preparation I was ably aided by the staff of the Institute of Judicial Administration under the guidance of Mrs. Fannie J. Klein, Research Coordinator and Librarian of the Institute. I appreciate the generous Foreword by Judge Laurance M. Hyde, the Institute's President for 1958-1959. I wish also to acknowledge my indebtedness to the editors of the *American Bar Association Journal*, the *Annual Survey of American Law, State Government*, and *Wayne Law Review* for their permission to reprint the articles which originally appeared in their respective publications.

Shelden D. Elliott

FOREWORD

by

Judge, Supreme Court of Missouri

When the history of judicial administration of the twentieth century is written, surely two dates will be remembered. The first in 1906, when Roscoe Pound made his great address, at the American Bar Association Meeting in St. Paul, entitled "The Causes of Popular Dissatisfaction with the Administration of Justice." The second in 1938, when under the leadership of Arthur T. Vanderbilt, as president of the American Bar Association, and with the thorough research work organized by Judge John J. Parker, as chairman of the Section of Judicial Administration, a comprehensive set of 66 recommendations, for improvements in the operation and administration of our courts, was approved by the House of Delegates at the Association's Cleveland meeting. These recommendations provided remedies for many of the causes of dissatisfaction stated by Dean Pound in his 1906 address; and have ever since been the foundation of the program of the American Bar Association for improving the administration of justice. The extent to which the standards, established by these recommendations, were accepted throughout the nation, during the next decade, was shown in the outstanding book of Chief Justice Arthur T. Vanderbilt, entitled "Minimum Standards of Judicial Administration," published in 1949.

This book, entitled "Improving Our Courts," by Shelden D. Elliott, Director of the Institute of Judicial Administration, Professor of Law, New York University, and former Dean of the University of Southern California School of Law, shows the progress made throughout the country generally since 1906 and in detail since 1952, which was the year the Institute of Judicial Administration began to function. The Institute is another result of the inspirational leadership of Chief Justice Vanderbilt and Dean Elliott has been its competent and able Director from the start. Under the direction of Dean Elliott, the Institute has aided in improvements made in many states, and even in other nations, by making available its research and information on all phases of judicial administration and organization and operation of the courts; perhaps the most important being very helpful assistance in the preparation of the Constitution of our new state of Alaska, which was adopted with an excellent judicial article, well suited to modern needs.

It is really remarkable how indifferent many lawyers seem to be to the basic problems of judicial administration but this is no doubt mainly due to the press of everyday work and problems of their practice. It should not be forgotten that the interest and support of laymen has often been essential to the accomplishment of great improvements in the courts. That was true in the nineteenth century struggle in England for procedural reform and court reorganization. It was also true in Missouri in obtaining the adoption of an effective nonpartisan plan for selection and tenure of judges. The helpful aid laymen may give in improving the administration of justice has not been overlooked by Dean Elliott in this book.

It is important to realize that most of our state judicial departments were organized during pioneer days when our country was constantly expanding into unsettled territory. Their development was on a haphazard basis, of adding unrelated, separate, new courts as population increased. In pioneer times, local communities had to be self-sufficient and people had few contacts with other parts of the country. Thus courts and judges were isolated from each other and most state judicial departments were composed of a group of completely separate courts. Court systems lacked unity and flexibility. There was no real responsible head to the system, and provisions for transfer of judges were lacking or inadequate. If some courts were unable to keep up with their dockets, while others had insufficient work, there was neither responsibility nor authority to do anything about it. The usual remedy was to add more local or specialized courts but this only added to the inefficiencies and inequalities of a hodgepodge of separated courts. These conditions were the principal causes of many cases being decided on technicalities of jurisdiction, venue, and trial and appellate procedure, instead of on the merits. In many states, courts have continued to operate without coordination or supervision so as to be almost as completely separated and unrelated as in pioneer times; and this has usually resulted in congestion of dockets causing unnecessary expense and delay to litigants. Modern conditions require a coordinated, flexible, unified system and that is the real remedy. Our courts should no longer be handicapped in efforts to maintain public respect for the law by being forced to attempt to keep up with the pace of modern business and industry without the organization and facilities necessary to do so. This book will serve a most useful purpose in showing both lawyers and laymen what has been done and what needs to be done to improve the administration of justice throughout the nation.

ARTHUR T. VANDERBILT:

Administrator of Justice

(From *State Government*, Vol. XXXI, p. 224, Autumn 1958)

A little more than a year ago occurred the death of the Chief Justice of New Jersey, Arthur T. Vanderbilt. The fruits of his labor—as lawyer, leader, educator and judge—continue to grow, to the benefit of his state, nation and world. Mr. Elliott, who gives us the following paper on those labors and their results, is Director of the Institute of Judicial Administration and Professor of Law at New York University. He long worked with Chief Justice Vanderbilt for the advance of the courts.

Anyone who knew Arthur T. Vanderbilt and was associated with him in one or more of the various activities that comprised the wide spectrum of his remarkable career was privileged indeed. The late Chief Justice of New Jersey was an inspiring individual with a rare blend of human qualities: relentless vigor and patient persistence, keenness of mind both in depth of perception and in breadth of intellectual grasp, personal charm that combined forthrightness of purpose with a leaven of gentle good humor. His capacity as an able advocate and a successful administrator is attested by the many accomplishments for which he has attained lasting fame. As aptly expressed by President Charles S. Rhyne of the American Bar Association at a memorial convocation held at New York University's Vanderbilt Hall in October, 1957:

> Occasionally there lives a man who walks as other men walk, who talks as other men talk, but who is endowed with such an indomitable spirit, such a dynamic heart and such a tremendous capacity for leadership and creative productivity that he is not as other men. To know Chief Justice Vanderbilt was to see this combination in a perfect blend. His supreme monument will always be that built by the stories of his own accomplishments.

It is my endeavor here to review briefly some of the significant contributions of which that monument was built.

Lawyer, Leader, Educator, Judge.—Arthur Vanderbilt's agile mind, his broad knowledge of legal principles, his ability to forecast the trends of the law, his gift of expression aided by his subtly sharp wit, and his thorough preparation of each case, combined to guarantee the enviable reputation and financial reward he enjoyed for thirty-five years as a practicing lawyer. Both as trial counsel and as appellate advocate he represented with equal skill and equal success large corporations, particularly in insurance matters, and individuals whose civil rights were at stake. Thus when Norman Thomas was "deported" from Jersey City by Mayor Hague it was Arthur Vanderbilt who, at his own expense, successfully represented Thomas before the United States Supreme Court. It was Vanderbilt, too, who secured reversal of the conviction of Roger Baldwin of the American Civil Liberties Union on a charge of "unlawful assembly" during the Paterson mill strike.

In an essay in 1953 he enumerated the "Five Functions of the Lawyer" as: (1) To counsel clients wisely, not only from a thoroughgoing knowledge of the law in operation, but also with a perceptive ability to forecast its trends; (2) to be skilled in advocacy, with the capacity to write and speak effectively, and with training in the art of asserting and defending the rights of men; (3) to do his part in improving his profession, the courts and the law; (4) to lead in moulding public opinion; and (5) to seek office in the service of the public.

As a political leader, it was Arthur Vanderbilt who conceived and headed the Republican Clean Government Movement in Essex County, New Jersey, and succeeded in ousting the entrenched public officials of the corrupt and incumbent political machine. It was this experience, and the convictions born thereof, that led him years later in 1947 to found the Citizenship Clearing House at New York University to instill in colleges and universities throughout the country a realization of the need for scientifically and effectively educating students regarding politics and their duties as citizens.

Concurrent with his other activities, Arthur Vanderbilt was a professor of law at New York Univerity, and his appointment as Dean of the Law School in 1943 gave a further opportunity to carry forward his ideals. His views on the existing methods and scope of pre-legal and law school education, and the deficiencies therein, were attuned to the needs of successful advocacy and the fivefold functions of the lawyer in society. He envisioned a law school not as just an institution for the teaching of prospective attorneys, but as a legal center for continuing scientific study of all aspects of the law, to simplify, modernize and keep dynamic its evolutionary growth. New York University's Law Center, named in his honor, is both the product of his genius for securing adequate financial support and an embodiment of his concepts. With a fully implemented program and facilities for the training of lawyers-to-be, are brought together an equally extensive program for the continuing education of practicing lawyers at the graduate level, institutes for foreign lawyers, seminars for appellate judges from all over the country, seminars for law teachers, and institutes for the intensive study and improvement of law and legal institutions in selected and important fields. The dedication of the Law Center in 1951 was but another milestone of achievement in Vanderbilt's career.

Meanwhile, the adoption of New Jersey's new and modern constitution, in 1947, called him into yet another field of public endeavor through his appointment as Chief Justice and head of that state's modernized and streamlined judicial system. It was here that he put into prompt and effective action the improvements of judicial administration he had so long championed and the reforms he had so long advocated—reforms that had their origins in the inspiration which Arthur Vanderbilt received from others as well as in his own activities in agencies and programs for the betterment of government.

For Law Reform and The Courts.—Among those for whose inspiration Arthur Vanderbilt often expressed his admiring acknowledgment were Lord Mansfield and Roscoe Pound. The former, as Lord Chief Justice of England in the eighteenth century, was noted for his great reforms in bringing the complex area of mercantile law and practice into simplified uniformity within the structure of the common law and in contributing to the synchronization of law and equity. Pound, as a comparatively young lawyer in 1906, set forth in a famous address to the American Bar Association at St. Paul a forthright analysis of "The Causes of Popular Dissatisfaction with the Administration of Justice" in which the basic shortcomings were pinpointed and the clarion call for their rectification was sounded. Vanderbilt was of the view that Pound's address should be required reading for every lawyer and he set for himself the task of seeing to it that everyone with whom his own far-reaching activities brought contact should be aware of the needs and means for improvement and reform of the machinery of justice.

One of his earliest opportunities came in 1930 when he was appointed to the newly created New Jersey Judicial Council, a state body of lawyers, judges and laymen to study the New Jersey judicial system and recommend means for its improvement. With Arthur Vanderbilt as chairman, the council's first report enumerated the "fundamental rights of a litigant" as

"(1) A prompt and efficient trial of his case; (2) At reasonable cost; (3) Represented by competent attorneys; (4) Before impartial, experienced and competent judges; (5) With the privilege of a review of the trial court's determination by an appellate tribunal composed of similar judges who will render a final decision within three to four months after the appeal is initiated."

In 1932 the council's third annual report proposed a new judiciary article for the state's constitution, a significant forecast of things to come some fifteen years later. Among other things, it embodied the principles of a simplified court structure, of centralized administrative authority in the Chief Justice of the Supreme Court, and of vesting in the Supreme Court the power to regulate civil and criminal procedure by court rule.

Arthur Vanderbilt's early interest and experience in the council led him to participate in the activities of the National Conference of Judicial Councils, of which he was chairman from 1933 to 1937, and which contributed much toward the growth of interest and improvement in judicial administration, both through encouraging the formation of councils in many other states and through the publication of noteworthy books on such subjects as court organization, appellate procedure, criminal procedure, traffic courts, judicial selection and tenure, and the basic standards of judicial administration.

At the same time his genius for leadership began to assert itself in the American Bar Association, where he served as first chairman of the Insurance Section in 1933, later as a member of the association's Board of Governors, and, in 1937-38, as President. It was during his presidency that the association developed its vigorous interest in judicial administration, and the year was marked by progress toward solution of the problems noted by Roscoe Pound some thirty years earlier. With Judge John J. Parker as chairman of the newly designated Section of Judicial Administration and its organization into subcommittees, and with the aid of state advisory committees, there emerged a set of proposed standards for court organization, administration and procedure embodying substantial reform in many areas. With Vanderbilt's endorsement, and the approval of the association's House of Delegates, these became the Minimum Standards of Judicial Administration toward which all states were urged to strive. In them, as he pointed out, were the means of achieving the protection of the "fundamental rights of a litigant," earlier noted in the first report of the New Jersey Judicial Council.

Widening Efforts and Results.—With no let-up in his determination and drive, Arthur Vanderbilt swung his attention and support to improving procedure in the federal district courts and a centralized administration for the federal judicial system. The Federal Rules of Civil Procedure, which have been a model for similar improved and simplified procedures in the states, were adopted in 1938. And in the following year, with Vanderbilt as chairman of the Attorney General's Committee to Cooperate with the Committee of Senior Circuit Judges, there was enacted by Congress in 1939 the law creating the Administrative Office of the United States Courts. For the first time, principles of sound public administration were introduced into the theretofore unsystematic and uncoordinated operations of the judicial branch of the federal government: centralized budgeting, collection and publication of uniform statistics on court business, supervision and coordination of court facilities and non-judicial personnel, and staff services for the Conference of Senior Circuit Judges. This enactment, too, became a model for state governments to emulate.

At the same time, he maintained an active interest in the courts at the lowest level in the judicial hierarchy, the local traffic courts in which the great preponderance of our citizens encounter their only direct relation with judicial machinery in action. In 1939, Vanderbilt became chairman of the National Committee on Traffic Law Enforcement, and the impetus he gave was to culminate in 1951 in a set of resolutions adopted by the Conference of Chief Justices and approved by the Governors' Conference for effective traffic law enforcement. One of the many features of this program was the "non-fixable" traffic ticket, so effectively used in New Jersey, Michigan, Puerto Rico and other jurisdictions.

The oldest and best known private national organization dedicated to improving the administration of justice is the American Judicature Society, and in 1939 Arthur Vanderbilt became its third President, succeeding former Chief Justice Charles Evans Hughes and former Secretary of War Newton D. Baker.

At the federal government level again, as a member of the Attorney General's Committee on Administrative Agencies, he applied his genius to the problems and procedures of administrative agencies, joining with the minority of that committee's 1941 report, and it was the minority's views that were to emerge in the subsequently enacted Administrative Procedure Act of 1946.

Following the earlier adoption of rules of civil procedure for the federal district courts, Arthur Vanderbilt was chosen by the United States Supreme Court in 1941 as chairman of an advisory committee to prepare comparable federal rules of criminal procedure. The rules proposed by his committee for modernizing procedure in federal criminal cases were adopted, and became effective in 1944.

In yet another area his talents and experience were called upon in 1946 when, at the request of the Secretary of War, the American Bar Association nominated the membership of the War Department Advisory Committee on Military Justice, with Arthur Vanderbilt as chairman. The committee's assignment was to hold hearings and to formulate recommendations for improving the system of military justice, and its labors resulted in substantial amendments to the Articles of War by the Elston Act of 1948, and laid some of the groundwork for the Uniform Code of Military Justice of 1950.

The year 1952 marked another of Arthur Vanderbilt's many accomplishments, the establishment of the Institute of Judicial Administration, a non-profit corporation chartered under the laws of New York, and charged with the task of conducting a continuing study, on a nationwide basis, of the problems of court organization, administration and procedure with a view toward developing an art as well as a science of judicial administration. With Chief Justice Vanderbilt as its first president, and financed by a grant which he was successful in obtaining from the Rockefeller Foundation, the institute's staff, with the aid of its membership of some 600 leading lawyers, judges and laymen, embarked on a program of studies and projects that were to touch on almost every phase and level of judicial matters. Its comprehensive library of source materials in the New York University Law Center, and its research facilities and personnel, have made possible the publication of numerous studies and surveys as well as the providing of advisory service and assistance to states and jurisdictions from Florida to Washington, Maine to California, and Alaska to Puerto Rico. The Institute's work has broadened to include the judicial administration problems of other lands, through programs for visiting jurists from more than fifty foreign countries seeking information on how to improve their court systems and procedures.

Thus has the creative genius and vision of one great man extended his influence throughout the nation and the world, stimulating momentum which others will endeavor to carry forward toward the ultimate goal of effective administration of justice everywhere.

Tenets for Effective Judicial Administration.—In the volume entitled *Minimum Standards of Judicial Administration,* compiled and edited by Arthur Vanderbilt and published by the National Conference of Judicial Councils, are set forth the fundamental requirements of a modern judicial system, together with an analysis of the extent of their adoption in the forty-eight states. Stemming from the principles and standards approved by the American Bar Association in 1937 and 1938, the recommendations embody specific proposals for the nonpartisan selection of judges, a simplified and integrated court structure, the vesting of responsibility and authority in the Chief Justice for over-all supervision with power to assign judges where needed, an administrative office to provide statistical information and housekeeping services for the judicial system, modernized and simplified trial and appellate procedures promulgated by rules of the supreme court rather than by the legislature, effective pretrial conferences to clarify issues and reduce the length of trials, efficient and impartial methods for the selection of qualified persons to serve as jurors, and improvements in traffic courts and traffic law enforcement.

In his later writings, Arthur Vanderbilt enumerated specific areas for initial concentration. The opening chapter of his book *The Challenge of Law Reform,* published in 1955 and based on lectures delivered at the University of Virginia, concludes its introductory analysis with the following summary of needs in the order of their importance today:

1. *The improvement of judicial personnel, including jurors as well as judges.* This is an exceedingly crucial problem in many jurisdictions, but one that is really capable of solution anywhere.

2. *The simplification of the judicial structure and of procedure,* so that technicalities and surprise may be avoided, and so that procedure may become a means of achieving justice rather than an end in itself.

3. *The elimination of the law's delays by modern management methods and effective leadership.* Without these a judicial establishment cannot hope to function efficiently any more than any other statewide business. This calls for an administrative head of the courts in each jurisdiction and an administrative office of the courts to assist him.

The end of trial delay and court congestion was the motif of an article completed shortly before his death. He advocated the following steps as the solution: improved pretrial conferences and calendar practices; modernization of trial procedure; elimination of partisan politics in judicial selection; centralized administrative control to facilitate the effective mobilization of judicial manpower; and improvement in appellate practices and procedures.

The remedies that Arthur Vanderbilt advocated were not pure Olympian theory. They have been tried and their effectiveness has been amply demonstrated. But any campaign to secure their adoption may require a long, persistent and arduous effort in which the role of the layman plays an extremely essential part. The story of judicial reform in New Jersey is proof of that. Vanderbilt was fond of saying that "judicial reform is no sport for the short-winded." But the results in New Jersey are also proof that a prophet can be a prophet with honor in his own state, if he is willing to help by leading in the fray.

The Tenets in Application: New Jersey Justice.—The structure of the New Jersey courts was of ancient origin. For the most part established under the state's first constitution in 1776, and little changed under the constitution of 1844, the complex judicial system included at least eight constitutional courts and some nine types of courts created by legislative enactment. There was no independent court of last resort, but instead a Court of Errors and Appeals consisting of a Chancellor, the Justices of the Supreme Court, and six judges, specially appointed, who under the provisions and prevailing public opinion of 1844 could be, and for the most part were, laymen. A separate Court of Chancery, created by ordinance of the royal Governor in 1704, was augmented in 1871 by the addition of Vice-Chancellors and Advisory Masters. Delays and confusion resulting from the system and its antiquated procedures were notorious, and the term "Jersey justice" became a symbol of inefficiency and frustration. Scarcely less notorious was the apathy of a great preponderance of the lawyers and judges toward reform and improvement, at least until growing public sentiment and provident leadership began to turn the tide.

Arthur Vanderbilt's determination to change the system was manifested, as noted above, with the first report of the Judicial Council of which he was chairman in 1930. The proposals in the Council's third annual report of 1932 for a new judiciary article were documented by detailed supporting memoranda prepared for the most part by Vanderbilt himself. There followed some fifteen years of political opposition and legislative discouragement, against which the "vexatious activity" of Vanderbilt and his small group of proponents for reform was gradually but surely building public support and demand for improvement. Undaunted by his nonreappointment to the Judicial Council through the influence of Mayor Hague, Vanderbilt continued his efforts with increasing vigor, and his campaign induced Governor Edison, a Democrat, not only to secure the legislative creation of a Constitution Revision Commission, but also thereafter to appoint Vanderbilt, a Republican, to its membership. Although the first draft of a model constitution was defeated at the polls in 1944, a constitutional convention in 1947 revitalized the proposal, and the new constitution was ratified by the people in 1947 by a vote of four to one.

In place of the multiple courts with overlapping jurisdictions, New Jersey now has five clearly defined levels of courts: three under the constitution—a Supreme Court with broad rule-making and administrative powers; a Superior Court with state-wide trial jurisdiction in civil and criminal matters and with intermediate appellate jurisdiction; and County Courts with countywide jurisdiction in civil and criminal matters. Under the legislative authority there are also County-District Courts with minor jurisdiction of a predominantly civil nature, and Municipal Courts with jurisdiction over minor criminal offenses and special civil matters. Justices of the Peace were eliminated by constitutional omission and by legislation, and the police courts and other local magistrates' and recorders' courts were constituted Municipal Courts.

The constitution declares that "The Chief Justice of the Supreme Court shall be the administrative head of all the courts of the state" and that "He shall appoint an administrative director of the courts to serve at his pleasure." It also provides that the Supreme Court shall make rules governing the administration of all courts in the state, and, subject to law, the practice and procedure of all such courts.

Under Chief Justice Vanderbilt's leadership, the new Supreme Court moved with swift efficiency to implement its powers. Rules of civil, criminal and appellate procedure were devised, studied, prepared in final form, and promulgated within a remarkably short span of time, in readiness for the new court system's effective date. An administrative office was created, with an administrative director at its head; it proceeded promptly to collect complete and up-to-the-minute statistics on the work loads of judges and the state of judicial business, and to take over the housekeeping functions and the supervision of non-judicial personnel. As the case-load statistics disclosed the need therefor, judges were assigned from underworked courts to those where help was needed. Pretrial procedures were devised and put into effect; and traffic law enforcement was improved and modernized. Also established by court rule in 1949 was a broadly representative judicial conference of judges, lawyers and laymen, to maintain a continuing and observant study of the work of the courts, and to advise on needed rules for further improvement.

Has the new system worked? The answer is a definite and overwhelming "Yes." Pre-existing accumulated backlogs of untried cases have been disposed of, and current cases are brought to trial within a few months instead of years. Appeals are heard and decided promptly. With the "non-fixable" traffic ticket, the evils of favoritism and special influence in traffic law enforcement have been substantially eliminated. In short, "Jersey justice," no longer a term of opprobrium, has become an enviable synonym for modern and efficient judicial administration.

His Legacy to Better Courts.—The enduring and tangible structures that Arthur Vanderbilt's genius has created for New Jersey and for the nation are visible evidence of his exemplary contribution to the cause of improving the administration of justice. But of equal significance for the future are the blueprints delineated in his many writings, such as *Minimum Standards of Judicial Administration, The Challenge of Law Reform, The Five Functions of a Lawyer, Report on Prelegal Education,* and a host of others. In years to come, other states and other nations will increasingly acknowledge the richness of Arthur Vanderbilt's bequest to posterity—a bequest that gives strengthening assurance and hope of achieving justice as humanity's and government's greatest asset.

IMPROVEMENTS IN JUDICIAL
ADMINISTRATION: 1906-1956*

Among the defects and shortcomings of the administration of American justice to which Roscoe Pound called attention in his St. Paul address of 1906 to the American Bar Association, there were several that stood out then, and still stand out, beacon-like in their challenge as needing correction in our judicial system. We have made progress in the past 50 years—but far short of enough to give cause for complacency.

I should like, first, to indicate those areas in which Pound's prophetic emphasis clearly foresaw and stressed basic problems. Then I shall venture a brief addendum, with the benefit of a half-century of hindsight, of other areas not included, or at least not underscored, in the 1906 address—areas nevertheless significant in present-day programs for improvement of judicial administration. With this two-fold frame of reference as background, it will, I think, be not too difficult to review in chronological sequence the major events that have occurred in the United State marking progress here and there toward solution of the problems.

THE POUND POINTS

Among the points most strongly emphasized in the St. Paul address—and I document the selection in each case with supporting quotations—were

a. The need for a simplified and integrated court system:

> "Our system of courts is archaic in three respects:
>
> (1) in its multiplicity of courts, (2) in preserving concurrent jurisdictions, (3) in the waste of judicial power it involves."
>
> • • • •
>
> "Multiplicity of courts is characteristic of archaic law."   • • • •
>
> The plan of the British Judicature Act, as originally proposed in 1873 "deserves the careful study of

*Paper presented at the Jurisprudence Symposium, Ninth Conference of the Inter-American Bar Association, Dallas, Texas, April 20, 1956.

American lawyers as a model modern judicial organization. Its chief features were (1) to set up a single court, complete in itself, embracing all superior courts and jurisdictions, (2) to include in this one court, as a branch thereof, a single court of final appeal."

b. The need for flexibility in the assignment of judges and the distribution of judicial business

"Judicial power may be wasted . . . by rigid districts or courts or jurisdictions, so that business may be congested in one court while judges in another are idle."

c. The need for taking the selection of judges out of the arena of partisan politics

"Putting courts into politics, and compelling judges to become politicians, in many jurisdictions has almost destroyed the traditional respect for the Bench."

d. The need for reform of procedural law to eliminate or minimize its obstruction to the decision of controversies on their basic merits

"The New York Code Commission was appointed in 1847 and reported in 1848. If we except the Connecticut Practice Act of 1878, . . . American reform in procedure has stopped substantially where that commission left it."

. . . .

"Uncertainty, delay and expense, and above all, the injustice of deciding cases upon points of practice —have created a deep-seated desire to keep out of court, right or wrong, on the part of every sensible business man in the community."

. . . .

"[W]ith the passing of the doctrine that politics, too, is a mere game to be played for its own sake, we may look forward confidently to deliverance from the sporting theory of justice."

e. The need for improving popular interest in jury service

"Popular lack of interest . . . makes jury service a bore and the vindication of right and law secondary to the trouble and expense involved."

f. The need for strengthening bar association responsibility.

"... [W]ith active Bar Associations in every state to revive professional feeling and throw off the yoke of commercialism . . . we may look forward to a near future when our courts will be swift and certain agents of justice, whose decisions will be acquiesced in and respected by all."

THE ADDENDUM

To the foregoing enumeration of needs foreseen by Roscoe Pound in 1906, we can add, in 1956, several others. Some of them are, however, merely secondary or ancillary to the basic requirements singled out by him. Others are of fairly fundamental significance in their own right. For example . . .

g. The need for restoring, or re-asserting, the fundamental rule-making power of the courts, to supplant and simplify legislature-made codes of practice and procedure

If procedural rules are to be effectively simplified, with a view toward eliminating the "sporting theory of justice", the proper branch of government to do it is the courts themselves, rather than the legislatures.

h. The need to develop pre-trial and discovery procedures to reduce lawsuits to their basic issues, to minimize the elements of surprise, and to shorten the overall time of trial by stipulations as to evidence and witnesses

This is a further incident, but an essential one to procedural reform.

i. The need for a centralized administrative office, functioning under a responsible head of the judicial system, such as the chief justice

Such an office would perform essential house-keeping functions for the judicial system, and would collect and make available current statistics on the state and volume of judicial business, in order to facilitate efficient assignment of judicial manpower and the redistribution of workload.

j. The need for adequate judicial salaries and retirement benefits

Taking the courts out of politics will not alone induce competent and qualified candidates to become available for judicial office. There must be sufficient compensation and retirement security to make the position economically possible for the lawyer who must sacrifice the greater rewards of private practice to accept appointment to the bench.

k. The need for judicial councils and judicial conferences
The establishment, on a permanent and continuing basis, of an agency representing the courts, the bar and the lay public, or a conference of representative judges of all the courts, is a highly valuable means to insure continuing surveillance and improvement of judicial administration.

l. The need for more effective organization and functioning of traffic courts and justices of the peace
Certainly in 1906 one could not have been expected to anticipate the key role that the automobile was to play in both civil and criminal litigation within the next few decades. It is in the operation and enforcement of our traffic laws that most citizens encounter the administration of justice in action, and the need for strengthening the courts at this level is a vital one.

THE CHRONOLOGY OF EVENTS
AND ACHIEVEMENTS

(1)   1912

A major step in a significant series of strides toward simplifying procedure and eliminating the "sporting theory of justice" was taken in 1912. In that year the American Bar Association's Committee on Uniform Judicial Procedure, under the chairmanship of Thomas W. Shelton, launched a long crusade to gain for the United States Supreme Court the power to prescribe rules of procedure in actions at law. The proposed legislation granting such power, supported by the Committee, met determined opposition in the United States Senate for many years. It was not until 1934 that Congress enacted the statute which paved the way for the adoption and promulgation in 1937 of the Federal Rules of Civil Procedure. These were followed by comparable developments in the criminal field, culminating in the Rules of Criminal Procedure in 1944. The resultant modernization and improvement of pleading and procedure in the federal courts have prompted a growing number of states to follow the lead of the federal system, so that today it can no longer be said as it could in 1906 that American reform stopped substantially where it had been left in 1848. Recent achievements and current proposals all point toward the attainment of justice by simplicity and openness in procedure, so that cases will be adjudicated on their merits, rather than on technicalities and defects of process.

(2)   1913

While bar association committees have played an increasingly important role in improving judicial administration, they have not provided the only leadership in this field. The establishment of the American Judicature Society in 1913 marked the founding of a national agency which through the years and through its tireless efforts has built an impressive record of championing its avowed objective "to promote the efficient administration of justice." The eminent lawyers who have headed and invigorated it are all deserving of honorable mention. And its Journal has for many years been looked to throughout the nation, and indeed throughout the world, for guidance and information concerning programs of judicial improvement and court reform.

(3)   1918 - 1921

It was in 1918 that the *Journal of the American Judicature Society* first published a model bar association act designed to create a state-wide all-inclusive organization of the bar. Three years later, in 1921, North Dakota became the first state to establish such an integrated state bar, and thus to take an important forward step in both broadening and strengthening bar association responsibility. North Dakota's lead has been followed by other jurisdictions so that today at least half of the states as well as the Commonwealth of Puerto Rico and the Territory of Alaska have integrated bar organizations. In some states integration has been achieved by statute, in some by rule of court, and in some by a combination of statute and court rule. But however established, the integrated bar association, speaking as it effectively does for the entire lawyer population of the state, can and does provide responsible support for improvement in the administration of justice.

(4)   1923

The State of Ohio is generally credited with being the first to create by statute another type of agency, the judicial council, and thereby in 1923 marked the inception of a movement which was to spread through a majority of the states. In many such councils, members of the bar work together with representatives of the courts and the legislature, and often with laymen members, to devise programs for improving the administration of justice. Some of the accomplishments of such organizations have been notable, as for example, the California Administrative Procedure Act of 1945. In some states, they have accomplished little; and in some they have been supplanted by judicial conferences. But the movement as a whole still has vigor, as witness recent and current activities of the new Judicial Council of Florida, and deserves to be counted as a solid contribution to progress in overcoming deficiencies of the American system of justice.

(5)   1929

The first systematic use of pre-trial as a device for expediting, clarifying and simplifying the disposition of civil lawsuits was inaugurated in 1929 in Detroit, Michigan, by Chief Judge Ira W. Jayne and his associate judges of the Wayne County Circuit Court. Pre-trial has been described by Harry D. Nims, a leading authority on the subject, as follows:

"This procedure consists of conferences between the attorneys for the parties to a law suit and a judge of the court, the chief purpose of which, as stated by Chief Justice Vanderbilt of New Jersey: 'is to prepare the case for an effective trial by formulating the issues, not in abstract legal terms but with the specific facts of the particular case in mind, and stating them in the pre-trial order, which then in effect becomes the chart for the trial.' "

Incorporated in the Federal Rules of Procedure, in the procedure rules of New Jersey, and in the practice of a growing number of states, the use of pre-trial together with broadened discovery procedures is another noteworthy step toward eliminating some of the causes of popular dissatisfaction with the traditional techniques of secrecy and last-minute surprise in the trial of lawsuits, or as one commentator has put it, "trial from ambush."

(6) 1931

Ohio again achieved distinction in 1931 with the adoption of the so-called "Cleveland Plan" for the selection of persons to serve as jurors. In its essence the statutory plan, based on a recommendation of the Cleveland Bar Association, devolves upon impartial jury commissioners appointed by the courts the responsibility for selecting those to be called upon for jury service. As recommended by the American Bar Association, and as described in "Minimum Standards of Judicial Administration", the plan operates as follows:

". . . Its main feature is the key-number system. The registration list of voters forms the basis of the jury list. The number of jurors required for the year is estimated by the court, and to this is added a number equal to that which past experience has shown probably will be eliminated upon examination. The resultant figure is divided into the entire list of voters, the quotient then being used as a key number in selecting jurors' names from the polling list. The citizens whose names have been chosen according to the key number are required to answer questionnaires, then are summoned to appear before the jury commissioners and be personally examined, until the requisite number of prospective jurors is selected. The purpose of the examination is to secure jurors who are 'physically and mentally healthy, possessing good reputation for honesty and morality, with at

least enough education to be able to read, write and
understand English; and finally of sufficient intelligence
and experience in life to be able to understand the various problems presented in both civil and criminal litigation.' "

The plan, in its original or in variant form, has been adopted
in a number of metropolitan court jurisdictions, and is proving
its value as one method of tending to alleviate the traditional
civilian antipathy, or even downright opposition, to jury service.

(7)   1934

We have already mentioned 1934 as the year in which Congress
authorized the Supreme Court to establish rules of civil procedure. The year was also significant in that it witnessed what
was probably the first major shift away from the Jacksonian
theory of direct popular election of state court judges, a theory
that has widely prevailed since the mid-nineteenth century. California in 1934 adopted a constitutional amendment providing for
the filling of judicial vacancies in the appellate courts by gubernatorial appointment subject to approval by a commission on
qualifications, the appointee so selected being required to run
solely on his own record and not against any opposition candidate. This latter feature, the periodic submission to the voters
of an unopposed incumbent, on the question as to whether or
not he shall be retained in office, was to become, as will be noted,
one element of the American Bar Association and Missouri plans
for judicial selection a few years later.

(8)   1937 - 1938

The American Bar Association, under the leadership and guidance of Arthur T. Vanderbilt and John J. Parker, adopted in
1937 and 1938 the group of recommendations that were to become the basic frame of reference for improvements in court
organization, administration and procedure. They embodied
proposed minimum standards or fundamental criteria for judicial systems, by postulating the desired ideal factors in such matters as judicial selection, business management of the courts, rule-
making, jury selection and service, pre-trial conferences, trial
practice, traffic courts and justices of the peace, law of evidence,
and appellate practice. These nine topics, with the addition of a
tenth, "administrative agencies", became the chapter headings
in a widely-used book published by the National Conference of
Judicial Councils in 1949 under Chief Justice Vanderbilt's edi-

torship, entitled "Minimum Standards of Judicial Administration." They constitute the most generally-acknowledged definitive and incisive presentation of goals toward which the bench, the bar, and indeed all the citizenry of America should strive, if we are to overcome the challenge of 1906 that "our system of courts is archaic."

(9) 1939

If courts are to be made more efficient, business methods must be introduced into their traditionally un-businesslike customs of operation. An implementation of the American Bar Association's recommendation along these lines came in 1939 with the setting up of the Administrative Office of the United States Courts. The duties and functions of such an office have been described by Chief Justice Vanderbilt as follows:

> "The duties of an administrative director and his staff are numerous: they include the purchase of law libraries, supplies and equipment for the judges; the establishment and maintenance of court rooms and chambers; the supervision and direction of court clerks and their offices; the preparation and administration of judicial budgets; the supervision of stenographic reporters, probation officers, sergeants at arms, constables and other court personnel; the investigation of complaints against the operation of the judicial system; the collection and analysis of statistical data concerning the status of judicial business and the publication of periodic reports based thereon."

The economies effected and improvements achieved have amply justified the founding of such an office for the federal courts, and it has set the pattern for a growing movement among the states to establish administrative offices in their respective systems.

(10) 1940

One of the boldest movements in the direction of taking judges out of politics was Missouri's 1940 constitutional amendment adopting its now-famous plan for the non-partisan selection of judges. It represents an adaptation of the American Bar Association proposal of 1937, and its functioning has been described as follows:

> "In Missouri the plan is applicable to all appellate judges and to the trial judges in Kansas City and St.

Louis. Under the plan the governor makes an appointment from a list of three names submitted by a selection
commission. For appellate judges the commission consists of the chief justice as chairman, three lawyers
elected by the bar, and three laymen appointed by the
governor. Aside from the chief justice each member is
appointed for a term of six years so arranged that the
term of one member expires each year. Members are
not eligible for reappointment, and are selected by districts to ensure geographical representation. For the trial
judges, the commission consists of five members made
up of the presiding judge of the court of appeals of the
district where the vacancy exists as chairman, two laymen appointed by the governor and two lawyers elected
by the bar. Since the term of the governor is only four
years and he cannot succeeed himself, he would ordin-
arily never control the appointment of a majority of
the commissioners.

"After serving one year, on the filing of a declaration
by the judge of his desire for another term, the name of
the judge is placed on a separate judicial ballot at the
general election, without any party designation, the only
question presented being: 'Shall Judge ....,
of the .... Court, be retained in office? Yes. No.' Under this system the judge is not com-
peting with any opponent, is not involved in any local
or national political controversies, and stands for election solely on the basis of his own record. If a majority
of the voters favor him, an appellate judge is given a
full term of twelve years and a trial judge one of six
years. If he is rejected, the governor appoints a new
judge and the process is then repeated a year later.
After a full term a judge again comes up for election."

Certainly the Missouri precedent, which has been featured in
many proposals for judicial reform in other jurisdictions, deserves
inclusion in any chronology of major events in the history of
what has been done to improve our courts.

(11)   1947

Even more far-reaching and impressive was the thorough-going
revision of New Jersey's judicial system under the state's new
Constitution of 1947 and the leadership of Arthur T. Vanderbilt, who became Chief Justice of the New Jersey Supreme

Court. Here we have dramatic proof of what can be accomplished when an aroused and determined citizenry decides that the time has come for bringing an outmoded judicial system up-to-date, and when at least some members of the bar and bench are willing to recognize, stimulate and give guidance to such public demand. Here too we have convincingly demonstrative proof that a modern judicial system can accomplish its objective: the swift and certain disposition of judicial business. New Jersey's system embodies a combination of the features proposed as models: an appointive judiciary, responsibility and authority vested in the Chief Justice of the Supreme Court as head of the judicial system, an administrative office to assist and guide the Chief Justice in determining the state of judicial business and to aid him in expediting it, the vesting of rule-making power in the Supreme Court, and the adoption of rules of procedure including an effective and careful pre-trial conference program. These are some of the features that have placed New Jersey in the vanguard of the states that are moving toward the goals prescribed as "Minimum Standards of Judicial Administration."

(12) 1951

The need for improvement of our courts at the basic level, that of traffic law enforcement tribunals and justices of the peace, has been increasingly recognized and stressed. But it remained for the Conference of Chief Justices in 1951 to formulate the basic principles to guide such improvement—principles of traffic law enforcement set forth in a set of sixteen resolutions. Among them, the integration of traffic courts into the state's judicial system, the provision of suitable courtrooms, the separation of traffic cases from other criminal business, the elimination of traffic ticket "fixing" and the non-partisan selection of local judges, are objectives toward which the several states are urged to strive. And unless and until the basic problem of traffic law enforcement can be effectively solved, the vast complex of civil litigation arising out of automobile accident personal injury litigation will dominate unabated the entire field of judicial administration at all levels.

(13) 1952

The year 1952 is significant in that it witnessed the adoption of a constitution establishing the Commonwealth of Puerto Rico and embodying a judicial article that in many respects marks a dramatic achievement in modern court structure and administration. It creates a completely unified court system, "consisting of the Supreme Court as the court of last resort, and the Court of First Instance, which together shall constitute the General Court of Justice." Although the trial court is organized into two general divisions, the Superior Court and the District Court, there are no hard and fast limitations of jurisdiction and venue, but rather a flexible adaptability within the general concept of "competencia." The Constitution, as supplemented by the Judiciary Act of 1952, invests the Supreme Court with broad rule-making power over procedure, both civil and criminal, as well as over the rules of evidence, and it establishes a strong administrative office to function closely with the Chief Justice in supervising the operations of the court system of Puerto Rico.

(14)   1955

In the United States, where judges are customarily selected from among the members of the bar rather than trained specifically for judicial careers, the inadequacy of judicial salaries and of pensions and retirement provisions has made it difficult to induce outstanding lawyers and successful practitioners to become candidates for judicial positions. As of 1953, the median pay of state trial court judges was $11,000 per year, and that of state appellate court judges, $12,500. The year 1955 is significant in that it brought the enactment of legislation by Congress which substantially raised the salaries of federal judges, and thereby set a standard and example for state legislatures to follow. For justices of the United States Supreme Court, the increase was from $25,000 per year to $35,000; for judges of the Courts of Appeal, from $17,500 to $25,500; and for District Court judges, from $15,000 to $22,500. While in one or two states, such as New York, the maximum paid to trial court judges is higher than in the federal system, the prestige that attaches in the appointive method of selection with lifetime tenure, as against New York's politically dominated system for choosing its judges, considerably enchances the comparative attractiveness of federal judgehips. In any event, a generally adopted combination of improved salaries and improved methods of judicial selection would do much to raise the standards of quality and performance of the American judiciary.

(15)   1956

The most recent event deserving inclusion in this fifty-year review occurred on February 5 of this year. On that date, the delegates of the people of Alaska, in convention asssembled, approved a proposed constitution for submission to the voters of the territory and, if adopted by them, to become effective upon the admission of Alaksa to statehood. The new constitution's article on the judiciary is noteworthy in several respects. It proposes a unified judicial system, a non-partisan method of judicial selection embodying the nominating commission features of the American Bar Association and Missouri plans, a provision for the advance retirement of judges who become incapacitated during incumbency, a vesting of rule-making power in the supreme court, and a designation of the chief justice as administrative head of the courts, with an administrative director appointed by him to supervise the administrative operations of the judicial system. When and if Alaska becomes a state, it may well be looked to as a proving ground for modern principles of court organization and administration.

THE CONCLUSION

The foregoing chronology is neither exhaustive nor all-inclusive. In a time span from 1906 to 1956, and a geographic range from arctic Alaska to tropic Puerto Rico, I have chosen those highlight events which seem to me to be most significant. Other reviewers would doubtless have their own choices at variance with mine. Nevertheless, I am confident we can all agree that it was Roscoe Pound in 1906 who set the sights for our present-day perspectives—perspectives that will ultimately insure a sound, effective and certain administration of justice throughout the entire United States.

JUDICIAL ADMINISTRATION — 1952 *

Tangible progress in the improvement of state court organization and administration is apt to be more marked in odd-numbered than in even-numbered years. The reason is obvious. Most state legislatures hold biennial sessions in the former and what is accomplished in the alternate years, except for constitutional amendments at the general elections and for court-enacted reforms through rule-making and internal administration, is largely groundwork for legislative sessions ahead. Nevertheless, there were noteworthy accomplishments in the year just past. Each in its way marked a step, and sometimes a major one, toward achievement of the objectives enumerated in *Minimum Standards of Judicial Administration.*[1]

One was the appearance of a new and different casebook on the subject of modern procedure and judicial administration.[2] It combines an analytical and up-to-date coverage of the Federal Rules of Civil and Criminal Procedure, and relevant cases and text discussion, with material designed to introduce law students to the field of judicial administration. To this latter end, there are chapters devoted to judicial selection and related matters,[3] to jury selection and service,[4] to the legal profession,[5] and to the problems of judicial administration and their proposed solutions.[6]

Among other developments of significance during the year 1952 a few are comprehensive in nature but many are directed toward specific reforms. The following review will serve in summary form to indicate by way of illustrative example that progress toward efficient organization and administration of the judicial system, sporadic though that progress may seem to the casual observer, is a growing tribute to the untiring efforts of bar associations, judges, and civic groups of lay and professional supporters.

---

* Reprinted from 1952 Annual Survey of American Law.

1. National Conference of Judicial Councils (1949). It is discussed in last year's Survey article on Judicial Administration by Professor Kharas, 1951 Annual Surv. Am. L. 893. For a recent review, see 68 L.Q. Rev. 254 (1952).

2. Vanderbilt, Cases and Other Materials on Modern Procedure and Judicial Administration (1952). Book Reviews: 13 Ala. Lawyer 409 (1952), 38 A.B.A.J. 754 (1952), 26 Conn. B.J. 397 (1952), 36 J. Am. Jud. Soc'y. 61 (1952), 5 J. Legal Educ. 265 (1952), 27 N.Y.U.L. Rev. 879 (1952), 27 St. John's L. Rev. 195 (1952), 16 U. Detroit L.J. 59 (1952).

3. Ch. XIII, pp. 1161-1189.
4. Ch. XIV, pp. 1190-1208.
5. Ch. XV, pp. 1209-1229.
6. Ch. XVI, pp. 1230-1265.

General Reforms and Surveys.—In terms of reorganizations effected, and effected in this case in a remarkably short span of time, the Puerto Rican Judiciary Act of 1952 is a notable accomplishment.[7] Implementing the Judiciary Article of the island's new Constitution,[8] it provides a unified and integrated court system, vests plenary power in the Chief Justice to supervise court operations and assign judges, and provides for an administrative director and an office of court administration. The Constitution authorizes the Supreme Court to adopt rules of evidence and procedure as well as rules for court administration. Both the Constitution and the Judiciary Act became effective July 24, 1952, the latter having been drafted, submitted to and passed by the Legislature in slightly over two weeks.

Even more far-reaching, although not yet a *fait accompli,* is the proposed new Judiciary Article for Illinois, prepared by a joint committee of the Illinois State Bar Association and the Chicago Bar Association for submission to the 1953 Legislature.[9] It would supplant the state's present complex court structure with a simplified and unified judicial system, empower the Supreme Court to supervise administrative affairs, vest rule-making powers in the courts, and substitute the Missouri plan of judicial selection for the existing method of popular election.

Among the general surveys giving an overall picture of judicial administration and recent improvements therein, the American Bar Association's handbook, now in its third edition, provides an invaluable summary and supplement to *Minimum Standards.*[10] Of similar value and comprehensive coverage is the section of the *Book of the States, 1952-53* devoted to judicial administration and procedure with both text and tabular information on the state judicial systems.[11]

Surveys of individual states are informative inventories both of results achieved and of programs pending. Among such local progress reports published in 1952 is one for Missouri, reviewing the history of that state's judicial system,[12] and one for New Jersey

7. Clark and Rogers, *The New Judiciary Act of Puerto Rico: A Definitive Court Reorganization,* 61 Yale L.J. 1147 (1952).

8. Approved by Congress as Pub. L. No. 447, 82d Cong., 2d Sess. (July 3, 1952), 66 Stat. 327 (1952).

9. Cedarquist, Explanatory Statement on the Proposed Judicial Article for the Constitution of the State of Illinois (1953); Cedarquist, *The Need for Judicial Reform in Illinois,* 2 De Paul L. Rev. 39 (1952); Zacharias, *The Proposed Illinois Judicial Article,* 30 Chi.-Kent L. Rev. 252 (1952).

10. American Bar Ass'n, Sec. of Jud. Admin., The Improvement of the Administration of Justice (3d ed. 1952).

11. Council of State Governments, The Book of the States 1952-1953, 455-468 (1952).

12. Hyde, *Historical Review of the Judicial System of Missouri,* 27 Vernon's Ann. Mo. Stats. 1 (1952).

discussing the third year of operation under the new Constitution.[13] Typical of appraisals in other jurisdictions,[14] a Wisconsin committee has analyzed that state's standing with respect to each of the minimum standards of judicial administration.[15] Another approach is indicated by the action of the Maryland Legislature in requesting the Governor to appoint a commission to investigate and evaluate the working of the judicial process in that state, including the organization and compensation of the judiciary.[16] In Texas, a study and proposed revision of the judiciary sections of the state Constitution have become a joint project of the State Bar, the Civil Judicial Council, and the Southwestern Legal Foundation.[17]

That problems and proposals in the field of judicial reform are as pressing in England as in this country is demonstrated in an article by Sir Arthur Goodhart.[18] Considerable interest there centers around the reports of the Evershed Committee on the expediting of litigation and appeals, and its consideration of the subject of court costs which, in the present system and even in ordinary cases, can mount upward to forbidding totals.

Judicial Selection.—Both foresight and hindsight are evident in the 1952 developments pertaining to proposals for changes in the methods of selecting judges. Partisans of the Missouri and American Bar Association plans outnumbered, in print at least, the advocates of retention of the elective system. It is too early to foretell what measures, if any, among the several pending for the 1953 legislative sessions will survive the preliminary rounds and reach the finals of submission to popular vote or referendum. Certainly the vigorous support of bar association committees, organizations, and individual spokesmen has not been wanting, and the determination with which their support has been renewed and strengthened from year to year gives promise that the goals sought with Sisyphean perseverance may ultimately be attained.

Among others in process, proposals comparable to the Missouri

---

13. Vanderbilt, *The Record of the New Jersey Courts in the Third Year under the New Constitution,* 6 Rutgers L. Rev. 367 (1952). See, also, Butterfield, *New Jersey Puts its Judges to Work,* Sat. Eve. Post, May 17, 1952, p. 30.

14. For earlier similar surveys in other states, consult 1951 Annual Surv. Am. L. 894. See, also, Leflar, *Minimum Standards of Judicial Administration —Arkansas,* 5 Ark. L. Rev. 1 (1950-51); Holme, *Colorado and Minimum Judicial Standards,* 28 Dicta 1 (1951).

15. Report, *Minimum Standards of Judicial Administration in Wisconsin,* 25 Wis. Bar Bull. 17 (1952).

16. Md. Laws 1952, Sen. J. Res. 4.

17. 15 Tex. B.J. 107, 265 (1952). See, also, Stayton, *Court Reorganization,* 15 Tex. B.J. 553 (1952); Burney, *Texas Lawyers Take Time for Leadership,* 36 J. Am. Jud. Soc'y 13 (1952).

18. Goodhart, *Current Judicial Reform in England,* 27 N.Y.U.L. Rev. 395 (1952).

plan have been advocated, endorsed or groomed, during the past year, for legislative consideration in Arkansas,[19] Illinois,[20] Kansas,[21] Michigan,[22] Ohio,[23] Pennsylvania,[24] and Texas.[25] In New Mexico, a judicial selection plan modelled along similar lines was defeated by the voters in 1951, and the causes of its defeat, as analyzed in a post-mortem appraisal, appear to have been several-fold, including a provision in the measure that a vote against retention of a judge in office must be "at least fifty per cent of the total number of legal voters voting at the election," and the lack of adequate lay participation to support the bar's pre-election sponsorship and campaign.[26] Similar analyses of unsuccessful as well as of successful campaigns for the adoption of judicial selection plans were featured in an open forum discussion at a meeting of the American Bar Association's Standing Committee on Judicial Selection, Tenure and Compensation in Chicago in February, 1952.[27]

In New York, where new methods of selecting judges have been reviewed and recommended by a bar association committee,[28] the existing method of political election has also been stoutly defended by a Presiding Justice of the Appellate Division.[29] It is the latter's thesis that "political considerations are fair considerations in the nomination and election of judges, and that political leaders have a legitimate interest and responsibility in the matter."[30]

Judicial Salaries and Retirement.—The latest tabulation of state judicial salaries shows that at least half of the forty-four state legislatures meeting in 1951 enacted measures increasing

---

19. *Report of the Committee on Court Reorganization,* 6 Ark. L. Rev. 126 (1952).

20. Note 9 *supra.*

21. *Report of the Committee on Selection, Tenure and Retirement of Judges,* 21 J. Bar Ass'n State of Kan. 72 (1952).

22. *Report of the Committee on Judicial Selection and Tenure,* 31 Mich. State Bar J. 34 (1952).

23. *Final Report of the Committee on Ohio Judicial System,* 25 Ohio Bar Ass'n Rep. 649 (1952).

24. Kenworthey, *The Pennsylvania Plan to Divorce Judges from Politics,* 25 Temp. L.Q. 410 (1952).

25. Burney, *Judicial Selection,* 15 Tex. B.J. 144 (1952).

26. Winters, *The New Mexico Judicial Selection Campaign—a Case History,* 35 J. Am. Jud. Soc'y 166 (1952).

27. *How to Conduct a Judicial Selection Reform Campaign,* 36 J. Am. Jud. Soc'y 4 (1952).

28. Ass'n Bar City of N.Y., Committee on Law Reform, Report on Consideration of New Methods to Select Judges (adopted at a Stated Meeting of the Association held on December 9, 1952).

29. Peck, *The Bar, Politics and Judicial Selection,* 24 N.Y. State Bar Bull. 32 (1952).

30. *Id.* at 38.

the compensation of appellate or trial court judges.[31] It is pointed out that the result of such increases was to raise the median annual salary of supreme court justices to $12,000 and of trial court judges to approximately $9,000.[32]

State legislatures meeting in 1952 in Arizona,[33], Colorado,[34] Louisiana,[35] and New York,[36] enacted legislation providing salary increases for judges in those states. These increments, together with further changes to be expected in the 1953 sessions, will bring the national salary averages to upward levels. By way of comparison, the present salaries for the federal judiciary are as follows: $15,000 for District Court Judges, $17,500 for Circuit Judges, and $25,000 for Supreme Court Justices. These are still below the salaries paid to state judges in New York, Pennsylvania, and New Jersey, and legislation to increase the federal scale is under consideration.[37]

A tabulation as of 1951 shows that retirement and pension plans have been adopted for appellate judges and trial judges in forty-two states.[38] Typical plans provide for retirement on from one-half to three-quarters pay, at ages ranging from 60 to 70, and after periods of service of from ten to twenty years. During 1952, supplemental provisions were added by statute or amendment in Colorado[39] and Michigan.[40] In Kansas, one of the few states without a judicial retirement plan, the subject has been recommended for study and legislative action.[41]

Judicial Discipline and Removal.—A recently-published volume of the Survey of the Legal Profession provides an authoritative study of professional and judicial ethics.[42] In a chapter on "Judicial Selection and Conduct" the authors review briefly the general views on partisan selection, the adoption and rigid enforcement of more adequate statutes delineating causes of dis-

31. The Book of the States 1952-1953, 464-465 (1952).

32. *Id.* at 459.

33. Ariz. Laws 1952, c. 37.

34. Colo. Laws 1952, c. 43.

35. La. Acts 1952, No. 30.

36. N.Y. Laws 1952, c. 5, 6, 7, 88 *et passim.*

37. Mooney, *Federal Judges Compensation—Proposed Legislation,* 27 N.Y.U.L. Rev. 457 (1952).

38. Council of State Governments, The Book of the States 1952-1953, 466-467 (1952).

39. Colo. Laws 1952, c. 37.

40. Mich. Pub. Acts 1952, No. 261, amending Mich. Pub. Acts 1951, No. 198. A proposed constitutional amendment in Washington, prepared by the Judicial Council, was approved by the bar association and the Superior Court Judges' Association. *Judicial Retirement Approved,* 6 Wash. St. Bar News 44 (1952).

41. Kagey, *Retirement and Pensions of Judges,* Kan. Jud. Council Bull. 2 (26th Ann. Rep. 1952).

42. Phillips and McCoy, Conduct of Judges and Lawyers (1952).

qualification, the problems of personal relationships in court matters, the practice of law by judges, and the insufficiency of present cumbersome provisions for the removal of errant members of the bench.[43] Another author suggests that the solution lies, not in a revision of disciplinary methods, but in the effective use of supervisory powers through administrative control vested in the state supreme court and chief justice.[44]

Court Integration and Unification.—In order to make administrative control effective, it is apparent that the complex congeries of separate and often overlapping or conflicting courts in some of the states must be supplanted by a simplified and integrated structure. Such unification as that achieved in Puerto Rico[45] and proposed for Illinois[46] represents a logical solution.

Two plans under consideration in Connecticut point toward similar results but differ considerably in the scope of the reforms sought. A proposal by the Judicial Council concerns primarily the Court of Common Pleas, Municipal Courts and Trial Justices.[47] Much more sweeping in extent is the State Bar Association Committee plan, proposing an overall unification of all courts, both trial and appellate, with centralized administrative supervision and rule-making power.[48]

In an address to the Florida Bar at its 1952 Annual Meeting, Governor Fuller Warren pointed out that with nine separate categories of courts in that state it is essential that there be some responsible administrative head for control of overall operations and dispatch of judicial business.[49] He urged support of a constitutional amendment for a unified court system, with the Chief Justice of the Supreme Court as the administrative head, having authority to assign judges temporarily where needed, and being supplied with adequate current statistical information.

Court Administration and Statistics.—As above noted, reorganization plans pending in several states, as well as that adopted in Puerto Rico, make provision for centralized administration with an administrative officer empowered and directed to manage judicial business affairs, including the compilation of current statistics. During 1952, two more states joined the growing ranks of

43. *Id.* at 130-153.

44. Miller, *Discipline of Judges,* 50 Mich. L. Rev. 737 (1952).

45. Note 7 *supra.*

46. Note 9 *supra.*

47. *Reorganization of the Courts, The Judicial Council Plan,* 26 Conn. B.J. 373 (1952).

48. *A Proposal for Court Reorganization, The State Bar Committee Plan,* 26 Conn. B.J. 382 (1952).

49. *Address by Governor Fuller Warren at the Florida Bar Convention,* 26 Fla. B.J. 237 (1952).

those having centralized administrative offices for the management or supervision of court business. A Michigan act, approved in May, provides for a court administrator with extensive powers, including the making of recommendations as to assignment of judges, and the collection and compilation of statistics.[50] In Virginia, a statute provides for an executive secretary to the Supreme Court of Appeals, to serve as secretary of the Judicial Council and the Judicial Conference, and to assist the Chief Justice in the performance of such administrative studies as may be required of him.[51] Also, a 1952 Rhode Island enactment vests administrative authority in the Presiding Justice of the Superior Courts, provides him with the assistance of an administrative clerk, and requires the superior and district courts to submit statistical data as requested.[52]

Statistical reports for the federal courts for the fiscal year ending June 30, 1952, stress the need for additional federal judges to cope with the growing volume of civil cases.[53] It is pointed out that the number of civil cases filed in the district courts per judge in 1952 increased by 16 per cent over the previous year's figure, and that the arrearage is greatest in the Southern District of New York where the median interval from filing to disposition of civil cases tried was 41.2 months.[54]

Court Congestion and Pre-Trial.—That congestion of civil cases is a problem not confined to the federal district court in New York is evident from the calendar status of general trial courts in New York City and Chicago. The situation in the latter city has attracted popular, or perhaps more correctly unpopular, attention.[55] Recommendations to alleviate the four-year backlog of tort jury cases in the New York County Supreme Court include a proposal to shorten jury trials by separating the issue of damages from the issue of liability, the former to be determined in advance by the court without a jury, and the latter alone to be

---

50. Mich. Pub. Acts 1952, No. 269.

51. Va. Acts 1952, c. 506. See, Bowles, *The Course of Law Reform in Virginia,* 38 Va. L. Rev. 689 (1952).

52. R.I. Acts 1952, c. 3030.

53. Annual Report of the Director of the Administrative Office of the United States Courts (1952), 1. See, also Tolman, *The Administration of the Federal Courts: A Review of Progress During 1950-51,* 38 A.B.A.J. 127 (1952).

54. Annual Report, *supra,* Table C5. For discussions of the function of the Administrative Office and the value of judicial statistics, see Stephens, *The Administrative Affairs of the United States Courts: A Report to the Bar,* 38 A.B.A.J. 555 (1952); Speck, *Statistics for the United States Courts: An Indispensable Tool for Judicial Management, id.* at 936 (1952).

55. *Legal Log Jam in Chicago,* Life, Nov. 10, 1952, pp. 127-133. The calendar conditions in New York courts in 1950-1951 are summarized in N.Y. Jud. Council, 18th Annual Report and Studies 32 (1952).

left to the jury.[56] Another plan, and one that is being put into operation on an experimental basis with the cooperation of medical societies, makes available a panel of impartial medical experts to be drawn upon when there is conflict in the testimony of the parties' medical witnesses.[57]

The growth in the use of pre-trial procedures as an expediting device received added impetus in 1952.[58] In Louisiana, statutory provisions pertaining to pre-trial and adopting new rules for discovery and depositions were enacted by the 1952 Legislature.[59] Under authorization of the California Judicial Council a three-month pre-trial experiment was conducted in one of the counties of that state with encouraging success.[60] The use of pre-trial in Onondaga County, New York, was reviewed by a trial justice there,[61] and its use in Iowa has been similarly surveyed.[62] In Michigan, where pre-trial has had its longest experience, the Judicial Council's 1952 report shows that in the Wayne County Circuit Court the percentage of cases disposed of on pre-trial has increased from 40.6 in 1935 to 77.6 in 1951.[63] Amended rules in New Jersey governing pre-trial conference procedures and antecedent proceedings were made effective on January 1, 1953, and are published in a handbook containing valuable introductory and illustrative material that can well serve as a guide to practitioners in other states.[64]

If trial court congestion is a problem at the trial court level in New York and Chicago, there are indications that the reverse may be true in other states or at other levels. Associate Justice Rossman of the Supreme Court of Oregon has pointed to figures in that state showing that, apart from divorce matters, civil litigation has lagged far behind the increase in population over a quarter-century.[65] Even more marked has been the decline in appeals filed, from 331 in 1926 to 174 in 1951.[66] Partially ac-

---

56. Cuff, *Shorter Jury Trials*, 24 N.Y. State Bar Bull. 297 (1952).

57. N.Y. Times, Nov. 24, 1952, p. 1, col. 1.

58. American Bar Ass'n, Sec. of Jud. Admin., Report of Committee on Pre-Trial Procedure (1952).

59. The several acts are discussed in *Louisiana Legislation of 1952*, 13 La. L. Rev. 21, 45-56 (1952).

60. Kincaid, *Pre-Trial In Our Superior Court*, 27 Calif. State Bar J. 205 (1952); *Report of Committee to Assist the Judicial Council in the Study of Pre-Trial Procedure, id.* at 305 (1952).

61. Searl, *What of Pre-Trial?* 44 Syracuse L. Rev. 1. (1952).

62. Crary, *The Pretrial in Action.* 37 Iowa L. Rev. 341 (1952); *Pretrial in Iowa—Its Use and Disuse, id.* at 345 (1952).

63. Jud. Council of Mich., Judicial Statistics for the Year 1951, 58 (1952).

64. N.J. Sup. Ct., Manual of Pre-Trial Practice (1953).

65. Rossman, *Quo Vadis?* 32 Ore. L. Rev. 1 (1952).

66. *Id.* at 5. For comment on a similar decline in the work of the New York Court of Appeals, see Desmond, *Where Have the Litigants Gone?* 20 Fordham L. Rev. 229 (1951).

counting for the latter may be the increasing high costs of such appeals and the overall delays from initial filing of actions to ultimate decision, both subjects that have received the attention of commentators[67] and of amended rules of appellate procedure.[68]

Rule-Making and Procedural Rules.—Among the several extensive reorganization proposals such as those above noted for Connecticut and Illinois, a salient common feature is the supplanting of legislative control of procedure by the vesting of full rule-making power in the courts. Pursuant to a grant of such authority in 1951,[69] the Nevada Supreme Court appointed an advisory committee which presented a complete draft of rules patterened on the Federal Rules of Civil Procedure. These were approved by the Nevada Supreme Court on August 29, 1952, to become effective January 1, 1953.

The Kentucky Legislature empowered and directed the Court of Appeals to promulgate rules regulating pleading, practice and procedure in civil matters, such rules to be submitted for consideration of the bench and bar, and to be adopted after public hearing.[70] Initial rules so adopted were to become effective as of July 1, 1953. In California, a federal judge has advanced cogent arguments in behalf of adoption of the Federal Rules of Civil Procedure in that state, including a plea for wider judicial discretion than exists in present state practice as to jury instruction.[71]

Juries and Jury Selection.—The jurors, despite the needless complexity of the instructions to which they must patiently submit and despite the appellation given them by another federal judge, are not really "forgotten men" in all jurisdictions.[72] They have been interviewed, questionnaired and tested after selected trials to determine their reactions and motivations.[73] The methods of selecting jury panels in the federal courts, and the qualifications and grounds for disqualification as compared with state courts, have been analyzed in Tennessee.[74]

Few jurisdictions have accomplished anything approaching the District of Columbia's achievements in enlisting the interest of

---

67. Brand, *The Impact of the Increased Cost of Litigation,* 35 J. Am. Jud. Soc'y 102 (1952); and see Goodhart, note 18 *supra.*

68. McCaleb, *The New Rules of the Supreme Court of Louisiana,* 26 Tulane L. Rev. 491 (1952).

69. Nev. Laws 1951, c. 40.

70. Ky. Acts 1952, c. 18. See, Sims, *The Work of Kentucky's Civil Code Committee,* 40 Ky. L.J. 7 (1952).

71. Goodman, *Should California Adopt Federal Civil Procedure?* 40 Calif. L. Rev. 184 (1952).

72. *Cf.* Hulen, *"Twelve Good Men and True": The Forgotten Men of the Courtroom,* 38 A.B.A.J. 813 (1952).

73. Hoffman and Brodley, *Jurors on Trial,* 17 Mo. L. Rev. 235 (1952).

74. Wicker, *Jury Panels in Federal Courts,* 22 Tenn. L. Rev. 203 (1952); Baugh, *Selecting a Trial Jury in Tennessee, id* at 220 (1952).

citizens in jury service. The techniques by which this was accomplished make interesting reading. The facilities provided for jurors in the new United States Court House in the District make even more interesting viewing. Both are described in a 1952 pamphlet published by the Section of Judicial Administration of the American Bar Association, reprinting the substance of discussions at a 1951 meeting of the Section's Committee on Cooperation with Laymen.[75] This is strongly recommended as worthy of study for groups in other states concerned with the problem.

Traffic Courts and Justices of the Peace.—Last, but far from least, mention should be accorded to the omnipresent problems of the lower courts and magistrates dealing with traffic offenses and minor justiciable matters. An excellent and comprehensive study on traffic courts and traffic cases was prepared for the Conference of Chief Justices in September 1952, pointing out the diversity and autonomy of courts handling traffic matters, and the major problems needing attention.[76]

Integration, as proposed in some of the state overall reorganization plans and as advocated or achieved for the minor judiciary in others,[77] may provide a solution. But integration is apt to be, in fact has been, doggedly resisted by those who defend the justice of the peace courts as essential guardians of "grass roots" justice.[78]

In its broader aspects, the field of traffic administration includes ramified factors reaching beyond traffic courts into problems of safety, highway engineering, police organization, and public education.[79] It has been suggested that this broad area offers fruitful material for jurisprudential study looking toward development of legal controls through techniques comparable to those used in other sciences.[80]

The role of the justices of the peace and minor courts in this larger pattern is receiving, and will continue to receive, increasing attention in the several states. The importance of that role in the overall picture of judicial administration was significantly

75. American Bar Ass'n, Sec. of Jud. Admin., Cooperation with Laymen in Improving the Administration of Justice (1952).

76. Council of State Governments, The Administration of Justice in Traffic Cases (1952).

77. McKenna, *Justice in the Minor Courts,* 25 Temp. L.Q. 436 (1952); Haney, *The Ohio Municipal Court Act,* 21 U. of Cin. L. Rev. 285 (1952).

78. Smith, *Justice for Justice of the Peace Courts,* 23 J. Okla. Bar Ass'n 1028 (1952); Powers, *Should We Keep Justice of the Peace Courts? Id.* at 1029 (1952).

79. Economos, *Justice, Safety, and Traffic Courts,* 25 State Gov't 9 (1952). See, also, Hale, *Jurisdiction of Justices of the Peace Over Uniform Traffic Act Violations,* 25 Ohio State Bar Ass'n Rep. 951 (1952).

80. Beutel, *Traffic Control as Experimental Jurisprudence in Action,* 31 Neb. L. Rev. 349 (1952).

stressed by former Chief Justice Charles E. Hughes when he
stated:

> Justice in the minor courts—the only courts that mil-
> lions of our people know—administered without favor-
> itism by men conspicuous for wisdom and probity, is the
> best assurance of respect for our institutions.[81]

81. Quoted in McKenna, *Justice in the Minor Courts*, 25 Temp. L.Q. 436,
448 (1952).

JUDICIAL ADMINISTRATION — 1953 *

In terms of accomplished improvements in judicial administration, the year 1953 was steady but not spectacular. In terms of groundwork hopefully laid for future reforms, both in England and in this country, the record is more impressive. The long-awaited and comprehensive report of the Evershed Committee was presented to Parliament in July.[1] American state legislatures, traditionally inclined to be cautious when it comes to court reform, nevertheless showed venturesome willingness in some states —at least a willingness to appoint commissions, or to assign existing agencies, to study or prepare comprehensive proposals for court reorganization and improvement.

Highlights, and some shadows, in the general scene for 1953 appear in the following paragraphs. They have been grouped under specific headings for convenience in reference, a device that sometimes loses the woods for the trees. To see the picture in proper perspective, one needs to take the longer and larger view—an overall vista of progress measured in ratings and scores. The scoring system used in 1950 provided a relative ranking of states in the order of their respective degrees of adoption of at least minimal standards of judicial administration.[2] In the 1950 tabulation, New Jersey, California, Delaware and Wisconsin ranked as the top four, in that order.[3] A partial updating of that report, covering twenty-two of the states, shows that by 1953 Utah and Minnesota have moved into second and third positions, respectively, and Vermont and Virginia have considerably improved their standings.[4] As a measure of cumulative progress for all of the twenty-two states in the four-year period since 1949, including five that reported "no progress,"[5] the advance is impressive, more than doubling the earlier aggregate score. When the full tally for forty-eight states is recorded, the results will show the picture in complete, and it is hoped gratifying, perspective.

---

* Reprinted from 1953 Annual Survey of American Law

1. Final Report of the Committee on Supreme Court Practice and Procedure (1953).

2. Porter, Minimum Standards of Judicial Administration: The Extent of Their Acceptance, 36 A.B.A.J. 614 (1950).

3. Id. at 616.

4. American Bar Ass'n, Sec. of Jud. Admin., Report of Director of State Committees (Aug. 1953). This relative standing may be misleading, however, since California and Delaware were among the nonreporting states, and may actually have improved sufficiently to retain their former positions.

5. Maine, Mississippi, New Mexico, Tennessee, West Virginia.

General Reforms and Surveys.—Of the several proposals under
legislative consideration in 1953, the projected new Judiciary
Article in Ilinois was the most far-reaching in scope, and perhaps
the most widely publicized.[6] Although it passed the Senate, it was
defeated in the House. Less comprehensive, but still substantial,
proposals in Connecticut[7] and Ohio[8] were also blocked in the
course of passage by the legislatures.

A promising beginning toward major reform in New York
was inaugurated by the authorization and appointment of a
Temporary Commission on the Courts to survey and report to
the next Legislature on (1) means of relieving calendar congestion, (2) simplification of practice and procedure, (3) en-
largement of the rule-making power, (4) reduction of costs of
litigation and appeals, (5) improved methods of selecting judges,
(6) a uniform method of jury selection, and (7) changes in
substantive law to improve the administration of justice.[9] It has
been reported that somewhat similar though less extensive studies
have been authorized in Maine[10] and Maryland.[11]

The end product of six years of study of Supreme Court practice and procedure in England by the Evershed Committee was
submitted by the Lord High Chancellor to Parliament in July
1953.[12] The report and recommendations cover a wide range of
topics from initial approach and pleadings to execution of judg-
ments and procedure on appeal. There are sections of the report
dealing with "The Limitation and Assessment of Costs"[13] and
with "Counsel's Fees,"[14] as well as with "Litigation at the Public
Expense"[15] and with "Distribution of Business in the High
Court."[16] To those who anticipated proposals for drastic inno-
vations in the British system of judicial administration, the report may fall considerably short of expectations. In many instances the Committee, in lieu of basic changes, recommended
the "more robust" exercise of powers and authority already
conferred. Nevertheless, if all or a substantial number of the 229

---

6. 1953 Ill. Senate Joint Res. No. 23. For a brief summary of its provisions
see Elliott, Judicial Administration, 1952 Annual Surv. Am. L. 780, 28
N.Y.U.L. Rev. 779 (1953).

7. 1953 Conn. Senate Bill No. 692.

8. 1953 Ohio Senate Joint Res. No. 31.

9. N.Y. Laws 1953, c. 591.

10. Jones, From the State Capitals (Jan. 31, 1953).

11. Jones, From the State Capitals (April 11, 1953). And see Report of
Commission to Study the Judiciary of Maryland (Jan. 1953).

12. See note 1 supra.

13. Section X, p. 232.

14. Section XI, p. 268.

15. Section IX, p. 216.

16. Section XII, p. 298.

recommendations are put into operation, the resultant simplifications in procedure should be substantial in cumulative effect.

Less numerous, but possibly more fundamental, proposals for state court systems in the United States were advocated by the Conference of Chief Justices at their annual meeting in August 1953.[17] Their recommendations included the creation and functions of administrative offices, judicial conferences and judicial councils; the provision of minimum ten-year terms for all trial and appellate judges; permanent chief justices for courts of last resort; increases in judicial salaries; and the adoption of adequate judicial retirement systems.

Another and more comprehensive analysis of basic requisites for a sound judicial system provides a valuable checklist of essential factors for efficient court organization and administration.[18] It includes a simplified and unified court system, improved selection of judges and juries, competent court staffs and administrative supervision, expedition of judicial business, and the collection, dissemination and use of current statistics as a basis for efficient allocation of judicial manpower.

Among the surveys and reports of past accomplishments in judicial and procedural reforms, there have been summary reviews of measures and methods in Florida,[19] New Jersey,[20] New York,[21] Puerto Rico,[22] and Virginia.[23] Recommendations and proposals for revised judiciary articles have been delineated in Minnesota[24] and Texas.[25] Suggestions as to how to secure a judicial reform through enlisting public support have also been offered, based on the successful experience in securing such support in New Jersey.[26]

Judicial Selection and Tenure.—During the year, attention

17. 1953 Conference of Chief Justices, 26 State Gov't 241 (1953).

18. Vanderbilt, The Essentials of a Sound Judicial System, 48 Nw. U.L. Rev. 1 (1953).
1 (1953).

19. Feibelman, Florida Blazes the Path of Legislative and Judicial Reform, 53 Com. L.J. 237 (1953).

20. Vanderbilt, The Reorganization of the New Jersey Courts, 34 Chi. Bar Record 161 (1953).

21. Nims, New York's 100 Years Struggle for Better Civil Justice, 25 N.Y. State Bar Bull. 83 (1953).

22. Adler, The New Judiciary Act of Puerto Rico: A Definitive Court Reorganization, 8 Record of Ass'n of Bar of City of N.Y. 76 (1953); Snyder, New Puerto Rico Judicial System is Modern and Efficient, 36 J. Am. Jud. Soc'y 134 (1953).

23. Whittle, Streamlined Justice in Virginia, 10 Wash. & Lee L. Rev. 9 (1953).

24. Final Report of the Special Committee on Revision of the Constitution of the State of Minnesota, 10 Bench & Bar of Minn. 52 (Sept. 1953).

25. Proposed Judiciary Article, 16 Tex. B.J. 12 (1953).

26. Paul, How to Sell Judicial Reform, 42 Nat. Munic. Rev. 280 (1953).

has been sharply focused on the Missouri plan, or variants of it, for the selection of judges. In Kansas a proposal for the plan's adoption reached legislative consideration but died in committee.[27] Substantial support by members of the bar for similar plans in Michigan[28] and Nebraska[29] has been shown, and bar association committees in Georgia[30] and New York[31] have advocated its adoption in those states, although bar members in the latter have also favored retention of the present elective system.[32] Support for the Missouri or American Bar Association Plan has been voiced in Chicago[33] and Florida,[34] and for the elective system in Detroit.[35] Discussion of the proposed Pennsylvania Plan for judicial appointment by the governor from a selected panel has indicated similar divergence of viewpoints.[36] In Wisconsin, the Judicial Council has been directed to study methods of judicial selection and to submit to the 1955 Legislature a plan "offering the most acceptable substitute for direct election."[37]

A comprehensive survey of sources from which appellate judges are appointed, as between direct appointment from the bar and elevation from the trial courts, supports the desirability of a mixture of both methods.[38] In Indiana, a new law provides that only persons admitted to practice before the state supreme court or acting as judicial officers are eligible for judicial appointments.[39] A report on English methods reviews the tradition of nonpolitical appointments to the bench in that country and

27. 1953 Kan. Senate Concurrent Res. No. 6.

28. Bar Favors Change in Method of Judicial Selection, 32 Mich. State B.J. 30 (Oct. 1953).

29. Hastings, President's Address, 32 Neb. L. Rev. 142, 144 (1953).

30. Report of Committee of Georgia Bar Association on Jurisprudence, Law Reform and Procedure, 15 Ga. B.J. 445, 446 (1953). The report reaffirms previous support of "a modified form of the Missouri Plan concerning judicial tenure."

31. Association Activities, 8 Record of Bar Ass'n of City of N.Y. 1, 2 (Jan. 1953); Association News, 10 Bar Bull., N.Y. County Lawyers Ass'n 120, 122 (1953). And see, Gallantz, Judicial Selection—A Metropolitan Proposal, 25 N. Y. State Bar Bull. 101 (1953).

32. Runals, Judicial Selection—An Upstate View, 25 N.Y. State Bar Bull. 90 (1953).

33. Ewing, Non-Partisan Selection of Judges, 34 Chi. Bar Record 465 (1953).

34. Tucker, Judges—Selecting the Best Men, 6 U. of Fla. L. Rev. 195 (1953).

35. Comment, The Judiciary Re-Examined—How Do They Get There?, 16 U. of Detroit L.J. 180 (1953).

36. Fox, Judges and Politics, 27 Temple L.Q. 1 (1953); Dechert & Frankel, We Must Elect Bar-Approved Sitting Judges, 16 The Shingle 208 (1953); Clark, Sitting Judges, Governor Fine's Appointees and the 1953 Election, 16 id. at 214.

37. 1953 Wis. Assembly Joint Res. No. 79A.

38. Tunstall, Why Ignore the Bar?, 38 Va. L. Rev. 1091 (1952).

39. Ind. Laws 1953, c. 254.

suggests the desirability of eliminating politics from judicial selection in the United States.[40]

In the area of judicial tenure, Wisconsin has enacted a law that judges elected to fill vacancies shall serve full initial terms rather than merely the balance of unexpired terms, before running for re-election.[41] In Oklahoma, a proposal to extend the terms of district court judges from four years to eight years failed to secure legislative approval,[42] and a bill in New Jersey to extend initial terms of county judges from five years to seven years, with life tenure on subsequent reappointment, also failed.[43]

Judicial Salaries and Retirement.—Judicial salary increases, some of them substantial, were approved in more than half of the states whose legislatures met in 1953. For the highest appellate courts there were salary advances of $5,500 in Missouri, $5,000 in Nevada, $3,000 to $3,500 in Colorado, Oregon, Washington and Wyoming, and $2,000 to $2,500 in California, Maryland, New Hampshire and North Dakota.[44] For trial courts of general jurisdiction, increases of from $2,000 to $3,000 were approved in Missouri, New Hampshire, Oregon, Utah and Wyoming.[45] The previous median national salary levels for highest appellate court judges and trial court judges were $12,000 and $9,000 respectively.[46] As a result of 1953 increases, these median salaries are raised to $12,500 and $11,000. Although the 1953 Congress failed to act on pending legislation to increase the salaries of federal judges,[47] there has been growing support for favorable action.[48]

New retirement plans were adopted in Indiana[49] and Kansas.[50] The former will provide maximum annuities of $4,000 after sixteen years of service. The latter is to be financed by a combination of salary percentage contributions and special filing fees, and permits retirement at age sixty-five, with retirement at age seventy mandatory. A new retirement plan has been proposed

---

40. Erskine, The Selection of Judges in England: A Standard for Comparison, 39 A.B.A.J. 279 (1953).

41. Wis. Laws 1953, c. 606.

42. 1953 Okla. House Bill No. 609.

43. 1953 N.J. Senate Bill No. 329.

44. Inst. of Jud. Admin., Preliminary Check List of 1953 Legislation on Judicial Administration 7-10 (Aug. 15, 1953).

45. Ibid.

46. The Book of the States 1952-1953, 459-60. (1952).

47. 1953 Sen. No. 1663.

48. Getting Our Money's Worth, 36 J. Am. Jud. Soc'y 163 (1953); Hayes, Salaries—United States Judges and Members of Congress, 24 Okla. Bar Ass'n J. 1475 (1953).

49. Ind. Laws 1953, c. 157.

50. Kan. Laws 1953, c. 182.

for judges in Kentucky;[51] and the Tennessee requirement that periods of judicial service to qualify for benefits be consecutive has been eliminated by amendment.[52] In Wisconsin, county judges have been brought into the judicial retirement system.[53] Pension provisions for orphaned children of deceased judges were adopted in Connecticut,[54] and for widows of judges in Maine[55] and Oregon.[56]

Apart from direct salary increases and retirement benefits, several states took steps to facilitate future increases or to provide supplemental assistance. Thus, in New Mexico the voters approved constitutional amendments to permit the Legislature to fix supreme court and district court salaries,[57] and a proposed Arkansas constitutional amendment to enable legislative fixing of judicial salaries will be submitted to the voters in 1954.[58] Expense allowances for judges were approved in Indiana[59] and Georgia,[60] and Florida Supreme Court justices have been authorized to employ clerks or research assistants.[61]

Judicial Conduct, Discipline, and Removal.—A proposed method of removing district judges in Nevada for misconduct and malfeasance, after preliminary ruling by the supreme court on the charges, and assignment to a different district for hearing, was vetoed by the governor.[62] Present provisions and methods for the removal of judges in all of the forty-eight states have been comprehensively surveyed in a 1953 report of the Wisconsin Judicial Council.[63]

Limitations on the practice of law by judges of certain courts were enacted in Connecticut,[64] and Missouri has prohibited law practice by circuit judges.[65] New York, on the other hand, has expressly permitted New York City justices and magistrates to receive supplemental income for lecturing, instructing or writing, if it does not interfere with the performance of their judicial duties.[66]

---

51. Pension Plan for Judges, 17 Ky. State B.J. 147 (1953).
52. Tenn. Laws 1953, c. 61.
53. Wis. Laws 1953, c. 461.
54. Conn. Pub. Acts 1953, No. 260.
55. Me. Pub. Laws 1953, cc. 338, 339.
56. Ore. Laws 1953, c. 529.
57. 1953 N.M. House Joint Res. Nos. 15, 16.
58. 1953 Ark. House Joint Res. No. 5.
59. Ind. Laws 1953, c. 25.
60. Ga. Laws 1953, No. 487.
61. Fla. Acts 1953, c. 28115, Item 57.
62. Jones, From the State Capitals (March 7, 1953).
63. Wis. Jud. Council, 1953 Biennial Report, App. 10, p. 36.
64. Conn. Pub. Acts 1953, No. 261.
65. Mo. Rev. Stat. Ann. § 478.013 (Supp. 1953).
66. N.Y. Laws 1953, c. 395.

On the subject of judicial demeanor, as a matter more of dignity and decorum than of possible disciplinary concern, attention has been called to the need for proper bearing, manners and courtroom courtesy on the part of judges, particularly on the trial bench.[67] Such a requirement is also embodied in Canon 10 of the American Bar Association Canons of Judicial Ethics.[68]

Judicial Councils and Judicial Conferences.—Florida was added this year to the states having judicial councils. The 1953 Legislature authorized a Council composed of judges, the attorney general, four members of the bar, and nine laymen, to make a continuing study of the organization, procedure, practice and work of the Florida courts.[69] In West Virginia, however, the Legislature substantially impaired the work of that state's Judicial Council by repealing existing statutory provisions for a paid executive secretary, for travel expenses of Council members, and for office space in the state capitol.[70]

In its 1953 biennial report, the Judicial Council of Wisconsin has announced major studies projected for the 1953-1955 biennium on (1) court organization, and (2) the functioning of pretrial conferences.[71] In addition, as noted, the Council has been directed by the Wisconsin Legislature to make recommendations on a substitute for direct election of judges.[72] A history of judicial councils and a study of their functioning in Massachusetts, California, Kansas and New York is included in the 1953 report of the Kansas Judicial Council.[73]

Increased impetus to the growing judicial conference movement was given by the Tennessee Legislature's creation of a judicial Conference in that state, to meet annually to consider matters relating to official judicial duties and to recommend improvements in the administration of justice.[74] A Colorado enactment provides for the summoning of conferences of judges in the state's respective judicial departments,[75] and the Massachusetts Legislature has requested the Judicial Council to investigate and report on a suggestion for holding annual judicial conferences.[76]

Two reports have been issued by the Judicial Conference of

---

67. Vanderbilt, supra note 18, at 11.
68. For a recent reprinting of the Canons, see Canons of Judicial Ethics, 30 Dicta 333 (1953).
69. Fla. Laws 1953, c. 28062.
70. W. Va. Laws 1953, c. 142.
71. Wis. Jud. Council, 1953 Biennial Report 13.
72. See note 37 supra.
73. Nims, Four Judicial Councils, 27 Kan. Jud. Council Bull., pt. 2, 26 (1953).
74. Tenn. Pub. Acts 1953, c. 129.
75. Colo. Laws 1953, c. 82.
76. Mass. Resolves of 1953, c. 20.

the United States, one covering a special session in March 1953,[77] and the other the regular annual meeting in September.[78] Both reports, in addition to summarizing current docket status in the federal courts, deal with a number of topics pertaining to judicial administration in the federal system, stressing in particular the need for additional judgeships.[79]

Court Integration and Unification.—Major proposals for the integration and unification of the court systems in Illinois[80] and Connecticut,[81] respectively, failed to pass the legislatures in those two states, as did also a proposal to integrate the lower courts in New Jersey,[82] and one to reorganize the district courts in Massachusetts.[83] Something was salvaged from the defeats in Connecticut and Massachusetts, however, by the referral in one case to the Legislative Council[84] and in the other to the next session of the General Court,[85] for further consideration.

In Michigan, proposals to reorganize and integrate the courts of Wayne County into a single metropolitan court,[86] and one to replace justice courts with municipal courts in cities over 25,000 population[87] were unsuccessful. Meanwhile, in California, reorganization of the lower court system under the constitutional amendment adopted in 1950 was completed in January 1953, the consolidation of such courts resulting in an overall reduction of judicial positions therein from 838 to 505 in number.[88]

Groundwork for possible future unification of the Arkansas courts has been reportedly suggested to the Judicial Council

---

77. Report of the Proceedings of a Special Session of the Judicial Conference of the United States (1953).

78. Report of the Proceedings of the Regular Annual Meeting of the Judicial Conference of the United States (1953). For a discussion of the 1952 report, see Stayton, Modern Judicial Administration, 16 Tex. B.J. 205 (1953).

79. See also Shafroth, The Federal Courts Need More Judges, 37 J. Am. Jud. Soc'y 9 (1953).

80. This was included in the overall revision of the Judiciary Article submitted in Illinois. See note 6 supra.

81. See note 7 supra. And see Clark, Realistic Court Reform—A Study of Pending Proposals, 27 Conn. B.J. 11 (1953).

82. 1953 N.J. Assembly Bill No. 36.

83. 1953 Mass. Senate Bill No. 247. For a discussion of the bill see Urbano, Summary of the District Court Survey Committee's Report with Draft Act, 37 Mass. L.Q. 1 (1952).

84. 1953 Conn. Senate Joint Res. No. 44.

85. 1953 Mass. Senate Bill No. 784.

86. 1953 Mich. Senate Joint Res. K; 1953 Mich. Senate Bill No. 23. And see Langs, The Metropolitan Court Bill, 32 Mich. State B.J. 25 (March 1953); Langs, The Metropolitan Court, 21 Detroit Law. 29 (1953).

87. See Judicial Administration Legislative Summary, 37 J. Am. Jud. Soc'y 49 (1953).

88. Report on the Reorganization of the Lower Courts, Jud. Council of Cal., 14th Biennial Report 13, 21 (1953).

there,[89] and has also been initiated for the lower courts in Maine by the Municipal Judges Association of that state.[90] From these, as well as from renewed attacks on the problem in other states, it can be hoped that eventually the modernization and stream-lining of state courts will become a rule rather than the all-too-rare exception it is now.

Court Administration, Congestion, and Statistics.—Reports on court operations and caseloads show in general a continuing in-crease in the volume of litigation to be handled, particularly in the trial courts of the larger metropolitan areas. Superadded to the current backlog of pending cases, this increase puts to a severe test the already overburdened judicial machinery and poses a pressing challenge. Basic to any solution is the need for centralized collection and publication of current judicial statis-tics—a need that has been recognized and provided for in two more states, Colorado[91] and Oregon.[92] The usefulness of such statistical information is demonstrated in the first annual report of the Administrative Director of the Courts in Puerto Rico,[93] as well as in the reports for New Jersey[94] and for the federal courts.[95] In the latter, for example, the increase in civil cases commenced in the district courts is 9.5 per cent over the 1952 figure, bringing to 66 per cent the cumulative increase since 1941.[96]

A nation-wide survey of the status of trial court calendars in 1953 shows that the overall average time interval from "at issue" to trial of civil cases in the ninety-seven metropolitan courts covered was 11.5 months for jury cases and 5.7 months for non-jury cases.[97] The greatest delays reported were in New York City, Worcester County in Massachusetts, and Cook County, Illinois. In the Supreme Court of Kings County (Brooklyn), the average figure was fifty-three months, and in New York County (Man-hattan), forty-three months.

Efforts and proposals to solve the problem have been many

---

89. Jones, From the State Capitals (Sept. 29, 1953).

90. See Judicial Administration Legislative Summary, 36 J. Am. Jud. Soc'y 148, 149 (1953).

91. Colo. Laws 1953, c. 236.

92. Ore. Laws 1953, c. 34.

93. Informe Anual del Director Administrativo de los Tribunales 1952-1953.

94. See Vanderbilt, The Record of the New Jersey Courts in the Fourth Year under the New Constitution, 7 Rutgers L. Rev. 317 (1953).

95. See Annual Report of the Director of the Administrative Office of The United States Courts (1953).

96. Id. at 3. And see Report of the Proceedings of the Regular Annual Meeting of the Judicial Conference of the United States 4 (1953).

97. Inst. of Jud. Admin., Calendar Status Study—1953 (June 30, 1953).

and varied. The need for additional judges has been stressed for the federal courts,[98] and met in California by legislative authorization of thirty-three additional superior court judgeships.[99] A New York constitutional amendment, approved by the voters in November 1953, permits judges within New York City to be assigned to courts where needed.[100] Presiding Justice Peck of the New York Appellate Division has reported on other steps taken to alleviate delays, including the preference rule, pre-trial conferences, and the use of independent medical reports.[101] Other suggestions have been advanced, such as elimination of delaying tactics,[102] and the use of referees and mediation of tort cases.[103] Judge Holtzoff of the District Court for the District of Columbia has described procedural improvements and the responsibilities of judge and counsel to expedite trials.[104]

Elsewhere, the congestion problems in Connecticut[105] and Massachusetts[106] have been analyzed and proposals offered for their solution, and a Colorado Supreme Court justice has reportedly announced steps to reduce congestion in the Denver courts, including the temporary suspension of pre-trial conferences "for present expediency."[107] In Missouri, the flexible provisions of the 1945 Constitution permitting "temporary transfers of judicial personnel from one court to another as the administration of justice requires"[108] have been availed of to help cope with the crowded docket conditions in the Circuit Court of Jackson County.[109]

Pre-Trial.—Increase in the use of pre-trial procedures, despite possible contrary indications in Denver, may provide one step toward solution of the problem of court congestion and trial delays. The Georgia Legislature, in an act patterned in part on the pre-trial provisions of the Federal Rules of Civil Procedure,

---

98. See note 79 supra.

99. Cal. Stat. 1953, cc. 255, 1817-29.

100. N.Y. Const. Art. VI, as amended Nov. 3, 1953 (1953 N.Y. Senate Int. 101).

101. Peck, Report on Justice, 25 N.Y. State Bar Bull. 107 (1953).

102. Nims, The Cost of Justice: A New Approach, 39 A.B.A.J. 455 (1953).

103. McGrath, The President's Page, 4 Brooklyn Barrister 182 (1953).

104. Holtzoff, How Courtroom Procedure May Be Expedited, 14 F.R.D. 323 (1953).

105. Baldwin, How Can We Expedite the Business of the Courts?, 27 Conn. B.J. 1 (1953).

106. Dimond, Congestion in the Superior Court Since Its Creation in 1859 and Proposals for Relief, 38 Mass. L.Q. 95 (June, 1953).

107. Jones, From the State Capitals (Oct. 31, 1953).

108. Mo. Const. 1945, Art. V, § 6. See also § 16: "Any circuit judge may sit in any other circuit at the request of a judge thereof."

109. Ellison, Temporary Transfers of Missouri Judges, 9 J. Mo. Bar Ass'n 25 (1953).

has authorized its use in superior court civil cases there,[110] and New York has extended pre-trial both in the city court of New York and in the supreme court in additional counties.[111] Adoption of pre-trial procedures for the Superior Court of Rhode Island has also been reported to be heavily favored by the members of the bar in that state.[112]

Reviews of successful operations of pre-trial systems in Texas[113] and Ohio[114] add weight to the growing body of supporting data. Also of value are recent surveys of pre-trial conferences and procedure in Kentucky,[115] and Judge Murrah's pamphlet, published by the Administrative Office of the United States Courts for distribution to newly appointed judges of the federal district courts.[116]

Rule-Making and Procedural Rules.—The movement for transfer of the procedural rule-making power from legislatures to the courts is slowly gaining ground. Thus, a 1953 statute in Connecticut yields to the judges the authority to adopt rules regulating pleading, practice and procedure in all courts of the state, such rules when adopted to be submitted to the General Assembly, which has power to disapprove them.[117] Similar legislation has been urged by the Judicial Council in Vermont,[118] and a committee of the Missouri Bar has recommended the enactment of a constitutional amendment to vest full rule-making power in the Supreme Court of Missouri, to cover all procedural law, including the law of evidence, and oral examination of witnesses.[119] Meanwhile, under its existing and more limited authority, the Missouri Supreme Court has formulated proposed new rules of civil procedure to supersede procedural provisions in the statutes and present rules.[120]

Kentucky's new rules of civil procedure, adopting substantial

---

110. Ga. Laws 1953, No. 319.

111. 19 N.Y. Jud. Council Rep. 28 (1953).

112. Jones, From the State Capitals (Aug. 15, 1953).

113. Hughes, Pre-Trial Progress in Texas, 16 Texas B.J. 131 (1953).

114. Pre-Trial Operation Termed Successful, 24 Cleveland Bar Ass'n J. 181 (1953). And see Norris, Results of Pre-Trial Procedure in Domestic Relations Court, 24 id. at 105.

115. Dow, The Pre-Trial Conference, 41 Ky. L.J. 363 (1953); Patterson, Pre-Trial Procedure in Practice, 41 id. at 383.

116. Murrah, Pre-Trial Procedure—A Statement of Its Essentials (1953).

117. Conn. Pub. Acts 1953, No. 214. The act continues in force existing statutes on the subject until modified or repealed by the proposed new rules.

118. Vt. Jud. Council, Fourth Biennial Report 9 (1953).

119. Report of Evidence Code Committee, 9 J. Mo. Bar 143 (1953).

120. Comment, The Proposed Rules of Civil Procedure for Missouri, 18 Mo. L. Rev. 280 (1953).

portions of the federal rules, became effective July 1, 1953,[121] and
New Jersey has undertaken and completed the first overall revision of its rules since their original adoption in 1948.[122] The
Federal Rules of Civil Procedure, it has been announced, will
be again re-examined by the Advisory Committee with a view
toward possible revision or expansion in the light of developments since the last major restudy that resulted in the amendments of 1946.[123]

Jurors and Jury Selection.—Despite the doubting view of some
commentators as to the future of jury trials in civil cases,[124] there
are evidences of effort to preserve and strengthen juries as an
institution. Against the oracles of obsolescence, there are those
who view the right of trial by jury, civil or criminal, as an essential safeguard of justice.[125] And there are those, also, whose interest urges them to probe deeper into the psychological workings
of a system so fundamentally established in Anglo-American
tradition.[126]

Improved methods of jury selection are anticipated in New
Jersey through the recent transfer from the governor to the
supreme court of the authority to appoint and remove jury commissioners.[127] In California, suggested model rules for the testing
and selection of prospective jurors would accomplish desirable
advancements in the caliber of those ultimately chosen for jury
duty.[128] But the discouraging obstacles of low pay, exclusion of
women in some states, and lack of public enthusiasm for jury
service remain to be surmounted. It is true that states from time
to time take cognizance of, and seek to improve, the low per diem
and mileage allowances for jurors—witness recent legislative action in Arkansas,[129] Idaho,[130] Iowa,[131] Minnesota,[132] and New
Hampshire.[133] It is true that the possibility of women jurors in
still-resistant states moves one step nearer through proposed con-

---

121. Judicial Administration Legislative Summary, 36 J. Am. Jud. Soc'y
148, 150 (1953).

122. New Jersey Court Rules, 1953 Revision.

123. The United States Supreme Court Advisory Committee on Rules for
Civil Procedure, 39 A.B.A.J. 754 (1953).

124. See, e.g., Peck, Report on Justice, 25 N.Y. State Bar Bull. 107 (1953).

125. See Bok, The Jury System in America, 287 Annals 92 (1953).

126. Meltzer, A Projected Study of the Jury as a Working Institution, 287
Annals 97 (1953).

127. N. J. Laws 1953, c. 240.

128. Comment, Jury Selection in California, 5 Stan. L. Rev. 247 (1953).

129. Ark. Acts 1953, No. 46.

130. Idaho Laws 1953, c. 88.

131. Iowa Code § 607.5 (1950), amended by Iowa Laws 1953, c. 248.

132. Minn. Laws 1953, c. 478. The act increased jurors' pay, but reduced
mileage allowances.

133. N.H. Laws 1953, c. 18.

stitutional amendments in Texas[134] and West Virginia.[135] But a basic approach through stimulation of citizen awareness of the privileges and duties of jury service, such as the educational program undertaken in the high schools of the District of Columbia,[136] needs wider adoption, if the values of a system, otherwise doomed to possible desuetude, are to be preserved and vitalized.

Traffic Courts and Justices of the Peace.—Efforts to enhance the status of, as well as to establish minimum qualifications for, justices of the peace have met with varied success. Thus, a legislative committee in New York has recommended that minimum qualifications be established for the office of justice of the peace, and that the title of the office be changed "in order to get away from certain derogatory implications attached to the name 'Justice of the Peace.' "[137] The reorganization plan in California, featuring the consolidation of justice courts and their integration into the judicial system, includes a requirement that no one shall be eligible to become a judge of such court unless he "has passed a qualifying examination under regulations prescribed by the Judicial Council."[138] The examinations, which are written and which relate to the jurisdiction, practice and procedure of justice courts, and the duties of judges, are administered by local county committees.[139] In Pennsylvania, on the other hand, proposed requirements for the instruction and standard examination of all justices of the peace, other than those who have been admitted to the bar, failed to secure legislative approval.[140] While the Arkansas Legislature paved the way for possible reduction in the number of that state's justices of the peace, by approving a constitutional amendment to be submitted to the voters in 1954,[141] the California Legislature failed to approve a measure that would supplement the integration of justice courts by bringing the judges thereof into the state's judicial retirement system.[142]

A nation-wide survey presents for the first time a comprehensive and detailed picture of traffic law enforcement in the forty-

---

134. 1953 Texas House Joint Res. No. 16.

135. 1953 W. Va. House Joint Res. No. 3.

136. See Pub. Schools of Dist. Col., A Resource Unit on The Jury System and American Courts (1953).

137. Shultz Committee's Preliminary Report, 13 Justice Court Topics 1, 2, 3 (May 1953).

138. Cal. Stat. 1949, c. 1510, § 13. The act exempts incumbent judges for the duration of their present and subsequent consecutive terms of office.

139. Report on the Reorganization of the Lower Courts, Jud. Council of Calif., 14th Biennial Report 13, 22 (1953).

140. 1953 Pa. House Bill No. 1458.

141. 1953 Ark. House Joint Res. No. 5.

142. 1953 Calif. Assembly Bill No. 763.

eight states.[143] The report discusses each of the sixteen resolutions adopted in 1951 by the Conference of Chief Justices, and
portrays by means of maps the extent of acceptance by the states
of each of the resolutions. Integration of traffic courts into the
state's judicial system, the provision of suitable courtrooms, the
separation of traffic cases from other criminal business, the elimination of traffic ticket "fixing," and the nonpartisan selection of
local judges are among the topics covered by the resolutions and
toward which the states are urged to strive. If the goal is to be
attained, constant, vigorous, and widespread public support is
essential. Also essential is an up-to-date appraisal in each state
of the local needs and problems of the administration of justice
in traffic cases.[144]

Conclusion.—Ultimate success in improving the judicial system
rests, at base, on an understanding awareness of present needs
and shortcomings. The leadership in insuring that awareness
and in alerting the public to informed action rests, in turn, on
the entire legal profession and its constituent lawyers and judges.
That such broad leadership has too often been reluctant in
forthcoming is emphasized in an address by Chief Justice Vanderbilt of New Jersey delivered at Northwestern University School
of Law:

> Where thoroughgoing judicial reform has been achieved,
> as in England and in New Jersey, it has come, in spite of
> the bench and the bar generally, through the efforts of
> laymen led by a few brave lawyers. This is the darkest
> and most indelible spot on the escutcheon of our other-
> wise great profession. Perhaps (I wish I could be more
> confident) the great popular discontent that presently
> confronts government at all levels—national, state, and
> local—may inspire the bench and bar everywhere to un-
> dertake the task that is emphatically theirs, not only as a
> matter of professional duty but also as a matter of self-
> preservation, despite the inconvenience it will tempo-
> rarily cause them until they become accustomed to the
> improved judicial system that they know the public is
> entitled to.[145]

---

143. Vanderbilt, Traffic Law Enforcement and the Sixteen Resolutions of
the Chief Justices and the Governors (July 1953).

144. See, for example, Report on Survey of the Administration of Justice
in Traffic Cases, Jud. Council of Calif., 14th Biennial Report 29 (1953).

145. Vanderbilt, The Essentials of a Sound Judicial System, 48 N.U.L.
Rev. 1, 2 (1953).

JUDICIAL ADMINISTRATION — 1954 *

> Progress goes by fits and starts. We cannot hope to survive by stubborn adherence to a system devised for a different world. We cannot apply nineteenth century notions of judicial administration to twentieth century conditions any more than we can apply all of its substantive rules to them.[1]

Most of the more promising "starts" in 1954 were programs planned or revised by state groups with a view toward hoped-for future adoption. With legislative sessions held in only a minority of states, actual enactments toward improved judicial administration were relatively few. At the planning level, as will be hereinafter noted, there were broad-scale projects for subsequent implementation in several states, such as Florida and Illinois. A project for the study of the Kentucky judicial system by the State Legislative Research Commission was authorized by the Kentucky legislature.[2] In Minnesota, Nebraska, Ohio, and Pennsylvania, bar association committees concentrated on prospective constitutional amendments to improve the judiciary of their respective states. The New York Temporary Commission on the Courts issued its preliminary report in March,[3] followed by hearings on specific proposals. These are some, but by no means all, of the 1954 developments that should be mentioned in an inventory of the year's activities. Inevitably, there were some setbacks, but the total gains exceeded losses by a sufficient margin so that the net results can be definitely entered in the "plus" column.

General Reforms and Surveys.—The Judicial Council of Florida, established in 1953, has announced a statement of its objectives, including the study of (1) appellate courts and procedures to relieve the present congestion; (2) a nonpartisan plan for the selection and tenure of judges; (3) organization of and procedure in the trial courts; (4) most effective use of jurors and other laymen; and (5) administrative improvements in judicial systems.[4] Meanwhile, in Illinois, the far-reaching and widely-

---

* Reprinted from 1954 Annual Survey of American Law.

1. Sears, A New Judicial Article for Illinois: From the 1848 Horse and Buggy Days to 1955, 40 A.B.A.J. 755, 807 (1954).

2. Ky. Acts 1954, c. 268.

3. Preliminary Report of the Temporary Commission on the Courts (March 5, 1954). The final report came out on Feb. 17, 1955.

4. First Annual Report of the Judicial Council of Florida (1954). See also, Feibelman, Florida's Judicial Council, 28 Fla. B.J. 73 (1954). See also, 28 id. at 269.

publicized proposal for a new judicial article of the constitution has been readied for reintroduction in the 1955 session of the state legislature.[5] It will be recalled that the original proposal, vigorously supported by the Joint Committee of the Illinois State and Chicago Bar Associations, the press, and a statewide citizens committee, passed the state senate in 1953 with the required two-thirds majority and made a creditable showing in the house, with 77 of the needed 102 votes.[6] In other states less comprehensive projects were under bar association consideration, as will be later noted in connection with the specific topics to which they pertain.

Able spokesmen and national leaders have continued to stress the need and responsibilities for achieving modern and efficient court systems, and the methods of overcoming resistance to change of the present status quo.[7] The measure of such change as has been actually achieved is provided in summary tabulations on a topic-by-topic and state-by-state basis.[8] Viewed in perspective, the cumulative record of accomplishments to date is good, but more—much more—remains to be done.

During the year there have also been published over-all reports recounting or measuring the progress and status of judicial reform in individual states and jurisdictions, notably, Alabama,[9] New Jersey,[10] and the District of Columbia.[11]

Judicial Selection and Tenure.—While no major changes in existing methods of judicial selection were adopted by any of the states in 1954, plans and programs for securing such changes have continued with undiminished vigor in several jurisdictions. In the renewed proposal for amending the Illinois judicial article, previously mentioned, the basic elements of the original plan

---

5. Sears, supra note 1, A tentative draft of the proposed article, prepared by the Joint Committee of the Illinois State and Chicago Bar Associations, has been published in printed form, dated Dec. 1954.

6. Sears, supra note 1, at 806. See also, Elliott, Judicial Administration, 1953 Annual Surv. Am. L. 815, 29 N.Y.U.L. Rev. 155 (1954).

7. See, e.g., Medina, Procedural Reform and the Achievement of Justice, 11 Wash. & Lee L. Rev. 141 (1954); Vanderbilt, The Courts, the Public and the Bar, 11 B. Bull., N.Y. County Lawyers Ass'n 209 (1954), Vanderbilt, The Courts, the Public and the Bar II, 12 id. 11; Winters, Whose Job Is Judicial Reform?, 28 Fla. B.J. 230 (1954).

8. Inst. of Jud. Admin., Check-List Summary of 1954 Developments in Judicial Administration (1954); A.B.A., Section of Judicial Administration, Annual Report (1954).

9. Thornton, The Minimum Standards of Judicial Administration in Alabama, 15 Ala. Law. 373 (1954).

10. Vanderbilt, The First Five Years of the New Jersey Courts under the Constitution of 1947, 8 Rutgers L. Rev. 289 (1954); Karcher, New Jersey Streamlines Her Courts: A Revival of "Jersey Justice," 40 A.B.A.J. 759 (1954).

11. Laws, Improving the Administration of Justice in the District of Columbia, 21 J.B. Ass'n of D.C. 45 (1954).

for filling vacant judgeships by appointment from candidates nominated by judicial nominating commissions have been retained, but with certain modifications in prospect before the proposed article is put in final form.[12] A committee of the Pennsylvania Bar Association has been actively continuing its campaign to secure citizen interest in, and support of, the "Pennsylvania Plan" for nomination and appointment of judges.[13]

In Nebraska, a so-called "Merit Plan" for the appointment of supreme court justices, district court judges, and judges of certain local courts was approved by the state bar association, on the recommendation of its Committee on the Judiciary.[14] The proposed constitutional amendment, an adaptation of the Missouri Plan but with the use of *ad hoc* rather than continuing nominating committees, was prepared for circulaion on initiative petitions to secure the signatures needed to place it on the November ballot. The number of signatures secured fell short of the total required, and the measure failed to qualify, but it is planned to submit it to the Nebraska legislature for passage and submission to the people at a future election.[15]

A new "Ohio Plan," similar in many respects to the original proposal submitted to and rejected by the voters of that state in 1938, but with some modifications, was proposed by the Special Committee on Judicial System and approved by the Council of Delegates, with instructions to prepare appropriate constitutional amendments to be considered at a later meeting.[16] The proposal as preliminarily approved would include only the supreme court and court of appeals under the appointive system and would leave it optional with counties to come under the system if they wish. Meanwhile, in Wisconsin, the state bar association's Committee on Judicial Selection prepared both a proposed constitutional amendment and interim legislation to be submitted to the 1955 legislature, embodying features of the American Bar Association Plan, but to apply initially only to supreme court

12. Sears, supra note 1, at 806-07. The tentative draft of Dec. 1954, supra note 5, contains a provision in paragraph 12 of the schedule for submitting to the voters, as a separate proposition, the method of selecting judges, including the appointment, composition, and duties of the judicial nominating commissions.

13. Pennsylvania Plan for Selecting Judges, 25 Pa. B. Ass'n Q. 334 (1954); Harris, The Program of the Pennsylvania Plan, 17 The Shingle 83 (1954).

14. Nebraska State Bar Ass'n Annual Meeting 1953, 33 Neb. L. Rev. 141, 183 (1954).

15. Letter to Institute of Judicial Administration from Kenneth H. Dryden, Chairman, Nebraska Committee, A.B.A., Section of Judicial Administration (Dec. 23, 1954).

16. 1954 Annual Meeting Proceedings, 27 Ohio Bar 431, 434 (1954). For a criticism of the proposal, see Binns, Reorganization of Ohio's Judicial System, 27 id. at 977.

justices.[17] The committee's recommendations were approved by the association's House of Governors.[18]

The comprehensive program of the Florida Judicial Council contains as one of its objectives "a non-partisan plan for the selection and tenure of judges."[19] The council's first annual report states that "One study in progress is an adaptation of the American Bar Association or Missouri Plan, with a view to taking judges and their selection and continuance on the bench out of party or personal politics, but preserving to the people the right to vote on judges."[20]

In the Arizona legislature, a concurrent resolution proposing an extensive constitutional amendment, including longer tenure for judges, creation of a judicial council, and provision for judicial appointments by the governor from qualified persons nominated by the council died in the House Judiciary Committee.[21] And in Rhode Island, a constitutional amendment approved by the 1953 legislature for submission to the voters, providing tenure and retirement benefits for supreme court and superior court judges, was rejected by the voters in the November 1954 election.[22]

A change in the tenure of the chief justice of the Supreme Court of Michigan was affected by legislative enactment which provided that, when a vacancy occurs in such office, the justices of the court shall choose from among their own number a chief justice to serve until the expiration of the term for which he has been elected as a justice of the supreme court.[23] This supersedes the existing system of rotation in office of the chief justiceship.

Judicial Salaries and Retirement.—State action affecting judicial salaries during 1954 has been scattered and sporadic, as was to be expected in an off-legislative year. The principal focus of national attention was on the proposal for substantial salary increases for federal judges, as recommended by the Commission on Judicial and Congressional Salaries in a report submitted in January.[24] For judges of the several courts the commission recommended as follows: $40,000 for the chief justice and $39,500 for associate justices of the Supreme Court, $30,500 for judges of the Courts of Appeals, the Court of Claims, the Court of Customs and Patent Appeals and the Court of Military Appeals, and

17. 27 Wis. B. Bull., No. 3, p. 38 (1954).
18. 27 id., No. 4, pp. 21, 22.
19. First Annual Report of the Judicial Council of Florida (1954).
20. Id. at 11.
21. Ariz. H.C. Res. No. 11 (1954).
22. R.I. Acts and Resolves 1953, c. 3096.
23. Mich. Pub. Acts 1954, No. 142.
24. H.R. Doc. No. 300, 83d Cong., 2d Sess. (1954).

$27,500 for District Court, Tax Court and Customs Court judges. The increases were incorporated in amendments to measures then pending before the Senate[25] and the House of Representatives,[26] and were unanimously approved by the House of Delegates of the American Bar Association.[27] The new Congress provided for increases somewhat below those recommended by the Commission.[28]

Pointed emphasis was given to the need for state action in Ohio by the announcement in November by the chief justice of the supreme court of that state that he was resigning effective January 1, 1955.[29] His statement said in part: "It seems incredible that the salary I am drawing was fixed by the legislature 27 years ago before inflation and at a time when the salaries of public officials were not subject to the federal income tax."[30]

Major increases enacted by state legislatures and finally approved during the year were those in Mississippi and New York, respectively. In the former, the governor approved measures increasing the chief justice's salary from $11,000 to $13,500, and of the other supreme court justices from $11,000 to $12,500.[31] In New York, a number of measures granting increases ranging from $500 to $6,000 for county judges in designated counties were passed and approved.[32] In addition to these states, salary adjustment provisions were enacted in Kentucky and Michigan. In Kentucky, a previously approved increase for judges of the Kentucky Court of Appeals to $12,000 was, by supplemental act, made applicable to incumbent judges as of January 1, 1955, instead of on subsequent re-election.[33] A Michigan statute has increased the state's contribution to the salaries of circuit court judges, with a proviso that total compensation shall not exceed $22,500 per year.[34]

A New Jersey bill,[35] introduced in the 1954 legislature to increase judicial salaries both in the supreme court and in the superior and county courts, failed to pass; and in the Massachusetts legislature, bills proposing salary increases for district court

25. S. 1663, 83d Cong., 2d Sess. (1954).
26. H.R. 7510, 83d Cong., 2d Sess. (1954).
27. Proceedings of the House of Delegates: Mid-Year Meeting: Atlanta, Georgia, March 8-9, 40 A.B.A.J. 438, 439 (1954).
28. Pub. L. No. 9, 84th Cong., 1st Sess. (March 2, 1955).
29. Chief Justice Weygandt Resigns, 27 Ohio Bar 1085 (1954).
30. 27 id. at 1086.
31. Miss. Laws 1954, c. 212, See also, Judicial Administration Legislative Summary, 38 J. Am. Jud. Soc'y 82 (1954).
32. N.Y. Laws 1954, cc. 13, 299-304, 371, 372, 438, 635, 636.
33. Ky. Acts 1954, c. 234.
34. Mich. Pub. Acts 1954, No. 155. See also, Judicial Administration Legislative Summary, 38 J. Am. Jud. Soc'y 81, 82 (1954).
35. N.J. Sen. No. 211 (1954).

judges[36] and probate judges,[37] respectively, were defeated.[38] In Arkansas, a proposed constitutional amendment to enable legislative fixing of judicial salaries[39] was rejected by the voters in the November 1954 election.

By judicial interpretation of the state constitution, the Minnesota Supreme Court rescued from gubernatorial nonapproval the legislative enactment of 1953 prescribing salaries for state district court judges.[40] On an appeal from the granting of a writ of mandamus to compel the secretary of state to recognize the enactment as valid, despite failure of the governor to act on it prior to legislative adjournment, the supreme court noted separate provisions of the Minnesota constitution that " 'The judges of the . . . district courts . . . shall receive such compensation at stated times as may be prescribed by the legislature; . . . ' "[41] and that " 'The legislature shall consist of the Senate and House of Representatives. . . . ' "[42] Reasoning that these provisions placed measures prescribing compensation of judges in a separate category from ordinary bills, and thereby exempted them from the veto power, the supreme court held that the legislative act was valid without the governor's signature, and affirmed the decision of the trial court.

In the area of retirement provisions the Kentucky, Michigan, and Virginia legislatures, as well as the Congress, gave approval to new legislation. The Kentucky act provides retirement pensions for circuit court judges ranging from $3,500 upward, depending on length of service, and with a reserved authority in the chief justice to require retired judges to sit as special judges, health permitting.[43] The Michigan statute provides retirement benefits for probate judges at varying ages, according to length of service, with a maximum limit of $4,000 per year.[44] New legislation in Virginia provides for compulsory retirement at age seventy-five, with permissive retirement at age sixty-five after twelve years service, and with possible recall for ninety-day periods to assist in the expeditious disposition of court business.[45] The federal statute permits retirement with full pay at age sixty-five for judges with fifteen years of service, as well as at age

---

36. Mass. H. No. 2906 (1954).
37. Mass. H. No. 1222 (1954).
38. Jones, From the State Capitals, Supplemental Rep. 2 (March 24, 1954).
39. Ark. H.J. Res. No. 5 (1953).
40. State ex rel. Gardner v. Holm, 62 N.W.2d 52 (Minn. 1954).
41. Id. at 55, quoting from Minn. Const. Art. 6, § 6.
42. Ibid., quoting from Minn. Const. Art. 4, § 1.
43. Ky. Rev. Stat. §§ 23.300-23.380 (Legis. Supp. 1954).
44. Mich. Pub. Acts 1954, No. 165.
45. Va. Acts 1954, cc. 274, 634, 635.

seventy with ten years of service as formerly provided, and reduces from sixteen to ten years the service requirement at age seventy for district judges in the territories and possessions, with retirement at age sixty-five for those who have served fifteen years.[46]

In other jurisdictions, the Montana district court judges agreed to seek bar association support for a bill to provide retirement at age 65 on at least half pay after three terms of service;[47] and the president of the Texas State Bar called attention to the urgent need for legislative action to reinforce the judges' retirement fund in that state,[48] which need was thereafter met by special legislative appropriation.[49]

Judicial Conduct, Discipline, and Removal.—The matter of eligibility of judges to hold other office or to serve as members of constitutional conventions has been under consideration in New York. A proposed constitutional amendment to extend the prohibition against holding other than judicial and military office to judges in the larger counties was passed by the New York legislature in 1954 and will be presented again in 1955.[50] But a proposal to bar judges from eligibility to serve as members of constitutional conventions died in assembly committee after senate passage.[51]

Canons of judicial ethics, adopted by the Ohio Supreme Court, are patterned on those of the American Bar Association with certain modifications, including a provision permitting judges nominated as candidates of political parties to attend and speak at political gatherings and to make contributions to party campaign funds.[52] By way of contrast, the projected new judicial article for the Illinois constitution contained at one stage a direct prohibition against a judge's holding office in, or contributing to, any political party.[53]

The subject of courtroom decorum, including proposed rules of conduct for both judges and lawyers, has been under consider-

---

46. Pub. L. No. 294, 83d Cong., 2d Sess. (Feb. 10, 1954), 68 Stat. 6, 28 U.S.C.A. § 371 (Supp. 1954).

47. Judicial Administration Legislative Summary, 38 J. Am. Jud. Soc'y 22, 24 (1954).

48. Looney, The Judges' Predicament, 17 Texas B.J. 101 (1954).

49. Tex. Laws 1954, c. 7.

50. 1954 N.Y. Sen. Print No. 2891.

51. 1954 N.Y. Sen. Print No. 30, Assemb. Int. No. 397. For a critical discussion of the proposals, see 131 N.Y.L.J., No. 26, p. 4, col. 1 (1954).

52. 27 Ohio Bar 74, 85, 93 (1954).

53. Sears, supra note 1, at 804. However, the prohibition against contributing to a political party does not appear in a later draft. See tentative draft of Dec. 1954, Art. VI, § 18.

ation both in Minnesota[54] and Oregon.[55] One aspect of the subject, that of publicizing courtroom trials by photographs, radio, and television, and the proposals to liberalize Canon 35 which presently proscribes such publicity, has been discussed in several articles.[56] A somewhat related problem, that of the authority of a judge to exclude the press and spectators from a much-publicized trial in New York City, has been considered by the New York Court of Appeals, which held against the assertion of such authority.[57]

With respect to procedure for the removal of judges, one feature of the proposed new Illinois judicial article is the provision for a special tribunal, consisting of judges representing the several courts, to be convened by the chief justice by order of the supreme court or at the request of the senate. The tribunal would have power to retire any judge for disability or suspend or remove any judge for cause.[58]

Judicial Councils and Judicial Conferences.—The first annual report of the Florida Judicial Council, in addition to the statement of objectives for long-range study previously noted, contains statistical data on the caseloads of the appellate courts, circuit courts, and county and other local courts.[59] A still newer member of the judicial council family was added by the appointment of a twelve-member council by the governor of Maine, acting under the existing but heretofore unused authority of a 1935 statute.[60] The new council has been directed to study all phases of the state's judicial system, including the field of criminal indictments.[61] In Oregon a bill has been prepared to establish a judicial council composed of supreme court justices and judges of courts of record whose function would be to make a continu-

---

54. Mendow, Judicial Decorum, 11 Bench & Bar of Minn., No. 12, p. 45 (1954).

55. Rules for Court Conduct Readied, 15 Ore. St. B. Bull., No. 2, p. 1 (1954). See also, Hinshaw, Courtroom Decorum, 17 Texas B.J. 171 (1954).

56. Boldt, Should Canon 35 of the Code of Judicial Ethics Be Revised?, 16 F.R.D. 83 (1954). See also, Howard, A Newspaper Editor Looks at Canon 35, 37 J. Am. Jud. Soc'y 166 (1954); McCoy, The Judge and Courtroom Publicity, 37 id. at 167.

57. People v. Jelke, 308 N.Y. 56, 123 N.E.2d 760 (1954).

58. Sears, supra note 1, at 804. See tentative draft of Dec. 1954, Art. VI, § 20(b). For the story of a recent removal proceeding in Texas, see McDonald, Texas Removes and Replaces a Judge, 38 J. Am. Jud. Soc'y 47 (1954).

59. First Annual Report of the Judicial Council of Florida, pp. 1-4 (1954).

60. Me. Pub. Laws 1935, c. 52. See Jones, From the State Capitals, Supplemental Rep. 1 (April 9, 1954).

61. Judicial Administration Legislative Summary, 38 J. Am. Jud. Soc'y 22 (1954).

ous study and survey of court administration and procedure.[62] The New York Temporary Commission on the Courts is also proposing a bill to establish a judicial conference of nine judges to replace the judicial council in that state.[63] Meanwhile in Mississippi a bill to create a judicial council,[64] recommended by the state bar association, failed to emerge from committee in the 1954 legislature.

The number of articles commenting on the accomplishments and activities of judicial councils and judicial conferences, as well as their official published reports, attest to the scope and variety of their respective programs.[65] Some have been considerably more active than others, and some give promise of future accomplishment, such as in Louisiana where funds and a full-time administrator have just been provided in 1954.[66] On the other hand, the New York legislature, in an unexpected last-minute move, cut the budget of the judicial council of that state from $50,000 to $10,000, thereby threatening the continuance of the council's work in spearheading improvements in judicial administration for the past twenty years.[67]

Court Integration and Unification.—During the year programs of broad-scale unification and simplification of existing court systems as a whole were under consideration or discussion in Illinois, New York, and Wisconsin. The proposed judicial article for Illinois would divide the state into judicial circuits, each with a single trial court of unlimited jurisdiction and with three grades of trial judges, designated as circuit judges, associate, judges, and magistrates, respectively.[68] There would also be a single appellate court, initially of fifteen judges, to sit in divisions in three judicial districts.

While the need for simplification of New York's complex and cumbersome structure of courts has been recognized,[69] the atten-

---

62. Letter to Institute of Judicial Administration from Jonel C. Hill, Administrative Assistant to Chief Justice (Dec. 21, 1954). See also, Judicial Council Favored in Report, 14 Ore. St. B. Bull., No. 11, p. 1 (Aug. 1954).

63. See Preliminary Report, supra note 3, at 29.

64. Miss. H.B. No. 399 (1954).

65. See, e.g., Hudgins, The Judicial Council and Judicial Conference in Virginia, 27 State Gov't 17 (1954). See also, Judicial Conference Annual Meeting, 10 Mo. B.J. 97 (1954); Alessandroni, The Seventh Judicial Conference and the Law's Delay, 17 The Shingle 55 (1954); Report of the Proceedings of a Special Session of the Judicial Conference of the United States (April 15-16, 1954).

66. The New Louisiana Judicial Council, 2 La. B.J. 149 (1954).

67. N.Y. Laws 1954, c. 281; Karlen, Civil Remedies and Procedure, 1954 Survey of New York Law, 29 N.Y.U.L. Rev. 1705, 1707.

68. Sears, supra note 1, at 758. And see, tentative draft of Dec. 1954, Art. VI, § 9.

69. Karlen, supra note 67, at 1707; Webster, Hotchpotch or Integration, 9 Record 52 (1954).

tion of the Temporary Commission on the Courts has been more immediately concentrated on a plan for an integrated special court to handle matters of youthful offenders.[70] The broader problem of children and and families in the courts of New York City has been extensively studied and analyzed,[71] and a proposal for an integrated family court for the District of Columbia has been under consideration.[72] Similar plans are recommended for study in Kentucky[73] and Baltimore, Maryland.[74] In November, Minnesota voters gave approval to a constitutional amendment to permit improving the handling of juvenile matters in the probate courts, and integrating such court more closely into the state's judicial structure.[75]

A far-reaching program for reorganizing the Wisconsin court system is being embodied in proposed constitutional amendments to be submitted to the 1955 legislature by the judicial council of that state.[76] As initially planned, the measures would replace county and municipal courts and justices of the peace with new circuit court branches, resulting in a simplified structure comprising only the circuit courts and the supreme court. Under Wisconsin procedure for constitutional amendment, the changes would require approval by two successive legislative sessions, followed by a popular referendum.[77]

Previously defeated proposals to consolidate the metropolitan courts in Detroit, Michigan, again failed to pass the legislature in 1954; but the Metropolitan Court Plan will receive additional study with a view toward possible renewed efforts in 1955.[78]

Court Administration, Congestion, and Statistics.—Calendar congestion and trial delays continue to occupy the attention of judges and court administrators, public and private agencies, and individuals concerned with improving the machinery of jus-

70. A Proposal for Dealing with Youth in the Courts, Report of Subcommittee on Youth and Family in the Courts to the Temporary Commission on the Courts of the State of New York (Nov. 1954).

71. Gellhorn, Children and Families in the Courts of New York City (1954).

72. Alexander, The Integrated Family Court, 21 J.B. Ass'n of D.C. 5 (1954); Bindeman, Comment on the Family Court Bill, 21 id. at 121.

73. See Ky. Stats. 1954, c. 281, directing the judicial council to investigate the desirability of a family court system.

74. Jones, From the State Capitals, Supplemental Rep. 2 (May 11, 1954).
75. Minn. Const. Art. VI, § 7, as amended, Nov. 2, 1954.
76. Jones, From the State Capitals (Dec. 29, 1954). See also, Hallows & DeWitt, The Need for Court Organization, [1954] Wis. L. Rev. 376.

77. See Judicial Administration Legislative Summary, 38 J. Am. Jud. Soc'y 22 (1954).

78. Ibid. See also, Mich. Pub. Acts 1954, No. 195, authorizing and directing the court administration to call an annual statewide meeting of judges to study the state's judicial system.

tice.[79] Nationwide figures for the state trial courts of general jurisdiction and comparable statistics for the federal district courts show some gains in 1954, but they also disclose that in some courts the problem is becoming more acute. The over-all average time interval from "at issue" to trial of civil jury cases for ninety-seven state trial courts was 11.1 months as compared with 11.5 months in 1953, a decrease of approximately 3.5 per cent. Comparable figures for the federal district courts show an increase from 7.5 months in 1953 to 8.3 months in 1954.[80] In nonjury civil cases, the state court averages decreased from 5.7 months to 5.1 months, while the federal figures increased from 7.4 months to 8.0 months.

Severe problems of state court jury trial delay are evident in the folowing figures: Queens County Supreme Court, New York —49 months (an increase from 42 months in 1953); Kings County Supreme Court—45 months (a decrease from 53 months); Worcester County Superior Court, Massachusetts—42 months (no change); New York County Supreme Court—37 months (a decrease from 43 months); Chicago Circuit Court and Superior Court—36 months.[81] In the federal district courts, the reported delays are greatest for civil jury cases in the Southern District of New York (44months) [82] and for nonjury cases in the Eastern District of New York (45.5 months) .[83]

Comments on the problem and demands or suggestion for its solution are not confined to professional journal or the reports of official agencies. The press and popular magazines are voicing an increasing concern, and calling for measures that will enable the courts to cope with the ever-growing volume of work.[84] The heart of the matter in the state courts, most people agree, is the automobile accident personal injury suit. Among the proposed cures there is bound to recur the suggestion, long and strongly opposed by substantially all lawyers and judges, to establish

79. Inst. of Jud. Admin., Calendar Status Study—1954 (June 30, 1954).

80. Annual Report of the Director of the Administrative Office of the United States Courts A-11 (1954). The federal court figures are for median rather than average intervals.

81. The 1954 figure for New York County represents personal injury cases only. Calendar Status Study, supra note 79, at 3.

82. Annual Report, supra note 80, at A-26. The figure is for personal injury cases only.

83. Id., Table C6. For a recent study of congestion and delays in civil matters in the state courts of Texas, see Stayton & Eubank, A Studay of Pendency in Texas Civil Litigation, 33 Texas L. Rev. 70 (1954).

84. See, e.g., Is Justice Breaking Down in U.S.?, U.S. News and World Report, Dec. 24, 1954, p. 27. For a summary of articles published in the Hartford Courant and the Bridgeport Sunday Post, see Demeusy, Justice in a Jam, 28 Conn. B.J. 369 (1954). For other references, see Nims, The Cost of Justice, 28 id. at 1.

automobile accident compensation commissions and transfer
from the courts all jurisdiction over automobile negligence
cases.[85] But, as has been pointed out, administrative agencies
themselves have not always provided the answer of simple, inex-
pensive and expeditious justice, and the cure might be worse
than the malady.[86]

There are, of course, many other proposed solutions. Where
the need for additional judges has been clearly established, additional judgeships should be created. Congress moved a considerable distance in this direction when it provided, by a law approved in February, for thirty additional judgeships, including
three for the courts of appeal, and twenty-seven for the district
courts.[87] But it fell short of going all the way, as the Director of
the Administrative Office has pointed out, because it failed to
provide an adequate increase in appropriations for the courts for
1955, and it failed to meet the full need for additional judgeships in the Southern District of New York, the Eastern District
of Pennsylvania, the Northern District of Ohio, and the Territory of Alaska.[88] In Maryland, the voters in November approved
a constitutional amendment providing for additional county
judgeships.[89]

An alternative to appointing additional judges is increased
flexibility in the use of judicial manpower already available. A
New Jersey statute facilitates more efficient use of the county,
superior, and county district court judges in that state on temporary assignment by the chief justice to other courts or counties
where needed,[90] as does a plan adopted in Wisconsin to eliminate
the need for calendar judges by providing a lot system of assign-
ing cases, thereby releasing such judges for trial service.[91] Elsewhere, more efficient operation of court calendars has been advocated as a solution in several reports and articles.[92]

No judicial system can operate with full effectiveness, however,
unless and until there is established a court administrator with

85. Demeusy, supra note 84, at 375.
86. Barnes, A Nobler Challenge, 38 J. Am. Jud. Soc'y 6 (1954).
87. Pub. L. No. 294, 83d Cong., 2d Sess. (Feb. 10, 1954), 68 Stat. 9, 28
U.S.C.A. § 132 (Supp. 1954).
88. Annual Report, supra note 80, at 1, 2.
89. Md. Const. Art. 4, §§ 3, 21, as amended, Nov. 2, 1954.
90. N.J. Laws 1954, c. 104.
91. Jones, From the State Capitals, Supplemental Rep. 1 (June 15, 1954).
See Rules of Civil and Criminal Practice of the Circuit Court of Milwaukee
County (Oct. 22, 1954).
92. Calendar Congestion—A Solution, 17 Queens B. Bull. 101, 105 (1954);
Evans, Calendar Congestion—A New Approach, 26 N.Y. St. B. Bull. 368
(1954); Notes, Efforts to Alleviate Calendar Congestion in the New York
Supreme Court: Preference Rules and Calendar Classification, 54 Col. L.
Rev. 110 (1954); Trial Calendar Advancement, 6 Stan. L. Rev. 323 (1954).

authority to supervise the housekeeping functions of the courts and the collection and promulgation of up-to-date statistics on court business. This fundamental truth is amply demonstrated by the annual reports as well as the achievements of such administrative offices as those of the United States courts,[93] New Jersey,[94] and Puerto Rico,[95] respectively. Recognition of it is gaining increasing support for the creation of similar offices in other states, such as the recent statute in Kentucky authorizing the appointment of an administrative director by the court of appeals[96] and recommendations advanced in Alabama,[97] Maryland,[98] Mississippi,[99] Ohio,[100] and Texas.[101]

The approach of the New York Temporary Commission on the Courts has been to propose an amendment to the judiciary law to create both a statewide judicial conference and local committees for court administration in each judicial department.[102] While there would be a state administrator for the conference, there would also be a local deputy administrator assigned to each departmental committee. The proposed measure has been criticized as inadequate and as falling short of the American Bar Association's minimum standard.[103]

Oklahoma presents a somewhat unusual picture. Trial court dockets in that state are in an up-to-date status, but the supreme court is heavily overcrowded.[104] As a remedy, a special committee

---

93. Annual Report, supra note 80.

94. Vanderbilt, The Courts, the Public and the Bar, 11 B. Bull. N.Y. County Lawyers Ass'n 303 (1954); Woelper, Court Reform in New Jersey, 28 Conn. B.J. 398 (1954).

95. Segundo Informe Anual del Director Administrativo de los Tribunales 1953-1954.

96. Ky. Acts 1954, c. 238.

97. Patton, The Functioning of Court Administrators, 15 Ala. Law. 386 (1954).

98. Judicial Administration Legislative Summary, 37 J. Am. Jud. Soc'y 152, 153 (1954).

99. Bunkley, Some Observations on Our Judicial System, 26 Miss. L.J. 1, 3 (1954).

100. Harris, A New Approach to an Old Problem, 27 Ohio Bar 595, 597 (1954).

101. Jones, From the State Capitals (Nov. 3, 1954). On the need for effective collection of court statistics in Texas, see Pitts, Civil Judicial Statistics, 17 Texas B.J. 591 (1954). For a complete statistical report on the work of the Virginia courts in 1953, see Va. Sup. Ct. of Appeals, Annual Report of the Executive Secretary 1953 25 (1954).

102. Preliminary Report, supra note 3, at 29; The Temporary Commission Reports on the Courts, 26 N.Y. St. B. Bull. 77, 94 (1954).

103. Karlen, supra note 67, at 1706. See also, Temporary Commission on the Courts, Public Hearings on Proposals for a Judicial Conference and on the Structure of the Courts and Their Practice and Procedure, Albany, N.Y. (June 29, 1954), 126-35.

104. Gable, What About the Future of the Administration of Justice in Oklahoma?, 25 Okla. B.J. 1825 (1954).

of the state bar association has proposed, for introduction in the 1955 legislature, a bill to establish a commission of seven members to be appointed by the supreme court to assist the court in handling cases on appeal.[105]

Pre-Trial.—If one can judge from the journals and reports, much was written or spoken on the subject of pre-trial in 1954, and almost all comment was favorable. While, as Judge Alfred P. Murrah, himself a strong champion of pre-trial, has pointed out, there are still those who "complain that pre-trial deprives them of the weapon of surprise to the detriment of their client's cause,"[106] growing experience with pre-trial in actual use has convinced increasing numbers of lawyers and judges of its value when properly utilized.

There are reports of its successful operation in Minnesota,[107] New Jersey,[108] North Dakota,[109] Rhode Island,[110] and Wisconsin,[111] as well as in Cleveland,[112] Detroit,[113] and the Federal District Court for the Eastern District of Louisiana.[114] The report from Minnesota contains illustrative forms of pre-trial notices, orders, and verdicts used in a district court of that state.[115] The Wisconsin article analyzes a number of specific matters such as the advantages of holding pre-trial at least one week before trial,[116] what part the pre-trial judge should play in settlement discussion,[117] and whether the same judge should both pre-try and later try the case.[118]

In New York, the use of pre-trial on a "mass" basis as a means toward clearing court calendars by securing settlements was resorted to in the Supreme Court of Kings County late in 1953.[119] Regular trials were suspended for approximately a month and

---

105. 25 id. at 1828.

106. Murrah, Some Bugaboos in Pre-Trial, 7 Vand. L. Rev. 603, 606 (1954).

107. Keyes, Beginnings in Pre-Trial, 38 Minn. L. Rev. 236 (1954).

108. Karcher, supra note 10, at 761.

109. Grimson, A Progress Report on Pre-Trial Conferences in North Dakota, 30 N.D.L. Rev. 85 (1954).

110. Curran, Pre-Trial, 2 R.I. Bar J., No. 9, p. 5 (1954).

111. Ryan & Wickhem, Pre-Trial Practice in Wisconsin Courts, [1954] Wis. L. Rev. 5.

112. Booth, Hon. William K. Thomas Addresses Bar's Fifth Informal Conference, 25 Cleveland B. Ass'n J. 113 (1954). See also, Thomas, Pre-Trial Procedure in Common Pleas Court Revamped, 25 Cuyahoga County B. Ass'n Bull., No. II, p. 2 (April 1954).

113. Jayne, Discovery and Pre-Trial, 22 Detroit Law. 117 (1954).

114. Wright, Pre-Trial on Trial, 14 La. L. Rev. 391 (1954).

115. Keyes, supra note 107, at 240, 242, 244.

116. Ryan & Wickhem, supra note 111, at 12.

117. Id. at 15.

118. Id. at 23.

119. Karlen, supra note 67, at 1709.

judicial manpower was concentrated on holding pre-trial conferences, with the result that over 55 per cent of the cases pre-tried
were disposed of.[120]

Two jurisdictions, Kansas[121] and Virginia,[122] have reported
disappointing results in their experience with the use of pre-trial,
due predominantly to lack of interest or to lack of understanding as to its proper functions. As pointed out in a review of the
experiments being conducted in Los Angeles County to determine whether pre-trial should become an integral part of the
judicial process: "If the pre-trial conference is to reach its most
effective application . . . the full cooperation of the bar must first
be obtained. Only when the true purposes of the pre-trial are
fully understood by the bar may this cooperation be realized."[123]

Rule-Making and Procedural Rules.—As in the case with pre-
trial, the trend toward vesting in the courts the full power to
adopt rules of procedure is gathering both interest and support.
An analysis of the status and scope of such power and its rela-
tionship to legislative authority in those states where rule-making
has been either fully or partially given to the courts is presented
in a comment on the adoption of rules of criminal procedure in
Missouri.[124] In another article, suggestions are given as to the
methods by which states desiring to adopt the federal rules
might proceed in order to achieve that goal.[125]

In states where courts already have the rule-making power,
such as Arizona, Colorado, Missouri, Nevada, New Jersey, and
Virginia, the process of revision and improvement is a continuing
one and represents the combined efforts of the bench and bar.[126]
Among the states where practice and procedure are still in the
legislative domain, the vesting of rule-making authority in the
courts has been advocated in Illinois,[127] Kansas,[128] and Ver-

---

120. 20 N.Y. Jud. Council Rep. 73 (1954).

121. Stavely, Pretrial—Five Years After, 2 Kan. L. Rev. 360 (1954).

122. McCarthy, Pre-Trial in Virginia, 40 Va. L. Rev. 359 (1954).

123. Ross, Suggested Application of the Pre-Trial Conference, 30 Los
Angeles B. Bull. 7, 31 (1954).

124. Note, Missouri Rules of Criminal Procedure: Their Effect on Statutes,
19 Mo. L. Rev. 70 (1954).

125. Hawkins, Mechanics of Adopting the Federal Rules for State Practice, 38 J. Am. Jud. Soc'y 57 (1954).

126. Conference of Chief Justices, Memorandum Report of the Committee
on the Administration of a State Judicial System 8 (1954). See also, Stayton,
New Jersey Revises Her Rules, 17 Texas B.J. 111 (1954).

127. Sears, supra note 1, at 804. See also, tentative draft of proposed judicial article, Art. VI, § 3.

128. Griffith, Civil Procedure Study Suggested, 22 J.B. Ass'n of Kan. 191
(1954).

129. Fifth Biennial Rep., Vt. Jud. Council 4 (1955).

mont,[129] and was unsuccessfully attemped in the 1954 Mississippi legislature.[130]

A substantial revision of the rules of the United States Supreme Court, incorporating changes in appellate procedure and practice, went into effect on July 1, 1954.[131] Meanwhile the restudy of the Federal Rules of Civil Procedure by an advisory committee continues, with a view toward needed amendments.[132]

In Puerto Rico, under Section 6 of Article V of the new Constitution, the supreme court has the power to adopt rules of civil and criminal procedure and of evidence, such rules to be submitted to the legislature and thereafter to become effective if the legislature fails to act on them. Implementing the authority thus granted, committees appointed by the supreme court have drafted proposed rules of evidence[133] as well as proposed rules of civil procedure,[134] and the drafts have been submitted to the bar for criticism and suggestions.

Jurors and Jury Selection.—One of the weaknesses of the jury system in many states, as pointed out by Judge Florence E. Allen of the United States Court of Appeals for the Sixth Circuit, is the large number of exemptions granted by statutes to various categories of citizens.[135] A noteworthy remedial step was taken in Kentucky with the enactment of legislation ending the exemptions previously given to some sixty classes of citizens, and placing in the trial judges the discretion as to who shall be excused as well as the power to appoint jury commissioners and supervise their work.[136]

Signs of progress toward equality of the sexes were manifested in Texas, where the voters in November approved a constitutional amendment permitting women to serve on juries,[137] and in South Carolina where a similar step was urged by Governor Byrnes.[138] But a bill introduced in Congress to provide that no

---

130. Miss. H. No. 399 (1954).

131. Wiener, The New Supreme Court Practice: A Summary of the New Rules, 40 A.B.A.J. 659 (1954); Wiener, The Supreme Court's New Rules, 68 Harv. L. Rev. 20 (1954).

132. Wright, Amendments to the Federal Rules: The Function of a Continuing Rules Committee, 7 Vand. L. Rev. 521 (1954).

133. Comite Consultivo sobre las Reglas de Evidencia, Borrador del Proyecto de Reglas de Evidencia para el Tribunal General de Justicia de Puerto Rico (Oct. 1954).

134. Comite Consultivo sobre las Reglas de Enjuiciamiento Civil para el Tribunal General de Justicia de Puerto Rico (Oct. 1954).

135. Allen, Trial by Jury, 15 Ala. Law. 437 (1954).

136. Ky. Acts 1954, c. 7.

137. Tex. Const. Art. XVI, § 19, as amended, Nov. 2, 1954.

138. Jones, From the State Capitals, Supplemental Rep. 1 (Jan. 18, 1954).

citizen shall be excluded from service as a juror by reason of her sex[139] was not enacted into law.

Other steps to enhance the attractiveness as well as citizen understanding of jury service have been adopted or recommended. An increase in jury fees from $4 to $8 per diem was enacted in Michigan.[140] A similar doubling of the present fee from $3 to $6 is being recommended by the Judicial Conference in Missouri,[141] and an increase to $15 has been advocated by the Massachusetts Judicial Council.[142] To inform prospective jurors of their functions and duties, handbooks have been adopted for distribution in Florida,[143] Missouri,[144] and New York.[145]

New York's hitherto complex system of jury selection has been unified, on recommendation of the judicial council,[146] by adoption of a uniform provision comparable to that already in effect in New York City, providing for centralized selection in each county, administered by a jury commissioner under the supervision of a county jury board.[147] The enactment supersedes some 164 or more separate statutes dealing with jury selection.[148] The establishment of a jury commissioner in each county has also been recommended by the Judicial Council of North Carolina.[149]

An interesting survey of jurors has been conducted for the Annual Conference of the Tenth Judicial Circuit of the United States.[150] Questionnaires mailed to jurors who had served in that circuit included questions on the clarity and effectiveness of the judges' instructions, the possible impact of pressures to reach agreement, and factors considered by jurors in determining damages.

Traffic Courts and Justices of the Peace.—Much of the activity in 1954 in the area of traffic law enforcement centered in regional and statewide conferences of traffic court judges and prosecutors, under the auspices of the American Bar Association Special Committee on Traffic Court Program and the Northwestern Univer-

---

139. H.R. 7652, 83d Cong., 2d Sess. (1954).

140. Mich. Pub. Acts 1954, No. 57.

141. Letter to Institute of Judicial Administration from Judge Laurance M. Hyde (Dec. 23, 1954).

142. Report of the Special Committee on Court Congestion, 25 B. Bull. Boston B. Ass'n 219 (1954).

143. Fla. B. Ass'n, . . . and Justice for All (1954).

144. Missouri Supreme Court, Rule 3.30 (1954).

145. New York Supreme Court, A Handbook for Trial Jurors (1954).

146. 20 N.Y. Jud. Council Rep. 157 (1954).

147. N.Y. Laws 1954, c. 305.

148. Karlen, supra note 67, at 1711.

149. Third Rep., N.C. Jud. Council 17 (1954).

150. A Report on a Survey of Tenth Circuit Jurors, 25 Okla. B.J. 1434 (1954).

sity Traffic Institute.[151] Among the recommendations emphasized
at such conferences were the integration of traffic courts into the
state's judicial system[152] and the elimination of traffic ticket
fixing.[153] Similar conferences and groups in other states have
advocated uniform standards of court policy and standards of
enforcement in traffic cases;[154] the creation of a special traffic
court for Chicago;[155] and stricter methods of enforcement against
violators.[156]

Attempts to eliminate or supplant existing justice of the peace
systems continue to encounter determined opposition. A decision
of the Washington Supreme Court has held invalid certain provisions of recent legislation enacted to establish justice court
district committees with power to create new justice of the peace
districts in that state.[157] And justices of the peace in Michigan,
having defeated efforts to eliminate them, have formed an association to study methods of improving their procedures and
status.[158] Bar association and legislative committees are continuing to study the subject of needed changes to insure the capable
administration of justice at the basic level of the justice of the
peace court.[159]

Conclusion.—What does it all add up to? For the year 1954,
"something attempted; something done," but as yet no clear en-
titlement to a night's repose in the continuing and vigilant effort
to achieve the ideal of modern and efficient judicial administration in every jurisdiction. "Judicial reform is everybody's business, but leadership in judicial reform is your business—the
business of the lawyers and judges of America. . . . "[160]

151. A.B.A., Report of the Special Committee on Traffic Court Program,
A.B.A. Advance Program, 77th Annual Meeting 92 (1954).
152. Traffic Courts Conference, 17 Texas B.J. 705 (1954).
153. Ibid.; South Dakota's First Traffic Court Conference, 23 S.D.B.J. 16
(1954).
154. Traffic Enforcement: A Joint Enterprise, 39 Minn. Municipalities 210
(1954); Traffic Cases, 14 Justice Court Topics, No. 5, p. 5 (1954).
155. Scheffler, Traffic Courts and Their Role in Traffic Enforcement, 35
Chi. B. Record 229 (1954).
156. Minn. St. B. Ass'n, Report of Committee on Traffic Law Enforcement,
11 Bench & Bar of Minn., No. 11, p. 85 (1954).
157. Manus v. Snohomish County Justice Court, 44 Wash. 893, 271 P.2d
707 (1954).
158. Michigan Justices Are Winning, 14 Justice Court Topics, No. 9, p. 7
(1954).
159. N.Y. St. B. Ass'n, Report of Committee on Administration of Justices'
Courts 301 (1954); Justices of the Peace, Bull. Rep. by Ill. Legis. Council
(May 1954); Preparing for 1955 Legislation, 14 Justice Court Topics, No. 11,
p. 1 (1954).
160. Winters, supra note 7, at 237.

JUDICIAL ADMINISTRATION — 1955 *

For a year in which most of the state legislatures were in regular session, 1955 was disappointing to those who looked for accelerated nation-wide progress in judicial administration. But "disappointing" does not mean "discouraging" and there were sufficient achievements in several states to counterbalance setbacks or "no progress" in others.

Apart from legislative activity, however, there were signs of promise and revivals of interest in underlying concepts just as significant for their part in keeping alive public and professional interest in improving the fundamental bases of the administration of justice. In a provocative volume on law reform, comprising the William H. White Lectures delivered at the University of Virginia in 1954, Chief Justice Arthur T. Vanderbilt speaks out against abuses causing unreasonable court delays and outmoded theories of justice.[1] Among the needed improvements he particularly stresses are: the selection of judges and jurors, simplified court structure, better court administration, pre-trial and other procedures for clarifying issues and shortening trials, judicial conferences, and improved law-making techniques through the development of law centers.

The basic essentials of a modern court system were also reviewed and restated by Judge Laurance M. Hyde, one of the country's leaders in the field of judicial administration, whose summary discusses the need for centralized administrative authority, for an administrative office, for rules of practice and procedure, for judicial regulation of bar admission and discipline, for nonpartisan selection and tenure of judges, for adequate compensation and retirement, and for respectable courts of limited jurisdiction.[2] Also, former President McWilliams of the Pennsylvania State Bar Association has reviewed the history of Anglo-American judicial reform as exemplifying the dynamism of the legal profession.[3]

On the broader over-all subject of law and justice, there is a

---

* Reprinted from *New York University Law Review;* January 1956, Vol. 31, No. 1, pp. 162-181; 1955 Annual Survey of American Law. This Survey article represents the joint work of members of the Institute's staff in assembling, analyzing, and presenting the material covered.

1. Vanderbilt, The Challenge of Law Reform (1955).
2. Hyde, Essentials of a Modern State Judicial System, 30 Notre Dame Law. 227 (1955).
3. McWilliams, The Law: A Dynamic Profession, 41 A.B.A.J. 18 (1955).

continuing interest in the potentialities of a national ministry of justice, whose function it would be to concern itself with the whole problem of law reform. In articles describing the scope and approach of the proposal, Chief Justice Vanderbilt notes three major divisions comprising the problem: first, the shortcomings, either legal or social, of the substantive law; second, "procedure which should always be merely a means to an end, and that end the achievement of justice"; and third, "overcoming any deficiencies in personnel and the coordination thereof in an effective judicial establishment."[4] Dean Harno of Illinois has developed a similar thesis in outlining the function of a ministry of justice and the role of the law school in relation thereto.[5]

General Revisions and Surveys.—High hopes for legislative approval this year of a proposed new judicial article for the Illinois constitution were dashed in June. The house resolution, after having been voted out of committee, was tabled by a seventy-four to seventy roll-call vote in the closing days of the session.[6] This marks the second defeat of a far-reaching program for revising and improving the Illinois judicial system, despite stalwart support for it by citizen groups and by the Illinois State and Chicago Bar Associations.[7]

Meanwhile, Florida achieved substantial progress toward revision of its judicial article by the legislative passage of a proposed constitutional amendment to come before the voters in November 1956.[8] It would create intermediate district courts of appeal to lighten the supreme court's present case overload, empower the supreme court to adopt rules governing practice and procedure in all courts, establish machinery for removing judges for disability, and provide for mandatory retirement of judges at age seventy. Dropped from the proposed amendment, however, was a provision initially included by the judicial council to enable adoption of a plan for nonpartisan selection and tenure of judges.[9]

---

4. Vanderbilt, The Idea of a Ministry of Justice Considered and Its Functions Distributed, 22 D.C.B.J. 346, 351 (1955). See also his address at the Syracuse University convocation for the dedication of Ernest I. White Hall, College of Law, 6 Syracuse L. Rev. 225 (1955).

5. Harno, A Ministry of Justice, 39 J. Am. Jud. Soc'y 35 (1955). For a selected bibliography of materials pertaining to the purposes of and duties of such a ministry, see Inst. Jud. Admin., Ministry of Justice (June 25, 1954).

6. Ill. H.J. Res. 16 (1955). A companion measure in the Senate, Ill. Sen. J. Res. 17 (1955), was not brought up for action.

7. For an analysis of Illinois problems, and of the proposed amendment as offered in 1955, see Cedarquist, The Continuing Need for Judicial Reform in Illinois, 4 De Paul L. Rev. 153 (1955).

8. Fla. Proposed Const. Amend. No. 1, Committee Substitute for H.J. Res. 810 (1955).

9. Judicial Council Recommendations, 29 Fla. B.J. 384 (1955).

In Minnesota the 1955 legislature passed, for submission to the people next year, an extensive revision of the state constitution's judicial article.[10] If approved, it would abolish justice courts and transfer their jurisdiction to district courts; two additional supreme court judges would be authorized; district judges could be temporarily assigned to the supreme court; all judicial terms would be fixed at six years; and the legislature would be empowered to provide for retirement of judges. The amendment also omits the present requirement that "legal pleadings and proceedings in the courts of this State shall be under the direction of the legislature."[11]

Wisconsin also initiated steps toward revising its constitutional provisions on the judiciary. A proposed amendment passed by the 1955 legislature will, if passed again by the legislature in 1957 and approved by the people, vest all judicial power *in* the supreme court, circuit courts, and justice courts, with branches of the circuit court taking over work done by other lower or special courts.[12] While the proposal as originally introduced would have abolished the justice courts, they were restored by amendment in the course of passage.

In the realm of state-wide surveys published during the year, unquestionably the most graphic was issued by the Asociation of the Bar of the City of New York. Under the colorful title "Bad Housekeeping," it deals with the administration of the New York courts, and points up the evils and shortcomings of the present system.[13] It also offers a plan for administration of the New York courts,[14] as will be noted later.

Other and less extensive state surveys include a summary review of judicial-administration developments in Kentucky since 1950, with proposals for the future;[15] and a report on the operation of the New Jersey courts for the year 1953-54.[16] The latter report contains a discussion of proposals and progress in the field of criminal justice.[17]

With a broader outlook, the American Bar Association is planning to undertake a study of the operation of the system of criminal justice in the United States. The project will ultimately cover both state and federal jurisdictions, its purpose being "to

---

10. Minn. Laws 1955, c. 881.
11. Minn. Const. art. 6, § 14.
12. Wis. Sen. J. Res. 25 (1955).
13. Ass'n of B. of City of N.Y., Bad Housekeeping (1955).
14. Id. at 150.
15. Eblen, Judicial Improvement in Kentucky, 19 Ky. State B.J. 182 (1955).
16. Vanderbilt, The Record of the New Jersey Courts in the Sixth Year Under the Constitution of 1947, 9 Rutgers L. Rev. 489 (1955).
17. Id. at 493.

provide what will be accepted as an authoritative foundation upon which sound and lasting remedial measures may be based."[18]

Proposed official surveys have been authorized in several jurisdictions. For example, Governor Herter of Massachusetts has appointed a commission to conduct a survey of that state's judicial system.[19] The Pennsylvania legislature has directed a joint state government commission to study and report on the court system, problems of court administration, congestion of dockets, possible rule-making power for the supreme court in criminal cases, reduction of costs of litigation, and allied problems.[20] And in the United States Congress, the House Committee on the Judiciary has been authorized to conduct a study relating to administration and personnel of the federal courts and local courts in the territories and possessions.[21]

Judicial Selection and Tenure.—As previously noted, the Florida Judicial Council's original proposal with respect to nonpartisan selection and tenure of judges was not included in the measure ultimately passed.[22] Also, as noted, the projected new Illinois judicial article, even with amendments limiting the application of a commission method of judicial selection, failed of passage.[23] It is evident that resistance to adoption of the Missouri or American Bar Association plan, even in modified form, continues to outweigh the efforts of proponents of a change, not only in Florida and Illinois, but also in other states. Thus, proposed constitutional amendments for nonpartisan systems of judicial selection failed to receive legislative approval in Kansas,[24] New Mexico,[25] Oklahoma,[26] and Wisconsin.[27] On the other hand, a proposal to amend Missouri's constitution so as to remove appellate judges from that state's judicial selection plan, and to reduce their terms to six years, was not passed by the legislature.[28]

---

18. Survey of Criminal Justice: A Research Effort of the Legal Profession, 41 A.B.A.J. 827 (1955). For a detailed description of the project, see American Bar Foundation, The Administration of Criminal Justice in the United States, Plan for Survey (1955).

19. Commission to Conduct Survey of Massachusetts Judicial System Appointed by Governor Herter, 40 Mass. L.Q. 109 (1955).

20. Pa. H. Res. 62 (1955).

21. H.R. Res. 22, 84th Cong., 1st Sess. (1955).

22. Judicial Council Recommendations, 29 Fla. B.J. 384 (1955). On judicial selection at the supreme court level, see Parsons, The Selection and Tenure of Florida Supreme Court Judges, 9 Miami L.Q. 271 (1955).

23. See note 6 supra.

24. Kan. Sen. Con. Res. 3 (1955).

25. N.M. Sen. J. Res. 24 (1955).

26. Okla. H.J. Res. 525 (1955).

27. Wis. Sen. J. Res. 31 (1955).

28. Mo. J. Con. Res. 12 (1955).

And a legislative attempt in Montana to remove judges from the nonpartisan ticket and place them on a partisan ballot was similarly unsuccessful.[29]

Elsewhere, the matter of judicial selection and tenure was the subject of trenchant comment and concern. The Pennsylvania plan for selecting judges, supported by some bar leaders[30] and opposed by others,[31] languished in legislative committee.[32] Meanwhile a committee of the Michigan State Bar recommended that lawyers assist in the circulation of initiative petitions for constitutional amendment based on the American Bar Association Plan,[33] and the Colorado Bar Association, at its annual meeting, launched a new drive for the nonpartisan selection of judges. Legislative approval for the proposed new system in Colorado, based on the Missouri plan, probably will not be sought until the 1957 legislative session.[34] The president of the Association of the Bar of the City of New York has urged the adoption of a short ballot and the selection of judges by other means than popular election.[35] But the appointive method of judicial selection, particularly as exemplified by the federal system, has come in for its share of critical comment during the year.[36]

Judicial Salaries and Retirement.—The picture in respect to judicial salaries in 1955 is considerably more encouraging than that of judicial selection and tenure. Twenty-seven states enacted increases for at least some of their judiciary,[37] and, as stated in last year's *Survey,* salary increases for federal judges were enacted by Congress.[38]

Spurred by the pointed challenge of the chief justice of its supreme court in 1954,[39] Ohio has provided salary increases for its appellate and lower court judges. The salary of the chief jus-

---

29. Mont. Sen. B. 148 (1955).

30. Harris, Report of the Committee on the Pennsylvania Plan for Selecting Judges, 26 Pa. B. Ass'n Q. 355 (1955); Langdon W. Harris, Jr., 18 Shingle 126 (1955). See also McWilliams, On Selecting Our Judges, 2 Temp. L. Reporter 1 (Feb. 7, 1955).

31. Report, The Pennsylvania Plan for Selecting Judges, 2 Temp. L. Reporter 1 (Jan. 3, 1955).

32. Pa. H.B. 974 (1955).

33. Committee on Judicial Selection and Tenure, 34 Mich. State B.J. 43 (Sept. 1955).

34. Jones, From the State Capitals (Supp. Rep. Oct. 22, 1955).

35. Klots, The Selection of Judges and the Short Ballot, 10 Record B. Ass'n City of N.Y. 103 (1955), 27 N.Y.S.B. Bull. 38 (1955).

36. Bloch, The Selection of Judges: The Independence of the Federal Courts, 41 A.B.A.J. 507 (1955); Miller, Federal Judicial Appointments: The Continuing Struggle for Good Judges, 41 id. 125.

37. Inst. Jud. Admin., Check-list Summary of 1955 Developments in Judicial Administration 8-11 (Aug. 1, 1955).

38. 1954 Ann. Survey Am. L. 832, 30 N.Y.U.L. Rev. 969 (1955).

39. Chief Justice Weygandt Resigns, 27 Ohio Bar 1085 (1954).

tice is increased by $3,500, bringing it to $20,000, and that of the associate justices is increased $2,000 to a total of $18,000; court of appeals judges will receive $17,000, an increase of $2,500.[40] Perhaps a more important move than the isolated enactment of salary increases was the passage by both houses of a proposed constitutional amendment to remove the prohibition against increasing judicial salaries during term of office.[41] The amendment, however, was rejected by the voters in November.[42]

Among the more substantial increases were those enacted in Connecticut, Illinois, Kansas, Massachusetts, Oregon, Tennessee, and West Virginia. In Connecticut and West Virginia raises were as high as $5,000. Connecticut's chief justice of the supreme court of errors received an increase from $15,000 to $20,000 and the associate justices from $15,000 to $19,000. The superior court and common pleas judges were also the beneficiaries of salary increases in the same bill.[43] West Virginia gave a flat raise of $5,000 to the judges of its supreme court of appeals, bringing their salary to $17,500.[44] Both Kansas and Illinois provided salary increases for their judiciary. In the former the governor approved measures, to take effect in January 1957, increasing the chief justice's salary from $10,000 to $13,000, and that of the associate justices from $10,000 to $12,000.[45] District court judges[46] and certain minor court judges[47] also received increases. In Illinois increases of $4,000 for supreme court judges and $2,500 for the circuit and superior court judges were passed, bringing their salaries respectively to $24,000 and $15,000.[48] Massachusetts, although rejecting a bill which would have given all state judges a 25 per cent pay raise,[49] did enact increases of $3,500 for the supreme judicial court and $3,000 for the superior and land courts, bringing their totals to $23,000 for the chief justice, $22,000 for associate justices, $20,000 for the chief justice of the superior court, and $19,000 for associate superior court judges and land court judges.[50] The same measure provided varying increases for probate judges in designated counties. In another bill certain district court salaries were raised from $9,900 to $12,000.[51]

40. Ohio Sen. B. 219 (1955).
41. Ohio Sen. J. Res. 3 (1955).
42. Dayton Daily News, Nov. 9, 1955, p. 1, col. 7.
43. Conn. Pub. Acts 1955, No. 411.
44. W. Va. Acts 1955, c. 160.
45. Kan. Laws 1955, c. 374.
46. Kan. Laws 1955, c. 375.
47. Kan. H.B. 9, Sen. B. 117, 158, 196, 231 (1955).
48. Ill. Sen. B. 534 (1955).
49. Check-list Summary, supra note 37, at 12.
50. Mass. Acts 1955, c. 733.
51. Mass. Acts 1955, c. 334.

A Nevada bill,[52] proposing an increase from $15,000 to $20,000 for its supreme court justices, died in committee, but increased compensation was enacted for their duties performed in connection with the Statute Revision Commission.[53] In Arizona a proposed $5,500 raise for supreme court justices failed of enactment,[54] as did salary increases in Colorado,[55] New York,[56] and New Jersey (vetoed by governor).[57] The proposed salary raise in Pennsylvania[58] appears destined to die in committee. It would provide increases ranging from $12,750 for the chief justice of the supreme court to $11,500 for judges of the superior court.

Among retirement provisions, important changes were effected in Delaware, Florida, and Nebraska. The Delaware legislation, providing retirement pensions to members of the state judiciary, sets the amount of the annual pension by taking the average annual salary of a judge during his five highest paid years, multiplying it by 2 per cent, and then multiplying the product by the number of years he has served.[59] In Florida supreme and circuit court judges are now eligible for retirement at age sixty and after ten years of judicial service, or after twenty years service without regard to age.[60] The Nebraska measure provides for the retirement of district and supreme court judges, with mandatory retirement at age seventy. The retirement fund will be built up by contributions from judges' salaries and a percentage of court costs, with the legislature making up any deficit. A special board is created to administer the fund.[61]

In Wisconsin the proposed constitutional amendment to provide for mandatory retirement of supreme and circuit court judges at age seventy was ratified by the voters at an election in April 1955.[62] Provision is made for the temporary recall of retired judges to judicial service to relieve court congestion. Two other states, Georgia by constitutional amendment[63] and North Carolina by statute,[64] provide that retired judges may be called back for temporary service. In Massachusetts a resolution to provide

52. Nev. Sen. B. 204 (1955).
53. Nev. Stat. 1955, c. 248.
54. Ariz. H.B. 260 (1955).
55. Colo. H.B. 89, 102 (1955).
56. N.Y. Sen. B. 2533, 2570, 2723, 3358 (1955).
57. N.J. Assembly No. 431 (1955).
58. Pa. H.B. 775 (1955).
59. Del. Laws 1955, c. 119.
60. Fla. Laws 1955, c. 29838.
61. Neb. Legis. B. 38 (1955).
62. Wis. Sen. J. Res. 10 (1955).
63. Ga. H. Res. 13-34a (1955).
64. Jones, From the State Capitals 4 (Supp. Rep. April 22, 1955).

for temporary service of semi-retired judges of the superior court
was defeated.[65]

Widows of judges received the benefit of legislation in Colorado,[66] Maryland, and Oregon. Maryland, in the same bill
which increased judicial pensions, for the first time provides a
pension for the widows of judges.[67] In Oregon widows will receive pensions from the Judges' Retirement Fund if the judge
dies after more than six years of judicial service.[68]

In four states retirement provisions failed of enactment. Rhode
Island voters defeated a proposed constitutional amendment providing tenure for supreme and superior court judges up to the
age of seventy and after fifteen years on the bench.[69] The amendment would have assured pensions after the fifteen-year period.
Similar provisions for retirement and pension benefits were defeated in the Montana[70] and Vermont[71] legislatures. An Ohio
proposal, which would have established an independent judges'
retirement system, died in house committee.[72] Official results of
retirement measures in several other states, as of November 30,
1955, have not yet been reported.[73]

In Iowa a resolution was adopted directing the governor to
appoint a committee to study the retirement system of judges.[74]
At their second annual conference Michigan judges recommended that retired judges be available for recall.[75]

Judicial Conduct, Discipline, and Removal.—The American
Bar Foundation has announced a projected study of the Canons
of Professional Ethics and the Canons of Judicial Ethics,[76] with
the object of determining if any of them require rewriting in
the light of new conditions. Concerning the specific and controversial subject of Judicial Canon 35, publicizing proceedings, an
article has offered the suggestion that the filming or taping of
judicial proceedings for release *after* completion of a trial would

---

65. Mass. H. No. 2801 (1955).

66. Colo. H.B. 269 (1955).

67. Md. Laws 1955, c. 639.

68. Ore. H.B. 149 (1955).

69. R.I. Pub. Laws 1955, c. 3487; The Providence Journal, July 13, 1955,
p. 1, col. 8.

70. Mont. H.B. 157 (1955).

71. Vt. H. 424 (1955).

72. Ohio H.B. 538 (1955).

73. N.J. Sen. B. 342 (1955) and Pa. H.B. 774 (1955) are still pending in
committee.

74. Iowa Sen. Con. Res. 30 (1955).

75. Jones, From the State Capitals (Supp. Rep. Sept. 16, 1955).

76. American Bar Foundation Begins Canons of Ethics Study, 41 A.B.A.J.
805 (1955).

eliminate the serious objections to such publicity.[77] Opposing any change in Canon 35, Judge Florence E. Allen has expressed the belief that it should be strictly enforced.[78]

New York passed for the second time, and the voters approved, a constitutional amendment prohibiting judges of courts, other than justice or police courts, from holding other public office.[79] The amendment applies only to counties with a population of 120,000 or more, and does not extend to other judicial and military office. The former prohibition applied only to judges of the court of appeals and justices of the supreme court.[80] In Minnesota a constitutional amendment, now awaiting approval by the people, provides for the immediate termination of office of any judge upon his filing as a candidate for election to any other than a judicial office.[81] Legislation in New Jersey and Puerto Rico has not yet been given final action.[82]

Judicial Councils and Judicial Conferences.—New York has created a new judicial conference with the objective of improving its present system of judicial administration,[83] following the recommendation of the Temporary Commission on the Courts.[84] As adopted, the act falls somewhat short of providing the conference with the powers and duties recommended in the previously mentioned plan of the Association of the Bar of the City of New York.[85] The conference, to be composed of nine judges, replaces the judicial council, and will study and make recommendations concerning the organization, jurisdiction, rules and precedure, administration, judicial assignments, and preservation of records of all state courts. Collection of judicial statistics will be within its purview. The structure of the conference includes departmental committees for court administration and departmental conferences, and provides for the appointment of a state admin-

---

77. Shuman, Publicizing Judicial Proceedings, 1 Wayne L. Rev. 1 (1954). The author's approach seeks to explain away the arguments for the unrevised continuation of canon 35 of the ABA Canons of Judicial Ethics, which presently forbids the publication of judicial proceedings by photographs, radio, or television.

78. Allen, Fair Trial and Free Press: No Fundamental Clash Between the Two, 41 A.B.A.J. 897, 900 (1955).

79. N.Y. Sen. B. 31 (1955); N.Y. Times, Nov. 10, 1955, p. 1, col. 3.

80. N.Y. Const. art. VI, § 19.

81. Minn. Laws 1955, c. 881.

82. N.J. Sen. B. 263 (1955) would provide that municipal magistrates who have served for nine years shall continue to hold office during good behavior and shall not be removed except for good cause after a hearing on written charges. P.R. Sen. B. 571 (1955) provides that no supreme court justice, on resigning, can engage in the practice of law until eight years have elapsed from the date of taking office.

83. N.Y. Laws 1955, c. 869.

84. Report of the Temporary Commission on the Courts 11 (Feb. 17, 1955).

85. Ass'n of B. of City of N.Y., Bad Housekeeping 150 (1955).

istrator to assist the conference in executing its duties. Strong
criticism of the New York measure has come from several sources,
decrying the lack of real authority in the conference.[86]

An Oregon bill establishing a judicial council, prepared in
1954 and reported in last year's *Survey*,[87] was enacted into law.[88]
The council, consisting of the justices of the supreme court and
the judges of other courts of record, is charged with making a
continuous survey of the organization, procedures, and methods
of administration of the various courts of the state.

Delaware's newly created Council on the Administration of
Justice[89] has duties and powers similar to those enumerated
above. Ten of the places on the council are *ex officio* (e.g., chief
justice, speaker of the house, attorney general, and president of
the state university), and five will be filled by nonlawyers appointed by the governor.

Surprisingly, the elimination by Michigan of its judicial council[90] presents an encouraging move in unifying court administration. The chief functions of the council, including the collection
and publication of judicial statistics, will be assumed by the
office of the court administrator, which was granted authority for
such activities by its enabling statute.[91] With this step and the
annual conferences mentioned below, Michigan has completed
the centralization of the administrative duties of its courts,[92] long
a major goal of leaders in court reform.[93] In September of 1955
a comprehensive program of judicial reforms was adopted by
Michigan's ninety-five judges at their second annual conference
of judges.[94] Included were recommendations for the recall of
retired judges and the establishment of intermediate appellate
courts. The court administrator, in 1954, was authorized to call
annual conferences of the state judges, under the direction of
the chief justice, for the purpose of studying and making
recommendations for the improvement of the judicial system.[95]

Court Integration and Unification.—As discussed earlier, thor-

86. Vanderbilt, The Challenge of Law Reform 121-32 (1955); Nims, The
Bar: A Sleeping Giant, 41 A.B.A.J. 908, 911 (1955).
87. 1954 Ann. Survey Am. L. 836, 30 N.Y.U.L. Rev. 973 (1955).
88. Ore. H.B. 150 (1955)
89. Del. Laws 1955, c. 18.
90. Mich. Pub. Acts 1955, No. 180.
91. Mich. Stat. Ann. §§ 27.15 (1) -27.15 (7) (Callaghan Supp. 1953).
92. For a full description of the duties performed by the Michigan Court
Administrator, see Inst. Jud. Admin., Court Administration 16-18 (Aug. 1,
1955).
93. See Vanderbilt, Minimum Standards of Judicial Administration 29
(1949). See also Vanderbilt, The Challenge of Law Reform (1955); Hyde,
supra note 2.
94. Jones, From the State Capitals (Supp. Rep. Sept. 16, 1955).
95. Mich. Pub. Acts 1954, No. 195.

oughgoing plans for consolidation and simplification of existing court systems were adopted in Florida,[96] Minnesota,[97] and Wisconsin,[98] while Illinois rejected for the second time a proposed new judicial article for its constitution.[99] The amendment would have provided a modernized court structure consisting of a supreme court, appellate and circuit courts, and a centralized administrative authority. A Vermont resolution directs the governor to appoint a commission to review the justice of the peace, municipal, and probate court systems of the state, with a view to reorganizing the court structure.[100]

In New York there has been heavy resistance to a simplified court system proposed by a subcommittee of the Temporary Commission on the Courts.[101] If adopted, the new system would make sweeping changes in the present structure, combining some eighteen types of courts now existent[102] into a unified and flexible system of five state-wide courts.[103] Although receiving some support from citizens' groups and bar associations, vehement opposition to the plan has arisen from many jurists and lawyers throughout the state in a series of public hearings conducted by the Temporary Commission.[104]

Consolidation in Connecticut met defeat without even coming to a final vote in the legislature. A bill providing for an integrated court system consisting of five divisions died in the house,[105] after senate passage, and a proposal to combine the superior court and the court of common pleas died in committee.[106] Failing to pass in Maryland were bills proposing a constitutional amendment to consolidate the common-law, criminal, and equity courts of Baltimore into one court,[107] while Michigan's metropolitan court plan for Detroit, integrating inferior courts in Wayne County, was also rejected by the legislature.[108]

---

96. Fla. Proposed Const. Amend. No. 1, Committee Substitute for H.J. Res. 810 (1955).

97. Minn. Laws 1955, c 881.

98. Wis. Sen. J. Res. 25 (1955).

99. Ill. H.J. Res. 16 (1955).

100. Vt. Sen. J. Res. 45 (1955).

101. A Proposed Simplified State-Wide Court System, Report of the Subcommittee on Modernization and Simplification of the Court Structure (June 17, 1955). See also Loeb, A Proposal for a Simplified Court Structure, 27 N.Y.S.B. Bull. 266 (1955).

102. A Proposed Simplified State-Wide Court System, supra note 101, at 33.

103. Id. at 1-7.

104. N.Y. Times, Oct. 27, 1955, p. 24, col. 2; id., Oct. 25, 1955, p. 35, col. 1; id., Oct. 22, 1955, p. 20, col. 2; id., Oct. 21, 1955, p. 56, col. 7; id., Oct. 17, 1955, p. 29, col. 1; id., Oct. 12, 1955, p. 1, col. 2.

105. Conn. Sen. B. 52 (1955).

106. Conn. H.B. 1083 (1955).

107. Md. H.B. 257, 642 (1955).

108. Mich. H.B. 451 (1955).

In the federal sphere, President Eisenhower has given full support to a six-point program for reducing delays in the United States courts. Included are proposals to create some twenty new judgeships and to send legal "task forces" from Washington to help clear up backlogs in congested federal court districts.[109]

Youth and family courts were the subject of action and comment in several states. In Maine the judicial council was requested to study and report to the 1957 legislature the desirability of creating a district court system, one feature of which would be the removal of domestic relations problems from the jurisdiction of the superior court.[110] New Hampshire directed its judicial council to institute a study of the jurisdiction of municipal courts and inquire into the advisability of establishing special courts for the administration of juvenile cases.[111] Very well received in New York City was the creation, by court rule, of a new family part of the supreme court,[112] which became effective September 1, 1955. Its purpose is to have all phases of matrimonial or child-custody litigation in the supreme court considered by the justice holding the family part.

In an article recommending a youth court for Detroit, Michigan, on the theory that there already exists sufficient statutory authority to create the new court, special treatment was urged for offenders in the seventeen to twenty-one age bracket.[113] Commenting on the growing movement to establish juvenile and family courts, a sociologist, in discussing the socio-legal implications of such courts, suggested that a more cautious attitude be adopted—that bar associations require tangible proof of the effectiveness of family and youth courts before supporting their proponents.[114]

Court Administration, Congestion, and Statistics.—Of increasing concern in the picture of judicial administration is the growing congestion of cases in the federal courts. For the year ending June 30, 1955, the median time for disposition of civil cases in all federal districts rose to 14.6 months.[115] Tied directly to this problem is the declared need for additional federal judges, set forth in the President's previously mentioned support for the creation of new judgeships. Since 1941 the number of private

109. N.Y. Times, Oct. 22, 1955, p. 1, col. 8.
110. Me. Laws 1955, c. 77.
111. N.H. Laws 1955, c. 335.
112. Special Term Rule VIII-a, Supreme Court, New York County. See 134 N.Y.L.J. No. 51, p. 1, col. 3 (1955).
113. Skillman, Youth Court Proposed, 23 Detroit Lawyer 102 (July 1955).
114. Kephart, The Family Court: Some Socio-Legal Implications, 1955 Wash. U.L.Q. 61, 73.
115. N.Y. Times, Sept. 24, 1955, p. 16, col. 8.

civil cases filed annually has increased by 78 per cent and the number of cases pending has risen by 158 per cent,[116] but the number of judges has increased by only 27 per cent.[117] The resulting congestion could therefore be expected.

In respect to state courts, nation-wide averages show no appreciable change. For ninety-eight state trial courts, the over-all average time interval from "at issue" to trial for civil jury cases was 11.4 months, as compared to 11.1 months for 1954 and 11.5 months for 1953.[118] For nonjury cases, however, the figures show a continuing 10 per cent decrease each year, from 5.7 months in 1953 to 5.1 months in 1954 and to 4.6 months in 1955. In courts with jurisdiction over areas having more than 750,000 population, the average delay in jury cases is 22.5 months, ranging from 44 months in the Queens County Supreme Court, New York, to 9 months in the San Francisco County Superior Court. Courts for smaller population areas generally show a correspondingly shorter time interval, although this does not hold true in every case. For example, Worcester County Superior Court, Massachusetts, is in a county with a population of about 550,000, and yet it has the longest reported period of delay in the nation—46 months. Spotlighting severe problems of jury-trial delay are the following examples of disproportionate time intervals: Chicago Superior Court—40 months (an increase from 36 months in 1954); New York County Supreme Court—39 months;[119] Kings County Supreme Court, New York—38 months (a decrease from 45 months); Fairfield County Superior Court, Connecticut—30 months (an increase from 25 months). Commenting on the delay in Cook County, Illinois, after the second unsuccessful attempt to amend the judiciary article of the state constitution, a Chicago newspaper stated: "Apparently the members of the legislature—or, at any rate, a lot of them—think that the situation as it exists is just dandy."[120]

State action in creating new judges, as at least a partial palliative, was rather sporadic and localized,[121] and the reception of measures increasing the utility of judicial manpower already

116. Administrative Office of the United States Courts, Third Quarter Report of the Director 6 (May 15, 1955).

117. Ibid.

118. Inst. Jud. Admin., Calendar Status Study—1955 i (June 30, 1955). The 1954 and 1953 figures are for 97 trial courts.

119. The New York County figure is for personal injury cases only. Calendar Status Study, supra note 118, at 3.

120. The Press Is Saying, 3 ABA Coordinator 5 (Oct. 1, 1955) (excerpt from an editorial in the Chicago Tribune of Sept. 14, 1955).

121. Inst. Jud. Admin., Check-list Summary of 1955 Devolopments in Judicial Administration 6 (Aug. 1, 1955).

available was not wholeheartedly favorable. Arkansas,[122] Colorado,[123] and Connecticut[124] rejected bills which would have permitted the assignment of judges to areas outside their jurisdiction. Connecticut also refused to provide for the transfer of actions between her superior and common pleas courts[125]—a move which would have accelerated the disposition of cases. On the other hand Delaware,[126] Florida,[127] Minnesota,[128] and Nevada[129] did accept measures providing for assignment of their trial judges. The Delaware bill, a proposed amendment to the constitution, also gives the supreme court administrative and supervisory control over all the courts in the state.

In a recent decision the Supreme Court of Pennsylvania upheld a state statute permitting the adoption by county common pleas courts of compulsory arbitration for controversies involving $1,000 or less.[130] Enacted in 1952,[131] the new method has been adopted in some forty of a total of sixty-seven counties, and its effectiveness in speeding the administration of justice has been demonstrated.[132]

An additional way to aid in eliminating judicial delay is better management of the assignment of cases, which may be helped by more intelligent use of the pre-trial conference. This was one of several recommendations in a study of the Superior Court of Maricopa County Arizona, conducted on a two-month period early in 1955 by the Institute of Judicial Administration.[133]

As stated in last year's article,[134] full and effective judicial administration cannot be achieved without the creation of an office within the courts which would be concerned solely with administrative functions. Recognizing this need, seventeen states and

---

122. Ark. H.B. 2 (1955).
123. Colo. H.B. 94 (1955).
124. Conn. Sen. B. 259 (1955).
125. Conn. Sen. B. 1071 (1955).
126. Del. Sen. B. 19 (1955).
127. Fla. Proposed Const. Amend. No. 1, Committee Substitute for H.J. Res. 810 (1955).
128. Minn. Laws 1955, c. 483.
129. Nev. Stat. 1955, c. 440.
130. Application of Smith, 381 Pa. 223, 112 A.2d 625 (1955).
131. Pa. Laws 1952, No. 2087, now Pa. Stat. Ann. tit. 5, §§ 22, 30, 31, 71, 77 (Purdon Supp. 1954).
132. Westwood, The Law's Delay and the Pennsylvania Arbitration Plan, 39 J. Am. Jud. Soc'y 50 (1955).
133. Inst. Jud. Admin., Delay and Congestion in the Superior Court of Maricopa County, Arizona (April 12, 1955). See also Phillips, Better Court Administration . . . A Challenge to the Bench and Bar, 39 J. Am. Jud. Soc'y 9, 12 (1955). In New Jersey a summer part of the appellate division was set up in order to keep abreast of court business. For an appraisal of the work of the summer part, see Stoffer, The Work of the Judicial System: 1954-55, 10 Rutgers L. Rev. 381 (1955).
134. 1954 Ann. Survey Am. L. 829, 840, 30 N.Y.U.L. Rev. 966, 977 (1955).

Puerto Rico now have some type of administrative office of the courts.[135] Iowa, Maryland, New York, and Ohio created their offices this year. In Iowa[136] and Maryland[137] the statutes provide for broad authority to be given the administrative officer, particularly in Maryland.[138] The New York[139] and Ohio[140] offices, however, have a much more limited scope. Proposals to establish such offices in Indiana[141] and Texas[142] failed of enactment.

Additional evidence that we are living in an atomic age, if any is necessary, is an article dealing with legal planning in case of an atomic war, one section of which is devoted briefly to judicial administration.[143]

Pre-Trial.—Recent developments in pre-trial procedure have been the further recognition of its utility and the extension of its application. A subcommittee of the Pennsylvania state bar association's committee on judicial administration recommended that the trial courts throughout the commonwealth adopt rules making pre-trial conferences compulsory.[144] The California Judicial Council was given power through legislative enactment to promulgate rules governing pre-trial conferences in the superior and municipal courts,[145] while Wisconsin enacted into law a provision allowing a circuit judge to appoint a retired judge in his circuit to act in such conferences.[146]

In New Jersey, where pre-trial conferences are compulsory, further confidence in their usefulness was evidenced by an act permitting the transfer of a cause from the superior or county court to the county district court if the judge decides, as a result of the pre-trial hearing, that there is a reasonable probability that the final recovery will not exceed the statutory jurisdiction of

---

135. Inst. Jud. Admin., Court Administration (Aug. 1, 1955). For favorable comment by the Michigan State Bar on the work of their court administrator, see Committee on Court Administration, 34 Mich. State B.J. 35, 36 (Sept. 1955).

136. Iowa H. File 349 (1955).

137. Md. Laws 1955, c. 343.

138. For a description of the expected future performance of the Maryland administrative office, see Inst. Jud. Admin., Court Administration 11-14 (Aug. 1, 1955).

139. N.Y. Laws 1955, c. 869.

140. Ohio Sen. B. 51 (1955).

141. Ind. H.B. 319 (1955).

142. Tex. H.B. 195 (1955).

143. Cavers, Legal Planning Against the Risk of Atomic War, 55 Colum. L. Rev. 127, 151 (1955).

144. 27 Pa. B. Ass'n Q. 29, 33 (1955).

145. Cal. Stat. 1955, c. 632. For an excellent description of the procedure of, and benfits afforded by, pre-trial, see Kincaid, Pre-Trial Comes to California, 30 J. State B. of Cal. 414 (1955).

146. Wis. Sen. B. 171 (1955).

the latter court.[147] Effective for the September 1955 term, the Columbus, Ohio, Common Pleas Court adopted the pre-trial conference as part of its procedure,[148] with the expectation of materially shortening actual trials and settling more cases than it has in the past. But in Tennessee a bill designed to broaden that state's pre-trial deposition procedures failed of enactment.[149]

Articles written on the subject have been concerned mainly with general development. An appraisal of the effect of pre-trial procedure in Detroit, Michigan, indicates its success in speeding court calendars.[150] There have been recommendations that pre-trial calendars be set up exactly like trial calendars,[151] and that judges, lawyers, and students be educated in the method and value of the conference.[152] The latter was submitted on the basis that pre-trial is here to stay; therefore, we should make the most of it. In Kansas a recommendation that the state utilize a penalizing provision for failure to participate in the conference was submitted to the judicial council.[153] It was previously reported in Kansas that the lack of experience and interest in pre-trial methods had caused disappointing results.[154] A comprehensive note dealing with pre-trial procedures in Maine, New Hampshire, Massachusetts, and Rhode Island will be of interest to lawyers and students in those states.[155]

Rule-Making and Procedural Rules.—Should the right to promulgate judicial rules of practice and procedure belong to the courts or to the legislature? Six states, Arkansas,[156] Montana,[157] North Carolina,[158] Tennessee,[159] Texas,[160] and Vermont,[161] an-

---

147. N.J. Laws 1955, c. 7.

148. 11 Columbus B. Briefs 3 (July 2, 1955). See also 11 id. 3 (Sept. 10, 1955).

149. Tenn. H.B. 117 (1955).

150. Schureman, Discovery Docket Speeds Court Calendar, 23 Detroit Lawyer 54 (April 1955).

151. Hartshorne, To Help Both Bench and Bar at Pre-trial, 41 A.B.A.J. 66 (1955).

152. Rucker, A Practicing Lawyer's View of Pre-Trial, 38 J. Am. Jud. Soc'y 75 (1954).

153. Thompson and Holland, Adoption of Federal Discovery Procedure for Use in State Courts, 29 Kan. Jud. Council Bull. 6, 13 (1955).

154. Stavely, Pretrial—Five Years After, 2 Kan. L. Rev. 360 (1954).

155. Note, 35 B.U.L. Rev. 256 (1955).

156. Ark. Sen. B. 313 (1955).

157. Mont. H.B. 331 (1955).

158. Letter from the Administrative Assistant to the Chief Justice of the Supreme Court of North Carolina to the Institute of Judicial Administration, June 29, 1955.

159. Tenn. Sen. B. 150 (1955).

160. Tex. H.J. Res. 26 (1955). This bill would have authorized the criminal court of appeals to make rules of criminal procedure in place of the present statutory code.

161. Vt. H.B. 82 (1955).

swered this rather controversial question by rejecting measures that would have granted the rule-making power to the courts. The North Carolina bill, although passing the senate, was defeated by a close vote in the house committee; and the state judicial council and bar are preparing a constitutional amendment to be presented to the 1957 legislature. As a result of the failure of the Missouri Legislature to adopt a new code of evidence, a committee of the state bar has recommended a constitutional amendment giving the supreme court full rule-making power with reference to all procedural law (including the law relating to evidence) .[162] This power would be circumscribed by the right of the legislature to annul or amend any rule.

One reaction to the constitutional provision in New Jersey,[163] giving the courts the power to prescribe rules of pleading and practice, was an article suggesting that such an authorization might violate the Federal Constitution, which guarantees to all states a republican form of government.[164] The writer expressed the belief that the state legislature should have some control over the rule-making power of the court. Other articles on the subject reviewed the origin of the Federal Rules of Civil Procedure,[165] examined the new rules adopted in the federal northern district of Illinois,[166] and analyzed the effect and reception of the modern rules of civil procedure in New Mexico.[167] A comprehensive study of the rule-making power in all forty-eight states, Hawaii, and Puerto Rico presents the situation as of 1955.[168]

Jurors and Jury Selection.—Fines ranging from $10 to $100 and several ten-day jail sentences were meted out by a New York supreme court justice to a number of men who had ignored notices for jury service. Calling attention to the fact that ours is one of the few countries left in the world where a man is entitled to a trial by a jury of his peers, the judge sharply criticized the defendants for treating with contempt one of the "highest privileges of citizenship."[169] While disregard of a jury summons is not to be condoned, serious consideration should be given to low jury fees and the fact that many employers do not pay employees

162. Report of Evidence Code Committee, 11 J. Mo. B. 119, 120 (1955).
163. N.J. Const. art. 6, § 2.
164. Kearns, Rule-Making in New Jersey: Denial of a Republican Form of Government?, 41 A.B.A.J. 435 (1955).
165. Holtzoff, Origin and Sources of the Federal Rules of Civil Procedure, 30 N.Y.U.L. Rev. 1057 (1955).
166. Ragland, The New Federal District Court Rules, 36 Chi. B. Record 317 (1955).
167. Robertson, New Mexico Rules of Civil Procedure for the District Courts, 16 F.R.D. 489 (1955).
168. Inst. Jud. Admin., Rule-Making Power of the Courts (June 1, 1955).
169. N.Y. Herald-Tribune, Oct. 21, 1955, § 2, p. 1, col. 7.

for time spent away in jury service. It is encouraging to report that several states have increased fees paid to jurors, in some instances doubling them.[170] But a study of jurors' fees indicates that in New York City jurors are still receiving the $3 daily fee adopted fifty years ago,[171] although the New York State Legislature in 1950 authorized municipalities to double this fee.[172]

Improvement in the manner of jury selection and operation has been effected in several states,[173] and the status of women as jurors is being given attention.[174] A lively and detailed account of the judicial function in instructing the jury is presented in two articles by Professor Curtis Wright,[175] wherein the power of the judge to comment and methods of instructing the jury in the forty-eight states are analyzed.

In an effort to ease the jury-trial log jam in Pennsylvania, the Board of Judges experimented with various systems of assignment which would leave a sufficient number of cases ready for trial, yet relieve lawyers, litigants, and witnesses of the burden of unnecessary waiting. Through the operation of a "pool," some measure of success in disposing of a maximum number of jury cases appears to have been accomplished. One of the major problems to be surmounted has been caused by the concentration of negligence cases in the hands of a comparatively small group of trial lawyers.[176]

Traffic Courts and Justices of the Peace.—It appears that the bar is showing more concern for the problems involved in traffic law enforcement. The constantly increasing use of automobiles has made this an area of mounting importance, and has brought forth several recommendations for reform.[177] It is a developing

---

170. Colo. H.B. 36 (1955) (increased from $3 to $6) ; Mass. Acts 1955, c. 328 (grand and traverse jurors' compensation raised from $8 to $10) ; Ore. H.B. 301 (1955) ($5 to $7.50) ; Wis. Laws 1955, c. 187 ($8 to $16).

171. Low, Nationwide Survey of Jurors' Fees |1954). See also Inst. Jud. Admin., Jury Costs (Aug. 15, 1955).

172. N.Y. Laws 1950, c. 187.

173. Neb. Legis. B. 175 (1955) restates qualifications of jurors and grounds for exemption; N.Y. Laws 1955, c. 797 recodified provisions relating to jurors and jury commissioners in counties outside of New York City. The North Carolina Judicial Council proposed the establishment in 1957 of an office of jury commissioner for each county to prepare lists of prospective jurors. N.C. Jud. Council, Third Report 16 (Dec. 1954).

174. Tex. Laws 1955, c. 288 authorizes certain exemptions to women jurors; W. Va. Acts 1955, c. 22 provides for submission to the voters in 1956 of a proposed constitutional amendment to allow women to serve as jurors.

175. Wright, Adequacy of Instructions to the Jury, 53 Mich. L. Rev. 505, 813 (1955).

176. Lovitt, The Jury Trial Log Jam, 18 Shingle 5 (1955).

177. Halsey, Judicial Point System Plan, 3 Traffic Digest & Review 5 (Aug. 1955) ; Johnston, A Plan for the Hearing and Deciding of Traffic Cases, 33 N.C.L. Rev. 1 (1954) ; Putnam, Traffic Courts—An Answer?, 23 J.B. Ass'n State of Kan. 215 (1955) ; Scheffler, A Psychiatric Laboratory is Planned for New Centralized Traffic Court, 36 Chi. B. Record 399 (1955).

popular concept that primary responsibility for the public safety, in respect to automobile accidents and their prevention, belongs to the traffic courts.[178] To this end, traffic court conferences and institutes are more and more becoming an integral part of organized bar activity.

The Florida bar held its first traffic conference in 1955, and concluded with the suggestion that the conference become a permanent fixture of its program.[179] Last year the Kansas Bar Association held its first Traffic Court Institute, focusing attention on the traffic offense problem and inspiring a proposed plan for an independent traffic court system in Kansas.[180] The establishment of a legislative committee was proposed in New Mexico to study the possible creation of a state-wide system of traffic courts to replace the present handling of traffic cases by justices of the peace, but it failed to pass the legislature.[181] Under consideration in Chicago is a plan for the Chicago traffic courts to utilize a psychiatric laboratory. This plan gives a traffic court judge the power to refer a traffic violator, under certain conditions, to the laboratory for a medical and psychiatric examination to determine his fitness to operate motor vehicles.[182] Puerto Rico, already a model in court administration,[183] continues to move forward in reforming its traffic system. Under authority of a 1954 act,[184] the use of a multiform, nonfixable traffic ticket was inaugurated in March 1955, and it is reported that its results have surpassed all expectations.[185]

In another area, efforts are being made to bolster the "minimal nature" of justice of the peace courts. By statute Connecticut set up a committee of judges, appointed by the chief justice, to adopt rules of procedure for justices of the peace courts.[186] A constitutional amendment proposed by a joint resolution of the Idaho legislature provides for the selection, rather than election, of justices of the peace, and will be voted upon at the next general

---

178. Halsey, Court Support of Driver Licensing, 3 Traffic Digest & Review 13 (July 1955); Halsey, Judicial Point System Plan, 3 id. 5 (Aug. 1955); Hare, How Courts Can Help Driver Licensing, 3 Traffic Digest & Review 7 (Oct. 1955).

179. Special Committee on the First Florida Traffic Court Conference, Report, 29 Fla. B.J. 418 (1955).

180. Putnam, supra note 177.

181. N.M.H.J. Res. 5 (1955).

182. Scheffler, supra note 177.

183. See 1952 Ann. Survey Am. L. 779, 780, 28 N.Y.U.L. Rev. 866, 867 (1953). See also Snyder, New Puerto Rico Judicial System Is Modern and Efficient, 36 J. Am. Jud. Soc'y 134 (1953).

184. P.R. Laws 1954, No. 93.

185. Judicial Administration in the Commonwealth of Puerto Rico, Informal Report to the Institute of Judicial Administration (June 1955).

186. Conn. Pub. Acts 1955, No. 387.

election.[187] The amendment will permit the legislature to provide by law for the appointment of justices of the peace. Colorado has passed a bill providing for a uniform docket fee in the justice courts,[188] and in Ohio the fee system was abolished in favor of judicial salaries.[189] In the latter state an opinion by the state attorney general held that the jurisdiction of justices of the peace will terminate in those areas where the present municipal court authority was expanded or new municipal courts were created.[190]

Strong opposition arose in New York to the recommendation, included in the report made by a subcommittee of the Temporary Commission on the Courts, that the justice of the peace courts be abolished and a system of magistrates be established in their stead.[191] Present justices argue that some rural communities have no lawyers and would have to depend on magistrates who know nothing of the local population and their problems.[192]

Conclusion.—It is timely to remind ourselves that the bench and the bar of the entire country continue to share a heavy responsibility for failing to provide the answers to the questions of judicial reform. Some of these more pressing questions have been pointedly posed by Mr. Harry D. Nims of the New York Bar:

> Is it possible that in many, many years during which these conditions have persisted, this problem of better justice has grown so stale with many lawyers and judges that they no longer see the devastating effect, in human terms of the expense, the anxiety, the continuation of animosities, the straitened family circumstances, the distrust and lack of confidence in our courts, which result from the methods we use or permit to be used in litigation and which we could change easily if we had the will to do so? Can it be that we intentionally permit these hardships? Or are we asleep?[193]

---

187. Idaho Sen. J. Res. 5 (1955).

188. Colo. H.B. 275 (1955).

189. Ohio Sen. B. 319 (1955).

190. Syllabi of Opinions of the Attorney General, 28 Ohio Bar 885, 886 (1955); Jones, From the State Capitals (Supp. Rep. Sept. 7, 1955).

191. A Proposed Simplified State-Wide Court System, Report of the Subcommittee on Modernization and Simplification of the Court Structure, 7, 75, 92, 93 (June 17, 1955).

192. N.Y. Times, Oct. 12, 1955, p. 1, col. 7.

193. Nims, The Bar: A Sleeping Giant, 41 A.B.A.J. 908, 983 (1955).

JUDICIAL ADMINISTRATION — 1956 *

From the dedication of a new supreme court building in San Juan, Puerto Rico, to the approval by Alaska voters of a projected state constitution containing a modern judicial article, the progress of judicial administration in 1956 more than spanned a continent. It also marked the fiftieth anniversary of Roscoe Pound's famous address to the American Bar Association at St. Paul on "The Causes of Popular Dissatisfaction with Administration of Justice,"[1] thus giving occasion for memorializing the event, such as at the Jurisprudence Symposium in the Inter-American Bar Association's Ninth Conference at Dallas[2] and in a special republication of the original paper with a new introduction by Dean Pound himself.[3] The latter takes note of the need for reorganizing the machinery of justice along the lines of that achieved in New Jersey, with adequate administrative supervision and control.[4] It also advocates the

> establishment in all jurisdictions of a well organized ministry of justice insuring systematic study of the law in action to find gaps in the body of legal precepts . . and to watch for cases and situations in which the law does not function adequately and devise and promote effective remedial measures.[5]

In another of his analytical surveys of the field, delivered as a memorial lecture at Washington University in St. Louis, Chief Justice Arthur T. Vanderbilt of New Jersey noted that popular dissatisfaction with the law "centers around the techniques by which justice is administered—the organization of our courts and how they manage their business."[6] He pointed out that at the bottom of all the difficulties lies the equalitarian and anti-professional movement of the Jacksonian period and the failure

---

* Reprinted from *New York University Law Review;* January 1957, Vol. 32, No. 1, pp. 116-132; 1956 Annual Survey of American Law. The material for this article was assembled, classified, and analyzed by Jay A. Gaines, Research Assistant of the Institute.

1. 29 A.B.A. Rep. 395 (1906) , 40 Am. L. Rev. 729 (1906) .
2. See Inst. Jud. Admin., Improvements in Judicial Administration: 1906-1956 (April 20, 1956) .
3. Pound, The Causes of Popular Dissatisfaction with the Administration of Justice, 8 Baylor L. Rev. 1 (1956) .
4. Id. at 3.
5. Ibid.
6. Vanderbilt, Impasses in Justice, 1956 Wash. U.L.Q. 267, 268 (1956) .

of law schools to recognize and assume their responsibility for improving the administration of justice. The essentials of sound administration of justice are delineated as (1) a simple system of courts, (2) competent judges and jurors, (3) effective use of judicial manpower through an administrative head of the courts, (4) simplified procedure to secure decisions on the merits without delay, technicalities, or surprise, and (5) an effective appellate practice.[7]

In his contribution to a symposium on "Law and the Future,"[8] Judge Alexander Holtzoff, Chairman of the American Bar Association's Section of Judicial Administration, enumerated the problems confronting judicial administration in the future as, first, "creating a simple, unified judicial structure in every jurisdiction";[9] second, "the selection of judges who are not only well qualified by education, experience and character, but who also will be in a position of complete independence while in office";[10] and third, "the restoration of the rule-making power to the courts," and the implementation thereof by the adoption of "a simple, non-technical practice."[11] In another article he reports on a visit to the courts of England and the comparative features of their practice with those in this country.[12]

General Revisions and Programs.—With only a minority of state legislatures in session, there were no general revision plans submitted for legislative enactment or rejection. However, two significant proposals previously passed by legislatures were adopted by the voters in November 1956. One, the Florida constitutional amendment noted in last year's *Survey* article, creates district courts of appeal, gives the supreme court rule-making power, and provides for retirement and removal of judges.[13] Minnesota's amendment of its constitution's judicial article, also noted last year, modifies its court structure and provides a number of changes therein, including the status and jurisdiction of justice courts, elimination of the requirement for separate probate courts, a uniform six-year term for all judges, and authority

---

7. Id. at 285.

8. Law and the Future: Administration of Justice, 51 Nw. U.L. Rev. 163 (1956).

9. Id. at 166.

10. Id. at 167.

11. Id. at 169.

12. Holtzoff, A Visit to the London Courts: The Administration of Justice in England, 42 A.B.A.J. 29 (1956).

13. Fla. Proposed Const. Amend. No. 1, Committee Substitute for H.J. Res. 810 (1955). The amendment was approved by the voters on November 6, 1956. Jones, From the State Capitals 1 (Supp. Rep. Nov. 13, 1956). See 1955 Ann. Survey Am. L. 670, 31 N.Y.U.L. Rev. 163 (1956); Barns, Courts, Lawyers and Taxpayers, 30 Fla. B.J. 162 (1956).

to initiate changes in the methods of judicial selection.[14] Wisconsin's pending constitutional proposal, having passed in 1955, must again be passed by the legislature in 1957 before being submitted to the people.[15] In Illinois the Joint Committee on the Judicial Article is pointing toward its third attempt to secure legislative approval of a new judicial article for that state, and the board of governors of the state bar association has reaffirmed its adherence to the principle that some form of non-political selection and tenure of judges is necessary.[16]

In scope and design, however, the judicial article of Alaska's proposed new constitution deserves to rank with that of the Commonwealth of Puerto Rico as embodying truly modern concepts of a model judicial system. Approved by the voters of the territory on April 24, 1956, in anticipation of ultimate statehood, it includes a provision for a unified court structure comprising a supreme court, superior court, and other courts as established by the legislature.[17] It provides for appointment of judges by the governor under a modified Missouri Plan.[18] Provision is also made for early retirement of judges for incapacity and for normal retirement at age seventy.[19] Other features include the conferring of rule-making power on the supreme court, authority in the chief justice as administrative head, and the requirement of an administrative director.[20]

The New York Temporary Commission on the Courts issued, in February, a report to the governor and the legislature, including several topics and proposals touching on congestion and delay, the cost of administering justice, a youth court measure,

---

14. Minn. Const. art. VI (1956). At the November 6 general election the amendment was approved. Jones, From the State Capitals 2 (Supp. Rep. Nov. 13, 1956). See 1955 Ann. Survey Am. L. 670, 31 N.Y.U.L. Rev. 163 (1956); Howard, Proposed Amendment to Article VI of the Constitution Providing for Exercise of Judicial Power of the State, Bench and Bar of Minn., March 1956, p. 13; Palmer, A Look to the Future, id., Aug. 1956, pp. 7, 9; Pirsig, The Proposed Amendment of the Judiciary Article of the Minnesota Constitution, 40 Minn. L. Rev. 815 (1956).

15. Wis. Sen. J. Res. 25 (1955). See 1955 Ann. Survey Am. L. 671, 31 N.Y.U.L. Rev. 164 (1956); Hallows, Court Reorganization, Wis. B. Bull., Feb. 1956, p. 7; Court Reorganization Plan Details Submitted, id., June 1956, p. 14.

16. Judicial Article Committee Named, 44 Ill. B.J. 562 (1956).

17. Alaska Const. art. IV, §§ 1-3 (1956). See New Alaskan Constitution Ratified, 39 J. Am. Jud. Soc'y 175 (1956).

18. Alaska Const. art. IV, §§ 6-8 (1956). See text at notes 29-30 infra.

19. Alaska Const. art. IV, §§ 10, 11.

20. Id. §§ 15, 16.

21. 1956 Report of the Temporary Commission on the Courts to the Governor and the Legislature of the State of New York (Feb. 15, 1956).

and auxiliary and related matters.[21] On the sensitive subject of judicial selection, the report stated:

> Certainly there has been no convincing demonstration that the present elective method should be abandoned in favor of any of the modified or different proposals which have been advanced. The Commission recommends against the abandonment of the elective system and against the substitution of some new or different system for it.[22]

Reports and proposals by official bodies in other states dealing with matters of major concern include those of the Advisory Committee on the Judicial System in Kentucky[23] and the Massachusetts Judicial Survey Commission.[24] Bar associations in Iowa[25] and North Carolina[26] have announced the availability and projected use of funds to study the administration of justice in their respective states. Broad-gauge programs of court improvement in California and in Connecticut were launched at the annual meetings of the State Bar of California and of the Connecticut State Bar Association, respectively,[27] and Peter Holme, Jr., of the Denver Bar has analyzed the problems of judicial administration in Colorado and has suggested solutions therefor.[28]

Judicial Selection and Tenure.—Alaska's new constitution, previously noted, embodies a selection system by which the governor is to appoint one of two or more persons nominated by a judicial council of seven members, namely, three nonattorneys appointed by the governor with legislative approval, three attorneys appointed by the governing body of the state bar, and the chief justice ex officio.[29] The appointee is subject to approval or rejection on a nonpartisan ballot at the first general election after three years, and thereafter every ten years for supreme court justices and every six years for superior court judges.[30]

22. Id. at 71. Compare, however, the views expressed by Judge Harold R. Medina, and the subsequent storm of controversy ensuing therefrom. Medina, For Whom The Bell Tolls, 11 Record B. Ass'n City of N.Y. 223 (1956); Amicus Curiae, Our Judicial System, 14 B. Bull. N. Y. County Lawyers Ass'n 14, 15 (1956); N.Y. Times, April 25, 1956, p. 25, col. 1; id., April 24, 1956, p. 1, col. 3.

23. Report of the Advisory Committee on the Judicial System to the Legislative Research Commission and the 1956 General Assembly (1956).

24. The Report of the Commission to Survey the Judicial System of Massachusetts, 41 Mass. L.Q. 34 (1956).

25. News Bull., Iowa State B. Ass'n, Nov.-Dec. 1955, p. 2.

26. Among the States, 29 State Gov't 117 (1956).

27. Jones, From the State Capitals 1-3 (Supp. Rep. Oct. 5, 1956); id. at 1-2 (Supp. Rep. Oct. 26, 1956).

28. Holme, The System for Administration of Justice in Colorado, 28 Rocky Mt. L. Rev. 299 (1956).

29. Alaska Const. art. IV, §§ 5, 8 (1956).

30. Id. § 6.

In Georgia, although the legislature turned down a proposed amendment to establish a judicial commission to make judicial nominations from which the governor's appointments would be made,[31] the charter of Atlanta was amended to provide for the appointment of judges to the municipal court of Atlanta, each such appointment to be by the mayor from among three candidates nominated by a majority of the superior court judges of Fulton County.[32] Thereafter, the appointee comes before the voters on the question of his retention in office.

Elsewhere, interest in the adoption of new systems of judicial selection continues. In Ohio the council of delegates of the state bar association has recommended that the Missouri Plan be submitted to the people as a constitutional amendment if the members of the association approve and has also appointed a committee to publicize the plan and conduct a referendum thereon.[33] The Pennsylvania Plan, unsuccessful last year, for nonpolitical selection of judges continued to draw support[34] as well as opposition.[35] An adaptation of the Missouri Plan is being developed for introduction in the legislature in Colorado for ultimate submission to the people,[36] and the merits of the American Bar Association Plan have been described in an address to the Wisconsin Bar Association by Glenn Winters, who noted that states in which proposals based on it have currently or recently been under active consideration include Michigan, Pennsylvania, Texas, New York, West Virginia, Wisconsin, Arizona, Florida, Iowa, Ohio, Oklahoma, Washington, and Wyoming.[37] The history and advantages of the Missouri Plan and the status of the Pennsylvania Plan were also discussed in addresses to the Baltimore regional meeting of the American Bar Association.[38]

Other writers and spokesmen have advanced their views and proposals. A writer for the *American Bar Association Journal* has suggested the establishment of a national judicial council for

---

31. Ga. H. Res. 69-200d (1956).

32. Ga. Laws Reg. Sess. 1956, No. 428, p. 3368.

33. Morris, President's Page, 29 Ohio Bar 565, 566 (1956).

34. See 1955 Ann. Survey Am. L. 672, 31 N.Y.U.L. Rev. 165 (1956); Harris, Who Pulls the Lever?, 27 Pa. B. Ass'n Q. 351 (1956); Harris, Politics, the Public, and the Pennsylvania Plan, 19 Shingle 62 (1956).

35. Heuges, Wanted a UNIVAC, 19 Shingle 88 (1956).

36. Holme, supra note 28, at 313.

37. Winters, How Should Judges Be Chosen?, Wis. B. Bull., April 1956, p. 7.

38. Fox, The Current Status of Pennsylvania Plan for Selecting Judges, Baltimore Daily Record, Oct. 13, 1956, p. 3, col. 1; Lashly, Missouri Plan for Selection of Judges, id., p. 5, col. 1.

the selection of all federal judges.[39] Another has advocated the inclusion, in the proposed new judicial article of Illinois, of provision for cumulative voting in the election of judges.[40] Assumption of greater responsibility by organized bar associations in judicial selection processes has been strongly urged in Ohio.[41] In line with this recommendation is the interest demonstrated by local bar associations in Milwaukee[42] and Columbus[43] in conducting polls of their members of lawyers on indorsement of judicial candidates. Objections to such a proposed plan in the latter city have been analyzed and summarized, following its rejection by the lawyers in county-wide balloting.[44]

Defects in the partisan election method of selecting judges have been pointed out by Chief Justice Vanderbilt.[45] In Rhode Island, where appointive methods are in effect, the legislature has passed a resolution proposing a constitutional amendment to grant life tenure to judges and to protect them from diminution of salary during office.[46] A comprehensive, nation-wide analysis of present provisions on selection, tenure and removal of appellate and trial judges in the states, territories and Puerto Rico, was published in August 1956 and has been widely distributed.[47]

Judicial Salaries and Retirement.—Salary increases for judges, or at least for some judges, were provided in each of nine states in 1956, namely, Alabama, Arizona, Louisiana, Maryland, Michigan, New Jersey, New York, Pennsylvania, and Virginia.[48] Of the more substantial raises, Pennsylvania granted general increases of $5,000 to its supreme court and superior court judges, and $4,000 to its common pleas judges in the first and fifth districts, with slightly smaller amounts in the less populous

---

39. Hartley, Taking Politics Out of Judicial Appointments, 42 A.B.A.J. 309 (1956). For a more recent article on the appointment of federal judges, see Miller, Politics and the Courts: The Struggle for Good Judges Goes On, id. at 939 (1956). And see Major, Federal Judges as Political Patronage, 38 Chi. B. Record 7 (1956).

40. Bairstow, Cumulative Voting for the Election of Judges, 44 Ill. B.J. 828 (1956).

41. Harter, Responsibilities of the Organized Bar to the Judiciary, 29 Ohio Bar 481 (1956).

42. Judicial Qualifications, Milwaukee B. Ass'n Gavel, Summer 1956, p. 20.

43. In re Judicial Endorsement Plan, 12 Columbus B. Briefs, July 14, 1956, p. 3.

44. Report of Judicial and Referendum Committee, id., Aug. 8, 1956, p. 2.

45. Vanderbilt, Judges and Jurors: Their Functions, Qualifications and Selection, 36 B.U.L. Rev. 1, 41 (1956).

46. R.I. H. Res. 955 Substitute "A" (1956). The resolution must be passed again by the legislature before submission to the people.

47. Inst. Jud. Admin., Selection, Tenure and Removal of Judges in the 48 States, Alaska, Hawaii and Puerto Rico (Aug. 10, 1956).

48. Inst. Jud. Admin., Check-List Summary of 1956 Developments in Judicial Administration 8-10 (Aug. 1, 1956).

counties.[49] As a result, the chief justice will receive $30,500 and his associate justices $30,000 a year. In Virginia the chief justice was increased from $13,250 to $16,000, his associates from $12,750 to $15,000, and lower court judges from $9,250 to $10,700.[50] Arizona raised salaries of supreme court justices from $12,500 to $15,000 and superior court justices from $10,000 to $12,500.[51] Judges in Maryland received salary increments ranging from $1,750 to $2,000,[52] but the Maryland legislature was also asked, unsuccessfully, by one of its members to declare a moratorium on such legislation in order to allow them a "breather" on judicial salary proposals.[53]

Increases were granted to certain county and lower court judges in Alabama,[54] circuit judges in Louisiana,[55] probate judges in Michigan,[56] and to judges of certain county courts in New Jersey[57] and New York.[58] Proposed increases for supreme court justices and superior court judges in New Jersey failed to pass,[59] and a New York measure to grant a $2,000 raise to supreme court justices was vetoed by the governor.[60]

Voters in Arkansas were offered a proposed judges' salary amendment to the constitution, to remove existing limitations and permit the legislature to increase the salaries and expenses of judges during their terms of office.[61] In Michigan, on the other hand, a proposal to remove the constitutional limitations on salaries of judges with terms of six years or more failed to pass the legislature.[62]

Three analytical and comprehensive studies based on state-by-state data and dealing respectively with salaries,[63] retirement,[64]

49. Pa. Laws 1955, No. 657.
50. Va. Acts 1956, c. 716.
51. Ariz. Laws 1956, c. 58.
52. Md. Ann. Code art. 26, § 48 (Supp. 1956).
53. Md. Sen. Res. 8 (1956).
54. Ala. Acts 1956, Nos. 75, 94, 95.
55. La. Acts Reg. Sess. 1956, Nos. 308, 315, 358.
56. Mich. Pub. Acts Reg. Sess. 1956, No. 228.
57. N.J. Laws 1956, c. 138.
58. N.Y. Laws 1956, cc. 82, 330, 327, 412, 501, 568, 675.
59. N.J. Assem. B. No. 272 (1956).
60. N.Y. Assem. Int. 2290, Pr. 4758 (1956); McKinney's 1956 N.Y. Sess. Laws 1761 (veto message, April 19, 1956).
61. Ark. Proposed Const. Amend. No. 46 (1956). Substantially complete returns from the November 6 election indicated that the amendment would be adopted. Jones, From State Capitals 1 (Supp. Rep. Nov. 9, 1956).
62. Mich. H.J. Res. "C" (1956).
63. Inst. Jud. Admin., Salaries of Judicial and Court-Related Personnel (Aug. 1, 1956).
64. Inst. Jud. Admin., Judicial Retirement, Statutory Provisions and Comment (May 8, 1956).

and survivors' benefits[65] were published by the Institute of Judicial Administration. During the year there were enactments or proposals to liberalize existing retirement and benefit pension provisions in Louisiana,[66] Maryland,[67] Michigan,[68] Pennsylvania,[69] and Rhode Island.[70] The latter state, for example, now allows supreme court justices and superior court judges to retire at age sixty-five with twenty years of service, or at age seventy with fifteen years of service, and to receive three fourths of their final pay.[71] Also enacted during the year, by the United States Congress, was a measure to provide the widows and surviving infant dependents of federal judges with annuities amounting up to 37½ per cent of the decedent judge's average federal salary.[72]

Judicial Conduct, Discipline, and Removal.—There is an apparent and growing awareness of the need for procedure to secure the removal of a judge when, as occasionally happens, his retirement for reasons other than age or misconduct becomes necessary to protect the administration of justice. The framers of the new Alaska constitution's judicial article vested initiating responsibility in the proposed new judicial council whenever a justice of the supreme court or judge of another court "appears to be so incapacitated as substantially to prevent him from performing his judicial duties."[73] In the case of a supreme court justice, the judicial council certifies the matter to the governor who appoints a board of three persons to inquire into the circumstances and on their recommendation the governor may retire the justice. In the case of judges of other courts, the council recommends to the supreme court which, after notice and hearing and by majority vote of its members, may retire the judge.

In California a committee of the judicial council has offered a tentative draft of a constitutional amendment to enlarge the functions of the commission on judicial qualifications to include the power to conduct hearings on citizen complaints as to judges, but with legislative action required for final removal.[74] A Maryland statute provides for the removal of full-time judges of the

---

65. Inst. Jud. Admin., Pensions and Benefits for Judicial Dependents Aug. 17, 1956).
66. La. Acts Reg. Sess. 1956, No. 481.
67. Md. Sen. B. 67 (1956).
68. Mich. Pub. Acts Reg. Sess. 1956, No. 224; Mich. Sen. B. 1168 (1956).
69. Pa. Sen. B. 318 (1955), vetoed June 1, 1956 (veto No. 46).
70. R.I. Pub. Laws 1956, cc. 3633, 3832.
71. Id. c. 3832.
72. Pub. L. No. 973, 84th Cong., Sess. (1956).
73. Alaska Const. art. IV, § 10 (1956).
74. Los Angeles Daily J., Sept. 21, 1956, p. 1, col. 8.

People's Court of Montgomery County after a finding, by the circuit court, of incompetency, physical or mental deficiency, willful neglect of duty, or other specified grounds of misconduct.[75]

Another feature of the Alaska constitution is the prohibition against the practice of law by an incumbent judge.[76] A Georgia act prohibits juvenile court judges from practicing law in their own courts or in any matter over which their court might have jurisdiction.[77] On the other hand, a proposal in Kentucky to prohibit county judges from practicing law[78] and one in Massachusetts that would have prevented a retired judge from practicing in the division of the court from which he had been retired[79] both failed to pass.

Meanwhile, the controversy over Canon 35 remains unabated and the question of publicizing courtroom proceedings continues to receive considerable publicity.[80] An editorial in the *New York Times* defends a recent supreme court decision in Pennsylvania upholding a lower court conviction of seven newspaper men for disobeying an express judicial prohibition against taking photographs of a murder trial.[81]

One aspect of courtroom decorum and dignity, the wearing of judicial robes, has been commented upon, with a summary of its history and a state-by-state tabulation of the extent to which judicial robes are in use in the various courts.[82]

Judicial Councils and Judicial Conferences.—The Supreme Court of South Carolina has directed the formation of an ad interim judicial council which is to serve until June 30, 1957.[83] The council is to be composed of twenty-one members representing the bench and bar of the state and including the dean or a faculty representative of the state law school. The council's task will be to conduct a study of the administration of justice in

---

75. Md. Laws Extraordinary Sess. 1956, c. 12.

76. Alaska Const. art. IV, § 14 (1956).

77. Ga. Laws Reg. Sess. 1956, No. 473, p. 799.

78. Ky. Sen. B. 164 (1956).

79. Mass. H.B. 2185 (1956).

80. See, e.g., Miller, Should Canon 35 Be Amended? A Question of Fair Trial and Free Information, 42 A.B.A.J. 834 (1956); Tinkham, Should Canon 35 Be Amended? A Question of Proper Judicial Administration, id. at 843; Wiggins, Should Canon 35 Be Amended? A Newspaperman Speaks for the News Media, id. at 838 (1956); TV—A Pressing Problem, 19 Texas B.J. 72 (1956); Courtroom Television, id. at 73; Press Photo Ban Still Favored, 24 Hennepin Lawyer 111 (1956).

81. N.Y. Times, Oct. 10, 1956, p. 38, col. 3.

82. Ferguson, To Robe or Not to Robe?—A Judicial Dilemma, 39 J. Am. Jud. Soc'y 166 (1956).

83. S.C. Sup. Ct. Order of July 10, 1956.

South Carolina, including practice and procedure in the courts
and before quasi-judicial bodies. It will also gather and analyze
statistics and will be authorized to recommend, on its own motion or on request of the court, changes in existing procedure.

The Oregon Judicial Council, formed in 1955 and noted in last
year's *Survey*,[84] issued its first annual report on August 1, 1956.
Among its seven recommendations is included a resolution to
consider the possibility of forming a regional organization of
state judicial councils, judicial conferences, and administrative
offices within the Ninth Judicial District of the United States.[85]
The recommendation takes note of the need for an effective body
for the exchange of ideas and experience in the area of operations
of such agencies.

The new Alaskan judicial council will conduct a study on the
improvement of the administration of justice and make reports
and recommendations to the supreme court and the legislature at
least once every two years.[86]

The Committee on Court Administration of the Judicial Conference of the United States has recommended that membership
in the Conference, currently consisting of the chief judges of the
several circuits, be expanded to include one district judge from
each circuit.[87] The district judges would be elected for three-
year terms in such manner that terms of one-third of such district
judge members would begin and end each year.

Court Integration and Unification.—Among the plans for
court integration considered during the year, that proposed by
the New York Temporary Commission on the Courts probably
attracted the most attention.[88] It would revise completely the
state's complex court system by consolidating its numerous parts
into a six-tiered structure, with the present court of appeals and
the appellate division remaining as the two upper levels. Beneath
them in New York City there would be, respectively, a supreme
court and a general court, absorbing the numerous general and
special trial courts into which the present system is divided. Outside of New York City, trial jurisdiction would be divided between the supreme court and county courts in each county, supplemented at the base by magistrates' courts in counties where
needed. There would be no separate surrogates' courts or courts
of general sessions or special session, as at present. These would

84. 1955 Ann. Survey Am. L. 677, 31 N.Y.U.L. Rev. 170 (1956).
85. Oregon Judicial Council, 1st Ann. Rep. 27 (1956).
86. Alaska Const. art. IV, § 9 (1956).
87. Report of Proceedings of Special Session of Judicial Conference of the
U.S. 11 (March 13-14, 1956).
88. The Plan of the Temporary Commission on the Courts for a Simplified
State-Wide Court System (July 2, 1956).

be incorporated into the proposed integrated state-wide system, which would be financed by a single budget, the cost being paid out of the state treasury with partial reimbursement by local units. Even in advance of the Commission's scheduled hearings on the proposed plan, there was anticipatory opposition, such as that from the local county courts,[89] although the state and New York City bar associations have expressed their support.[90]

Connecticut's plan for the reorganization of its court system, which passed in the state senate last year but failed in the lower house, has been redrafted for submission to next year's legislative session.[91] In South Dakota a state bar committee on the judicial system has recommended a constitutional amendment to simplify and unify the selection and functions of county district court judges,[92] and Oregon's judicial council has recommended that all judicial functions of courts with lay judges in that state be transferred as soon as possible to court having law-trained judges.[93] In Massachusetts[94] and Michigan[95] measures designed to consolidate minor court systems failed to pass.

In the area of specialized integration, New York adopted a Youth Court Act as proposed by the Temporary Commission on the Courts, its purpose being to place in one court jurisdiction over youths between sixteen and twenty-one who are eligible for youthful offender treatment.[96] In counties outside New York City it would be in county court, and in the City the Court of General Sessions would have jurisdiction. Because of critical reactions to the measure, particularly in its application to nonmetropolitan areas, there are indications that postponement of its effective date will be sought in the 1957 legislature.[97]

Recognizing the need for specialist judges and special procedures in domestic relations matters, Congress has created a domestic relations branch of the municipal court in the District of Columbia.[98] In Pennsylvania the counties of Philadelphia and lations branch of the municipal court in the District of Colum-

---

89. Knight, The Proposal to Abolish All Courts of the Towns, Villages and Counties, Bull. of Westch. County Magistrates Ass'n, Jan.-Feb. 1956.

90. N.Y. Times, Sept. 27, 1956, p. 41, col. 7; id., Oct. 1, 1956, p. 29, col. 1.

91. A Bill to Strengthen the Connecticut Court System, 30 Conn. B.J. 129 (1956).

92. Report of Committee on Judicial System, 25 S. Dak. B.J. 45 (1956).

93. Oregon Judicial Council, 1st Ann. Rep. 4 (1956).

94. Mass. H.B. 725 (1956).

95. Mich. H.B. 99 (1956).

96. N.Y. Laws 1956, c. 838; 1956 Report of the Temporary Commission on the Courts 29 (Feb. 15, 1956).

97. Updike, Comments on the Youth Court Bill, 16 Just. Ct. Topics, May 1956, p. 6; N.Y. Times, Aug. 5, 1956, p. 50, col. 1.

bia.[98] In Pennsylvania the counties of Philadelphia and
Allegheny have domestic relations courts, but a proposal to create
such courts in other judicial districts failed to pass.[99] Elsewhere,
as in Pennsylvania, there has been continued interest in the subject of juvenile courts and their important role in the administration of justice.[100]

Court Administration, Congestion, and Statistics.—The problem of court congestion and delay was the subject of a conference
called by the Attorney General in May and attended by some
ninety representatives of bar associations, courts, and agencies
concerned with improvement in judicial administration.[101] The
conference approved a report that it be established on a continuing and permanent basis, functioning through an executive committee, to receive and correlate information on projects for the
better administration of justice, including adequate judicial statistics, assignment of judges, use of discovery and pre-trial procedures, handling of court calendars, control of the progress of
litigation, and the professional responsibility of the bar to assist
in improving judicial administration.[102]

The annual Calendar Status Study for the year ending June 30,
1956, indicates that there has been little, if any, over-all improvement in the reducing of time from "at issue" to trial of civil jury
cases.[103]The court with the longest time interval from "at issue"
to trial, forty-six months, is the Supreme Court of Queens
County, New York. It is followed by the Supreme Court of New
York County, with forty-one months for personal injury cases,
and the Superior Court of Worcester County, Massachusetts, with
forty months.[104] Noteworthy among the courts showing a decrease

98. Pub. L. No. 486, 84th Cong., 2d Sess. (April 11, 1956). See Dalton,
New Domestic Relations Court in the District of Columbia, 23 J.B. Ass'n of
D.C. 414 (1956); Mittlebeeler, New Family Tribunal Eases Court Congestion
in Nation's Capital, 40 J. Am. Jud. Soc'y 19 (1956).

99. Pa. H.B. 1296 (1956); Smith, A Domestic Relations Court for Pennsylvania, 60 Dick. L. Rev. 181 (1956). See Note, The Family in the Courts,
17 U. Pitt. L. Rev. 206 (1956), for a comprehensive study of domestic relations jurisdiction in Allegheny County and the need for an integrated family
court.

100. Pound, The Juvenile Court in the New-Time America, 7 Juvenile Ct.
Judges J. 78 (1956); Alexander, A Legal Look at Juvenile Court, 27 Clev. B.
Ass'n J. 171 (1956); Busser, Citizens Look at the Juvenile Court, 19 Shingle
97 (1956); Kohler, The Courts for Handling Youth, 2 Nat'l Probation &
Parole Ass'n J. 123 (1956).

101. Proceedings of the Attorney General's Conference on Court Congestion and Delay in Litigation (May 21-22, 1956). See Rogers, Let's Eliminate
the Delay in the Trial of Cases, 28 N.Y. State B. Bull. 281-84 (1956).

102. Proceedings, supra note 101, at 138.

103. Inst. Jud. Admin., Calendar Status Study—1956 (June 30, 1956). The
study this year also includes figures showing time intervals from "first filing"
to trial.

104. Id. at iii.

in delay is the Supreme Court of Kings County, New York, where the time interval from "at issue" to trial dropped from thirty-eight months in 1955 to twenty-six months in 1956.

The Administrative Director of the United States Courts has noted "a gleam of light ahead" in the picture of congestion in the federal district courts.[105] In the southern district of New York, which last year reported the longest delays, a decrease of approximately 68 per cent in the pending backlog of cases on calendar was achieved during the year ended June 30, 1956.[106] This marked improvement has been attributed to a new system of calendar control by the judges and the elimination of "dead-wood" cases.

In New York an experiment in holding summer court sessions as a device to relieve congestion was undertaken on recommendation of the Judicial Conference.[107] In September the chief judge of the court of appeals reported that the experiment was sufficiently successful to justify its continuance in future summers in counties where conditions so warranted.[108]

Other devices for expediting trial calendars include the temporary transfer of judges to courts where congestion is greatest. Such a procedure has been adopted in Massachusetts[109] and has been effectively used in Missouri.[110] The device of compulsory arbitration as a remedy for congested calendars has continued to operate successfully in Pennsylvania.[111] In the area of appellate courts, the Oregon supreme court has held unconstitutional a provision that would allow circuit court judges to sit temporarily on the supreme court.[112] In Washington the judicial council has recommended that an intermediate appellate court be established, and that the supreme court be authorized to request aid from superior court judges in reducing appellate backlogs, and also that consideration be given to increasing the supreme court from nine to eleven justices.[113]

---

105. N.Y. Times, Sept. 24, 1956, p. 17, col. 6.
106. Id., Sept. 23, 1956, p. 42, col. 1.
107. Id., May 25, 1956, p. 1, col. 5.
108. Id., Sept. 17, 1956, p. 14, col. 2.
109. Mass. Acts 1956, c. 472. Massachusetts has also increased the number of full-time district court justices and has provided for trial by six-member juries in certain courts. Mass. Acts 1956, c. 738.
110. Leedy, Temporary Transfers of Missouri Judges in 1955, 12 J. Mo. B. 1 (1956).
111. Swartz, Compulsory Arbitration: An Experiment in Pennsylvania, 42 A.B.A.J. 513 (1956); Note, Compulsory Arbitration to Relieve Trial Congestion, 8 Stan. L. Rev. 410 (1956); 31 N.Y.U.L. Rev. 1316 (1956); Inst. Jud. Admin., Compulsory Arbitration and Court Congestion: The Pennsylvania Compulsory Arbitration Statute (July 1, 1956).
112. State ex rel. Madden v. Crawford, 295 P.2d 174 (Ore. 1956).
113. Among the States, 29 State Gov't 191 (1956).

The office of court administrator has continued to be a mile-stone in securing effective administration of the courts[114] with Massachusetts joining the ranks of those states which have such an office.[115]

Pre-Trial.—Pursuant to authority conferred by statute in 1955, the California Judicial Council has approved rules, effective January 1, 1957, requiring pre-trial conferences in civil actions in the superior courts.[116] In New York the Temporary Commission on the Courts has proposed a new technique for early pre-trial conferences in personal injury and death actions, in order to expedite and encourage settlement of such cases.[117] In the United States District Court for the District of Columbia, an amendment to the rules provides for settlement conferences after pre-trial or before pre-trial if the case has been at issue for six months or more and counsel are agreeable.[118] Among articles written on the subject of pre-trial have been discussions of its operations in Ohio,[119] Rhode Island,[120] and the federal courts,[121] Other discussions include federal discovery procedure[122] and New Jersey's mandatory pre-trial discovery and pre-trial conference procedures.[123]

Rule-Making and Procedural Rules.—In Massachusetts a judicial survey commission has recommended the vesting of rule-making power in the supreme judicial court.[124] The proposed draft of the legislation to implement this recommendation specifically reserves to the legislature the power to modify or repeal any such court rule.[125] The commission's recommendations were embodied by the legislature in a resolve to request the judicial council to investigate and report on the matter but the resolve

114. See Dixon, Judicial Administration in Maryland—The Administrative Office of the Courts, 16 Md. L. Rev. 95 (1956), id. at 185.

115. Mass, Acts 1956, c. 707.

116. California Judicial Council, Final Draft of Rules Relating to Pre-Trial Conferences (1956).

117. 1956 Report of the Temporary Commission on the Courts 76 (Feb. 15, 1956).

118. D.C. Dist. Ct. Local Civ. Rule 11 (h) (i) ; O'Connor, Settlement Procedure under Local Rule Eleven, 23 J.B. Ass'n of D.C. 611 (1956).

119. Pre-Trial—A Symposium, 7 Western Res. L. Rev. 367 (1956).

120. Mullen, More About Pre-Trial, R.I.B.J., May 1956, p. 1.

121. Clark, Objectives of Pre-Trial Procedure, 17 Ohio State L.J. 163 (1956) ; Pre-Trial Procedures in the Federal Court, 11 Record B. Ass'n City of N.Y. 180, 314 (1956).

122. Knepper, Some Aspects of Discovery Under the Federal Rules of Civil Procedure, 35 Neb. L. Rev. 258 (1956).

123. Remarks of Judge William J. Brennan, Jr., Proceedings, supra note 101, at 78.

124. Report, supra note 24, at 87. See Ford, Supreme Court Rule-Making Power, 27 B. Bull. (Boston B. Ass'n) 69 (1956).

125. Mass. H. Doc. 2620, at 7 (1956).

was recalled by the senate after passage and before the governor's approval.[126] Meanwhile, in New Jersey an effort to secure legislative passage of a constitutional amendment to subject the rule-making power of the supreme court to amendment by the legislature failed of passage.[127]

Further amendment of the Federal Rules of Civil Procedure has been advocated as essential to eliminate unsound results arising from interpretations in the administration of the rules.[128] In the states the movement for adoption of the Federal Rules in whole or in part continues to gain new adherents, and their adoption has been suggested in Ohio,[129] Georgia,[130] and North Dakota.[131] In Wyoming an advisory committee on rules of civil procedure has been appointed by the supreme court and is expected to consider the Federal Rules as a basis of study and recommendation.[132] The adoption of rules 7 to 25 and rule 42 has been tentatively considered by the Judicial Council in the State of Washington.[133]

Maryland has codified its rules of procedure which will go into effect on January 1, 1957.[134] In New York the Temporary Commission on the Courts has announced a tentative plan for revision of practice and procedure which would include, as one of its objectives, the shifting of responsibility for purely procedural regulation from the legislature to the courts.[135]

Jurors and Jury Selection.—Apparently as an aftermath of wide-spread publicity given last year to a jury research project involving wire-tap recording of jury deliberations, several states[136] and Congress[137] have either passed or considered measures de-

---

126. Mass. H. Res. 2862 (1956).

127. N.J. Assem. Concurrent Res. 13 (1956). See Meyner Asks Elimination of Winberry Case Rule, 79 N.J.L.J. Index, Feb. 2, 1956, p. 33.

128. Wright, Rule 56 (e): A Case Study on the Need for Amending the Federal Rules, 69 Harv. L. Rev. 839 (1956).

129. Shumaker, Should Ohio Adopt the Federal Rules of Civil Procedure?, Toledo B. Ass'n News Letter, Jan. 1956, p. 3.

130. Magruder, Why Adopt the Federal Rules?, 18 Ga. B.J. 297 (1956). Cf. Henson, Let's Quit Monkeying with Procedure, id. at 292.

131. Crum, The Proposed North Dakota Rules of Civil Procedure, 32 N. Dak. L. Rev. 88 (1956); Holtzoff, New Civil Procedure in North Dakota, id. at 81.

132. Jones, From the State Capitals (Supp. Rep. Oct. 19, 1956).

133. Letter from the Chief Justice of the Supreme Court of Washington to the Institute of Judicial Administration, June 8, 1956.

134. Maryland Rules of Procedure (1956); Order of the Maryland Court of Appeals, July 18, 1956.

135. 1956 Report of the Temporary Commission on the Courts 141 (Feb. 15, 1956).

136. Mass. Laws 1956, c. 48; Mich. Pub. Acts Reg. Sess. 1956, No. 47; N.Y. Sen. Int. 57, Pr. 57 (1956); Pa. Sen. B. 907 (1955).

137. Pub. L. No. 919, 84th Cong., 2d Sess. (Aug. 2, 1956).

signed to prohibit such recordings. In other states legislative attention has been given to the matter of compensation for jurors, and increases were enacted in Arizona,[138] Louisiana,[139] and Michigan.[140] In Michigan a measure designed to provide for payment of the difference between the juror's fee and his salary failed of passage,[141] as did a New Jersey measure concerning eligibility of unemployed jurors for unemployment insurance.[142]

The basic traits considered as prerequisite in evaluating the competency of jurors have been analyzed,[143] as have the function, qualifications, and selection of juries and the historical background and current aspects of the problem.[144] Difficulties inherent in the performance of the juror's task of attentive and objective fact determination have been noted by an analyst and by a juror.[145] From the standpoint of court congestion and delay, advocates of abolishing jury trials in automobile personal injury litigation continue to press their views.[146] Of the few states in which women are still ineligible for jury service, a constitutional amendment to remove the restriction failed to pass in South Carolina,[147] arguments have been advanced for its elimination in Alabama,[148] and a constitutional amendment in West Virginia on the subject was approved by the people in November 1956.[149]

Traffic Courts and Justices of the Peace.—The need for unremitting efforts to improve traffic-law enforcement was underscored by the fact that the nation-wide toll of traffic deaths has continued to rise.[150] A program on the subjects of traffic court procedures and the consideration of uniform traffic laws was held in Florida.[151] Other programs include those designed to educate

138. Ariz. Laws 1956, c. 91.
139. La. Acts Reg. Sess. 1956, No. 97.
140. Mich. Pub. Acts Reg. Sess. 1956, No. 64.
141. Mich. H.B. 78 (1956).
142. N.J. Assem. No. 187 (1956).
143. Note, Psychological Tests and Standards of Competence for Selecting Jurors, 65 Yale L.J. 531 (1956).
144. Vanderbilt, supra note 45.
145. McCarter, The Jury System: A Twentieth Century View, 4 Kan. L. Rev. 425 (1956); Confessions of a Juror, Wis. B. Bull., Aug. 1956, p. 21.
146. Delacy, Jury Trial of Auto Injury Claims Threatened, 35 Neb. L. Rev. 389 (1956); Hershman, The Jury—Yes or No, 3 Advocate 135 (1956); Peck, Do Juries Delay Justice?, 18 F.R.D. 455 (1956); Peck, System of Jury Trial Cause of Court Delay, Va. L. Weekly, Jan. 12, 1956, p. 1, col. 1.
147. Jones, From the State Capitals 2 (Supp. Rep. March 28, 1956).
148. See Jones, Trial by Jury in Alabama, 8 Ala. L. Rev. 274 (1956).
149. W. Va. Acts 1955, c. 22; 1955 Ann. Survey Am. L. 686, 31 N.Y.U.L. Rev. 179 (1956). The amendment was approved at the 1956 general election. Jones, From the State Capitals 2 (Supp. Rep. Nov. 9, 1956). However, it will need implementation by enabling legislation which is to be considered at the next legislative session.
150. May Traffic Toll Sets Record, Traffic Digest & Rev., July 1956, p. 17.
151. Greenberg, Our Highway Safety Program, 30 Fla. B.J. 439 (1956).

judges and prosecutors in traffic law enforcement[152] and to educate primary school children in safety awareness and the techniques of law enforcement.[153] One obstacle to the effective enforcement of traffic laws has been the lack of coordinated and centralized enforcement authority in many of the states and counties.[154] In Georgia the legislature approved a proposed constitutional amendment to authorize traffic courts in the larger cities with jurisdiction over traffic misdemeanors and drunk driving[155] but rejected an amendment that would have allowed the general assembly to create, in any city or county, traffic courts with jurisdiction to try both state and municipal offenses.[156] In Michigan the commissioner of state police received authority to promulgate a uniform traffic code which may be adopted by any city, town, or village, by reference and without publication.[157]

The movement toward supplanting justices of the peace by municipal or other local courts continues. Michigan has approved a uniform system of municipal courts to consolidate the justice courts in cities over 15,000 population.[158] Incumbent justices, even though not attorneys, may be candidates for municipal judgeships, but other candidates will be required to be members of the bar. Virginia revised its Trial Justice Act, designating its trial justices as municipal and county courts and providing that judges of the latter will be appointed by the courts of record while municipal judges will be elected.[159] The office of justice of the peace in wards with cities over 5,000 in population has been abolished in Louisiana and replaced by city judges who are required to be attorneys.[160] The Chief Justice of New Jersey has reviewed the history of justices of the peace in that state, the problems leading to the establishment of municipal courts, and some of the present shortcomings.[161]

In other states where the justice of the peace system is being retained, there are efforts to improve the system through programs of education. Thus in New York the state Department of Education and other agencies have developed a course of training for

---

152. The Esso Safety Foundation, Traffic Digest & Rev., July 1956, p. 15.

153. Primary School Safety Court, id., p. 28.

154. Traffic Court Problem Analyzed and Discussed, Va. L. Weekly, May 3, 1956, p. 1, col. 1.

155. Ga. Laws Reg. Sess. 1956, No. 79, p. 415.

156. Ga. H. Res. 168-477e.

157. Mich. Pub. Acts Reg. Sess. 1956, No. 62.

158. Id., No. 5.

159. Va. Acts 1956, c. 555.

160. La. Acts Reg. Sess. 1956, No. 326.

161. Vanderbilt, The Municipal Court—The Most Important Court in New Jersey: Its Remarkable Progress and Its Unsolved Problems, 10 Rutgers L. Rev. 647 (1956).

justices of the peace.[162] A Pennsylvaia proposal, designed to secure attendance at such an education program by limiting the
jurisdiction of justices who fail to participate, did not pass.[163]
Elsewhere the publication of manuals for use by justices of the
peace has been a significant development, notably in Georgia[164]
and Utah.[165]

Conclusion.—The problem of what is wrong with our courts
is still far from solved. Perhaps it will not be wholly solved by
human endeavor unless those who seek to achieve it are dedicated
to the task, and blessed with divine inspiration. Timely, in this
connection, is the language from a prayer offered at a special
service in New York City's Trinity Church in October 1956, designated as "A Service for the Blessing of God upon the Courts
of Justice":

> . . . We humbly beseech Thee to bless the courts of
> justice and the magistrates in all this land and give unto
> them the spirit of wisdom and understanding, that they
> may discern the truth, and impartially administer the
> law in the Fear of Thee alone . . . .

---

162. N.Y. State Univ. Outline of Course of Study for Justices of the Peace
(1956) ; Observations on Training Courses, Just. Ct. Topics, July 1956, p. 1.
See Shultz, The Future of the Justice Court, id., April 1956, p. 1.
163. Pa. H.B. 265 (1955).
164. Gibson, The Office of the Justice of the Peace in Georgia (1956).
165. Bodenheimer, Manual for Justices of the Peace in the State of Utah
(1956).

JUDICIAL ADMINISTRATION — 1957*

Far overshadowing other events in judicial administration during 1957 was the death of Chief Justice Arthur T. Vanderbilt last June. His vigorous leadership and outstanding contributions in the cause of improving the administration of justice were salient factors in whatever progress has been achieved and are monumental tributes to his memory.

One of the last articles completed before his death was an over-all review and appraisal of the past two decades of improvements in judicial administration.[1] In it, he noted the current evil of delay in litigation and the steps that can and should be taken to surmount it: improved pretrial conferences and calendar practices; modernization of procedure; elimination of partisan politics in judicial selection; simplification of court structure; centralized administrative control to facilitate the effective mobilization of judicial manpower; and improvement in appellate practices and procedures. Each of the topics is developed with the wisdom and experience of which the author had an unlimited store. His counsel and guidance will be sorely missed in the years ahead by everyone—and this means many, many individuals and organizations—who has an interest in seeing the attainment of the goals which he so clearly and steadfastly delineated.

General Revisions and Programs.—State-wide judicial revision proposals were given consideration in several states during 1957, and Illinois in particular achieved encouraging advancement. A constitutional amendment providing a comprehensive revision of the Illinois judicial system, passed by the legislature for submission to the voters at the 1958 election, incorporates much but not all of what the bar associations and local groups have been seeking for the past several years.[2] The amendment is being supported by the Chicago Bar Association and the Illinois State Bar Association, despite its differences from their original proposal.[3] If adopted, it will accomplish these far-reaching

---

*Reprinted from 1957 *Annual Survey of American Law,* p. 593. The material for this article was assembled, classified and analyzed by Philip S. Reiss, Research Assistant of the Institute.

1. Vanderbilt, Improving the Administration of Justice—Two Decades of Development, 26 U. Cin. L. Rev. 155 (1957).

2. Ill. S.J. Res. 17 (1957).

3. See Bar Activities, 43 A.B.A.J. 956, 957 (1957). Both associations feel the proposed judicial article has not gone far enough in that it fails to set up a nonpolitical system of judicial selection; it subordinates the supreme court's inherent rule-making power to future legislative action; it severely limits the general administrative control of the supreme court by not allowing it to assign judges in congested areas unless the trial courts request such aid; and it retains the counties as basic units for judicial administration.

changes: a simplified and consolidated court system comprising the supreme court, an intermediate appellate court, and all-inclusive circuit courts at the trial level; the vesting of broad administrative powers in the supreme court with an administrative officer and staff to assist the chief justice; the discontinuance of fee-paid judicial offices and the abolition of justice of the peace courts and other minor tribunals. Incumbent judges of certain courts would become circuit judges of the new circuit courts, municipal and city court judges would become associate judges of the new courts, and police magistrates and justices of the peace would become circuit court magistrates.[4] The principles of the proposed new judicial article have received wide-spread support in Illinois,[5] although there will undoubtedly be opposition from those who prefer the present system.

A proposed new judicial article for Kentucky, prepared for introduction in the 1958 legislative session, would extensively revise the judicial system of that state.[6] As drafted, the proposal would greatly simplify the present judicial structure by consolidating the judicial functions of all minor courts with those of the circuit courts, of which there would be one in each county, and the state would be divided into circuit court districts, each comprising one or more counties. A circuit court district would have a chief judge, and such additional circuit judges and associate circuit judges as prescribed by the legislature on certification by the court of appeals. The chief judge, with approval of the court of appeals, could designate circuit court commissioners as necessary, their qualifications and authority to be fixed by rule of the court of appeals. All judges would be elected on a nonpartisan ballot at the 1966 general election, and every eight years thereafter, so that all judges would come before the voters for election at the same time. The courts would constitute a unified judicial system for operation and administration, with centralized control vested in the court of appeals. Minor courts,

---

4. Explanatory Summary of Judicial Article, 39 Chi. B. Record 85 (1957).

5. Kohn, The 1957 Campaign for the Adoption of the Judicial Amendment: A Call to Action!, 45 Ill. B.J. 626 (1957); Sears, No Sport for the Shortwinded, id. at 252 (1957). See also Klockau, Some Thoughts on the Proposed Judicial Article, id. at 718; Zacharias, Judicial Reform for Illinois, 35 Chi.-Kent L. Rev. 87 (1957).

6. Legislative Research Comm'n, A Tentative Draft of Proposed Judicial Article (Nov., 1957). For background developments see Matthews, The Bar and a Study of the Kentucky Judicial System, 21 Ky. State B.J. 176 (1957); The March of Progress, 41 J. Am. Jud. Soc'y 85 (1957); The Kentucky Judicial System, An Institute for Members of the Kentucky Bar, 22 Ky. State B.J. 16 (1957).

such as the quarterly courts, justices' courts, police courts, and the office of police judge, would be abolished.[7]

In Iowa, substantial steps have been taken to implement the principles adopted by a committee of the state bar association and approved by its governing board. The proposed program embraces four integral parts: (1) a unified trial court; (2) managing judges; (3) current caseload data; and (4) a nonpolitical judiciary. Background material and plans for over-all improvement of the Iowa court system are being readied by the Iowa Council on the Judicial Article.[8]

Although not a state-wide program, an intensive and thorough-going survey of the metropolitan trial courts of Los Angeles County, California, published late in 1956, has provided one of the most complete studies yet available of the local courts of a particular area.[9] It contains a number of specific recommendations for improvement, many of which have subsequently been approved by the governing board of the Los Angeles Bar Association.[10] The California legislature, possibly stimulated in part by the Los Angeles report, has established a Joint Committee on the Administration of Justice, with an appropriation of $100,000, to study the entire California court system and to report thereon to the 1959 legislative session, with recommendations to improve the efficiency of the courts and expedite the administration of justice.[11]

Also, the Oregon legislature established a Legislative Interim Committee on Judicial Administration, composed of 21 members, and charged with making a study and written report with specific recommendations as to a number of topics pertaining to improvement of the administration of justice in that state.[12] A proposed new judicial article for Texas has been summarized and reviewed as part of an over-all study of needed revision of the state's con-

---

7. It is reported that on December 18, the legislative research commission eliminated two provisions from the plan. One would have removed judges' salaries from the $12,000 limit imposed by the constitution; the other would have empowered the legislature to enact a nonpartisan plan, other than by election, for the selection of judges. Jones, From the State Capitals 2 (Supp. Rep. Dec. 26, 1957).

8. Iowa Can Have Better Courts (1957) on file, Institute of Judicial Administration (hereinafter IJA) Library, New York University School of Law. See also Jones, From the State Capitals 1 (Supp. Rep. April 2, 1957); The Iowa State Bar Association, Annual Proceedings I-25, II-34 (1957).

9. Holbrook, A Survey of Metropolitan Trial Courts, Los Angeles Area (1956); Pirsig, Book Review, 45 Calif. L. Rev. 397 (1957).

10. Special Report on the Holbrook Courts Survey, 32 L.A. B. Bull. 149, 179, 207 (1957).

11. Cal. Stat. Reg. Sess. 1957, c. 349 (Res.). See Farley, Court Survey, 32 Calif. State B.J. 499 (1957).

12. Ore. Laws 1957, S.J. Res. 24.

stitution,[13] and a comprehensive study of the North Carolina judicial department by a state bar association committee in cooperation with the North Carolina Institute of Government is in progress.[14]

During 1957 there were also several important developments in the more specific area of court consolidation and simplification—among them the proposals and events in New York, Connecticut, and Wisconsin—as will be noted later in this article.

Judicial Selection and Tenure.—As nation-wide interest in the nonpartisan selection of judges continues to grow, attention is being increasingly directed to the Missouri Plan and its operation. That it has more than lived up to the expectations claimed for it in improving the administration of justice has been recently asserted.[15] Further impetus for the nominating-commission method was given in Kansas, where the legislature has passed a constitutional amendment, to be submitted to the people at the 1958 election, providing for the non-partisan selection of supreme court judges.[16] Under the Kansas plan, the governor will fill supreme court vacancies from a panel of three qualified candidates recommended by a thirteen-member nominating commission, and the justice so chosen will subsequently run against his record.

The Ohio Plan, noted in last year's *Survey*,[17] has received approval of both the Executive Committee of the Cleveland Bar Association[18] and the Ohio State Bar Association.[19] It would provide for a ten-member nominating commission, comprising five lawyers and five nonlawyers, appointed by the governor with the advice and consent of the senate. Judges appointed from

---

13. Stayton, The Proposed Judicial Department—Its Twenty-eight Principles, 35 Texas L. Rev. 954 (1957).

14. North Carolina Bar Plans Study of Courts, 40 J. Am. Jud. Soc'y 118 (1957). "An innovation in judicial administration research was a five-day workshop on techniques and methodology conducted for the staff of the North Carolina project by the Institute of Judicial Administration at the New York University Law Center." Ibid.

15. Crowdus, The Missouri Experience with Judicial Selection and Tenure, 21 Ky. State B.J. 186 (1957); Hyde, The Missouri Method of Selecting Judges, 41 J. Am. Jud. Soc'y 74 (1957). See also Elliott, Judicial Selection and Tenure, 3 Wayne L. Rev. 175, 182 (1957); Winters, Ideal Judicial Selection in a Practical World, 5 R.I.B.J. 1, 5 (1957).

16. Kan. Laws 1957, c. 234. As originally submitted, the proposal would also have applied to district court judges, but provisions including them were eliminated in the course of passage. See, Selection, Tenure and Retirement of Judges, 26 J.B.A. State Kan. 102, 103 (1957).

17. 1956 Ann. Survey Am. L. 598, 32 N.Y.U.L. Rev. 119 (1957).

18. CBA Resolution Approves Ohio Bar's Plan for Selection, Tenure of Judges, 29 Cleveland B.A.J. 4 (1957).

19. The Ohio State Bar Association Plan for Selection and Tenure of Judges, 30 Ohio Bar 376 (1957).

among the commission's nominees would periodically run against their records.[20] While there is vigorous support for the plan's ultimate passage and adoption, it is being opposed by the Cuyahoga County Bar Association.[21]

Meanwhile, comparable proposals in Colorado,[22] Michigan,[23] Montana,[24] Pennsylvania,[25] and Washington,[26] failed to secure legislative passage. However, the Nevada legislature gave initial approval to a constitutional amendment proposal to fill supreme court vacancies by gubernatorial appointment on recommendation of a nominating commission, the amendment to become effective after a second legislative passage in 1959 and subsequent approval by the people.[27] The Los Angeles metropolitan trial court survey recommends that appointment of trial court judges be made from a panel of three qualified persons nominated by a qualifications commission, and that such judges should thereafter run for re-election only against their records.[28] Disappointment has been expressed by bar associations in Illinois that the legislature failed to include a nonpartisan selection plan in their proposed new judiciary article,[29] and in New York a federal district judge has urged its inclusion in the court reorganization program of that state, commenting that: "The manner of their selection—that is, who selects the judges and how—is the key to the problem of winning public confidence."[30] An excellent summary of the status of judicial selection methods in the several states, and the outlook for improvement, was given in an address by the executive director of the American Judicature Society.[31]

In the selection of federal judges, a proposal drafted for consideration by the American Bar Association would establish an independent commission to advise the President on judicial appointments, and limit to not more than 60 per cent the num-

---

20. Id. at 376-77.
21. Cuyahoga County Bar Opposes Appointive Judiciary!, Cuyahoga County B. Bull. 3 (Nov. 1957). In Maryland, the state bar association failed to approve a comparable plan for that state, The March of Progress, 41 J. Am. Jud. Soc'y 55, 57 (1957).
22. Colo. S.C. Res. 2 (1957). See Holme, The Fate of the Court Bills in the Forty-First General Assembly, 34 Dicta 176 (1957).
23. Mich. S.J. Res. F. (1957).
24. Mont. H.B. 48 (1957).
25. Pa. H.B. 1030 (1957).
26. Wash. S.J. Res. 16 (1957).
27. Nev. Res. 1957, No. 21.
28. Holbrook, supra note 9, at 379.
29. See note 3 supra.
30. Lumbard, Plain Speaking About Courts and Lawyers, 12 Record B. Ass'n City of N.Y., 72, 85 (1957).
31. Winters, Judicial Selection Reform Today, 21 Ky. State B.J. 127 (1957).

ber of judicial appointees from his own political party.[32] Meanwhile, the Association's Committee on Federal Judiciary has continued to cooperate with the Attorney General and the Senate Committee on the Judiciary by making report on the qualifications of federal judicial nominees.[33]

Judicial Salaries and Retirement.—Proposals for judicial salary increases were quite prevalent in the various state legislatures this past year. Among the states giving approval to increased judicial salaries were Alabama, Arkansas, Delaware, Florida, Georgia, Idaho, Illinois, Maine, Minnesota, New Hampshire, North Carolina, Oregon, South Dakota, Texas, Utah, Vermont, Wisconsin, and Wyoming.[34]

Of the more substantial raises, Arkansas increased the salaries of supreme court justices from $9,000 to $15,000 per year and increased the salaries of the judges of the circuit and chancery courts from $7,200 to $10,800.[35] Georgia raised the salaries of associate justices of the supreme court from $14,500 to $18,000, judges of the court of appeals from $14,500 to $18,000,[36] and also raised the salaries of superior court judges from $10,000 to $12,500.[37] Idaho provided increases for the justices of the supreme court from $8,500 to $10,500, and for district court judges from $7,500 to $9,500.[38] Maine raised the salary of the chief justice of the supreme judicial court from $13,000 to $14,000 and gave the associate judges an increase from $12,000 to $13,000, while justices of the superior court were given salary increases from $11,500 to $12,500.[39] Minnesota raised the salary of the chief judge of the supreme court from $16,000 to $20,000 and the associate judges from $15,000 to $19,000.[40] Nevada increased their supreme court judges' salaries from $15,000 to $18,000,[41] while Oregon justices of the supreme court received an increase from $13,500 to $16,000,[42] and circuit judges from $11,000 to $13,000.[43] South Dakota gave their supreme court judges salary

32. New Formula Urged for Selecting Judges, A.B. News, June 1957, p. 1.

33. Fox, The Selection of Federal Judges: The Work of the Federal Judiciary Committee, 43 A.B.A.J. 685 (1957).

34. IJA, Check-List Summary of 1957 Developments in Judicial Administration 9-14 (July 17, 1957). See also The March of Progress, 41 J. Am. Jud. Soc'y 15, 17; id. at 85, 86-87 (1957).

35. Ark. Acts 1957, No. 17.

36. Ga. Laws Reg. Sess. 1957, No. 216, p. 205.

37. Ga. Laws Reg. Sess. 1957, No. 236, p. 273.

38. Idaho Laws Reg. Sess. 1957, c. 315.

39. Me. Pub. Laws 1957, c. 417, p. 575.

40. Minn. Laws 1957, c. 903.

41. Nev. Stat. 1957, c. 328.

42. Ore. Laws 1957, c. 685.

43. Ore. Laws 1957, c. 646.

increases from $8,000 to $11,000 and circuit court judges to $9,000.[44] Utah provided increased compensation for supreme court justices, raising their salaries from $10,000 to $12,000 annually,[45] and the district court judges also received increases from $8,000 to $10,000 per year.[46] In Washington, the salaries of supreme court judges were increased from $15,000 to $20,000, and of superior court judges from $12,000 to $15,000.[47] The Washington legislature also passed a state constitutional amendment, to be submitted to the people at the next general election, eliminating the prohibition against increasing judicial salaries during a term of office.[48] The chief justice of the Wisconsin supreme court received an increase from $14,500 to $18,000, the other six justices from $14,000 to $17,500.[49]

Judicial salary proposals in other states were less successful. In California provisions for over-all increases in judicial salaries failed to receive legislative approval,[50] and Colorado measures met with a similar fate.[51] Proposed substantial increases in Delaware for the chief justice and associate justices also failed to gain approval.[52] The New Mexico legislature did not approve a proposed increase for supreme court and district court judges,[53] and a bill for substantial judicial salary raises in Ohio also failed to pass.[54]

Increases were granted to certain county and local court judges in Maryland,[55] Montana,[56] and Oklahoma.[57] In Vermont, probate judges were changed from a fee schedule basis and provided instead with salaries ranging from $2,500 to $7,500, depending upon the population of the probate district.[58]

A recent study by the Council of State Governments tabulates the salaries for state appellate and trial court judges, and notes that the median salary for justices of the highest courts has risen from $10,000 in 1950 to $16,000 in 1957, an increase of 60 per

44. S.D. Laws 1957, c. 166.
45. Utah Laws Reg. Sess. 1957, c. 148.
46. Utah Laws Reg. Sess. 1957, c. 149.
47. Wash. Laws Reg. Sess. 1957, c. 260.
48. Wash. Laws Reg. Sess. 1957, S.J. Res. 9.
49. Wis. Laws 1957, c. 633.
50. Cal. S.B. 162 (1957).
51. Colo. H.B. 3, 5, 25, 38, 50, 303, 408 (1957); Colo. S.B. 115 (1957). See Holme, supra note 22, at 177.
52. Del. H.B. 154 (1957).
53. N.M. H.B. 126 (1957).
54. Ohio H.B. 486 (1957).
55. Md. Laws Reg. Sess. 1957, cc. 322, 343, 470, 683, 825.
56. Mont. Laws 1957, c. 47.
57. Okla. Laws 1957, tit. 19, pp. 108-11.
58. Vt. Laws 1957, No. 300.

cent.[59] The study points out, however, that by reason of decreased dollar value the actual increment in terms of constant dollars was considerably less, and in a few states there was practically no actual increase or even a slight decline.

State legislatures in 1957 also gave attention to various retirement and pension systems for members of the judiciary.[60] Arizona provides pensions for judges of the supreme and superior court who have served 20 years on either or both of these courts and have attained the age of 65. The retirement pension is to be two-thirds of the amount of the judge's salary at resignation or termination of his service. The measure also provides for retirement of judges with less than 20 years but not less than 12 years of service, the amount paid being prorated in accordance with length of service.[61] The Utah legislature took a similar step in providing a retirement plan for supreme and district court judges who have reached the age of 70 with 10 years service or have had 20 years service regardless of age. This bill also included a disability provision.[62] Oklahoma has set up a pension system whereby veteran judges may leave office and become supernumerary judges and be paid an income not to exceed 75 per cent of the former salary, and the chief justice of the supreme court may call upon the supernumeraries to serve as district or superior court judges if the need arises.[63] The Pennsylvania legislature has given legislative approval to a new retirement plan,[64] and other states either amended or made minor provisions in existent retirement and pension plans for the benefit of the judiciary.[65]

Judicial Conduct, Discipline, and Removal.—With respect to controversial Canon 35 of the Canons of Judicial Ethics, the American Bar Foundation special committee on canons has submitted its report. In substance, the committee has recommended that there be no relaxation of the present restriction against broadcasting or televising court trials but that the canon should be modified in order to permit photographing or televising of

59. Council of State Governments, Compensation of Judges of State Appellate Courts, Trial Courts of General Jurisdiction and Courts of Limited Jurisdiction (June, 1957).

60. IJA, Check-List Summary of 1957 Developments in Judicial Administration 14-17 (July 17, 1957).

61. Ariz. Laws 1957, c. 25.

62. Utah Laws Reg. Sess. 1957, c. 87.

63. Okla. Laws 1957, tit. 74, p. 548.

64. Pa. Laws 1957, No. 291.

65. Ind. Acts 1957, c. 234; Md. Laws Reg. Sess. 1957, c. 344; Neb. Laws Reg. Sess. 1957, c. 79; N.D. Laws 1957, c. 210; Wash. Laws Reg. Sess. 1957, c. 243.

ceremonial occasions in courtrooms.[66] The report gives five principal reasons for the recommendation: Judges should be left free from avoidable "distractions or disturbances that are inimical to judicious conduct;" trials have none of the attributes of ceremony spectacle or entertainment; trials are no less public because cameras and broadcasting equipment are excluded; photographic reporting introduces extraneous influences; and judges should not be placed in the position of censors.[67]

The survey of the Los Angeles metropolitan courts has recommended that a specially constituted body, consisting of appellate justices, be given disciplinary power over judges of the superior, municipal, and justice courts.[68]

With respect to suspension and removal of judges, section 16 of the proposed new judicial article for Illinois provides that

> . . . subject to rules of procedure to be established by the Supreme Court and after notice and hearing, any judge may be retired for disability or suspended without pay or removed for cause by a commission composed of one judge of the Supreme Court selected by that court, two judges of the Appellate Court selected by that court, and two circuit judges selected by the Supreme Court. Such commission shall be convened by the Chief Justice upon order of the Supreme Court or at the request of the Senate.[69]

Judicial Councils and Judicial Conferences.—The South Carolina legislature, by way of implementation of a supreme court order in 1956 forming an ad interim twenty-one-member judicial council to serve until June 30, 1957,[70] passed a bill creating a permanent judicial council, with the same general composition as the ad interim committee. The functions of the council will include a continuing study and survey of the administration of justice in the state and the practice, procedure and rules of the state courts.[71]

---

66. A.B.A. Coordinator and Pub. Rel. Bull., Nov. 1, 1957, p. 1; N.Y. Times, Nov. 2, 1957, p. 39, col. 1.

67. American Bar Foundation, Report and Recommendations on a Restatement of Canon 35 of the Canons of Judicial Ethics by the Special Committee on Canons of Ethics (1957). For earlier viewpoints see Cedarquist, The Case for Canon 35, 45 Ill. B.J. 698 (1957); McCandless, The Case Against Canon 35, id. at 544.

68. Holbrook, supra note 9, at 380-81. See also White, Should Judges be Subject to Disciplinary Action?, 32 L.A.B. Bull. 99 (1957).

69. Explanatory Summary of Judicial Article, 39 Chi. B. Record 85, 91-92 (1957).

70. See 1956 Ann. Survey Am. L. 603, 32 N.Y.U.L. Rev. 124 (1957).

71. S.C. Acts 1957, No. 41

A California proposal to enlarge the membership of its judicial council to include four members of the state bar appointed by the board of governors failed of passage.[72] The Ohio legislature increased from 15 to 16 the membership of its judicial council by adding to it the administrative assistant to the supreme court.[73]

In Washington legislation was enacted to authorize the supreme court in its discretion to provide by rule or special order for calling an annual judicial conference for the consideration of matters relating to judicial business, the improvement of the judicial system and the administration of justice.[74] Oklahoma provided by legislation that the district and superior court judges shall meet monthly with the other judges of the county for the purpose of discussing problems connected with civil and criminal trials.[75] The Ohio legislature failed to pass a bill to provide for annual meetings of probate, juvenile, and common pleas courts judges, attended also by the chief justice of the state supreme court.[76]

A comprehensive summary of state provisions pertaining to judicial councils, judicial conferences, and related organizations was prepared and published for the Washington State Judicial Council by the University of Washington Law Library in December 1957. It gives brief descriptions of their composition and functions, with supplemental references to their publications.[77]

Court Integration and Unification.—As mentioned above, the proposed new judicial articles for Illinois[78] and Kentucky,[79] respectively, would achieve complete integration and consolidation of trial court functions in the new all-inclusive circuit courts of general jurisdiction, supplanting justices of the peace and other local judicial tribunals. If ultimately adopted, these proposals would mark the farthest advances yet achieved by any states toward simplification and unification of their court systems.

The Iowa court plan now undergoing study and preparation by the Iowa Council on the Judicial Article contemplates a supreme court and a unified trial court, the latter to replace the present district, municipal, superior, justice of the peace, mayors', and police courts; the vesting in the chief justice of administra-

---

72. Cal. S. Const. Amend. 11 (1957).
73. Ohio S.B. 39 (1957).
74. Wash. Laws Reg. Sess. 1957, c. 259.
75. Okla. Laws 1957, Spec. Act, p. 680.
76. Ohio S.B. 27 (1957).
77. U. Wash. Law Library, State Judicial Councils, Judicial Conferences, Court Administrators and Related Organizations (1957).
78. See note 2 supra.
79. See note 6 supra.

tive authority over the entire court system, with power to assign judges as the necessity arises; and the requirement that all judges be members of the bar and serve on a full-time basis.[80]

The history of New York's effort in 1957 to achieve at least partial consolidation of its complex court system provides an interesting case study in successful opposition by defenders of the status quo. The plan proposed by the New York Temporary Commission on the Courts, and described in last year's *Survey*,[81] was introduced in the legislature[82] with the widespread backing of citizen groups throughout the state. At a hearing before the judiciary committees of the legislature in February, the chief judge of the court of appeals counseled that there should be a year's delay to permit further study of the proposal, while other witnesses opposed certain aspects of the plan, and still others stressed the need for urgent action during the present session.[83] On March 20, by way of concession to the opposition, certain changes in the original plan were agreed to, namely, the addition of a separate family court for New York City, the exemption of justices of the peace from the proposed plan, and the elimination of the recommendation for constituting Queens County a separate judicial district.[84] After passing the senate, the bill embodying the plan finally came up for action by the assembly in the closing hours of the legislative session on March 30, with a "compromise resolution," designed to effect the main features of the Commission's plan, and backed by leaders of the majority party in both houses. By a vote of 112 to 32, the compromise resolution was referred back to committee, and the other measures were allowed to die without action, thereby effectively terminating New York's hopes for court revision during 1957.[85] The legislature did, however, grant an appropriation of $125,000 to the Temporary Commission to continue its activities for another year.[86] As of December 31, the Commission had not yet officially announced a new plan of court reorganization, although supporters of the original plan were hopeful that a new proposal embodying substantially the same features would be ready for introduction in the forthcoming 1958 session. Meanwhile, at the state bar association meeting in June, the chief judge of the court of appeals had expressed the view that a plan for reorgani-

80. See note 8 supra.
81. 1956 Ann. Survey Am. L. 603, 32 N.Y.U.L. Rev. 124 (1957).
82. N.Y.S.B. 345 (1957).
83. N.Y. Times, Feb. 13, 1957, p. 1, col. 5.
84. Id., Mar. 21, 1957, p. 1, col. 1.
85. Id., Mar. 31, 1957, p. 1, col. 8.
86. N.Y. Laws 1957, cc. 258, 618.

zation and consolidation of the court structure in New York City "would provide an invaluable pilot study for the rest of the State."[87]

Several bills proposing court reorganization in Connecticut were introduced in the 1957 legislative session.[88] The most comprehensive proposal, prepared by a committee of the state bar association, provided for a five-court system comprising the supreme court of errors, the superior court, the court of common pleas, the family court, and the probate court, and would thereby have supplanted the justices of the peace, trial justices, and municipal courts.[89] All of the bills, however, failed of legislative passage.

In Wisconsin a constitutional amendment passed by the 1955 legislature providing for a reorganization of the court structure failed to get the required approval of the 1957 legislature necessary for its submission to the people.[90] However a resolution proposing a new study of the Wisconsin courts by the judicial council was approved by the legislature.[91]

Massachusetts legislation passed in 1956 but not effective until July 1, 1957, provides for the reorganization of the district courts and full-time judicial service for all district court judges. Under this act, 32 more of the court judges are to be placed on a full-time basis at a salary of $12,000 annually.[92]

The New Hampshire house of representatives rejected a proposed new system of district courts for the state. Under the plan, 32 district courts would have been substituted for the now existing 82 municipal courts.[93]

In Maine a legislative research committee has been directed to study the desirability of creating a district court system integrating the activities of the municipal court and trial justice systems.[94]

A proposal that all municipal courts of Los Angeles County be integrated into one Los Angeles County municipal court was

---

87. Conway, The Report of the Chief Judge, 29 N.Y. State B. Bull. 277, 287 (1957).

88. Conn. S.B. 408 (1957); Conn. H.B. 134, 1812 (1957). See Mars, Court Reorganization in Connecticut, 41 J. Am. Jud. Soc'y 6, 13-14 (1957).

89. Conn. H.B. 1812 (1957).

90. Wis. S.J. Res. 18 (1957). Under the proposed reorganization, only the supreme court, circuit court and justices of the peace would be retained. Probate, municipal and other inferior courts would have been abolished. Hallows, Court Reorganization, Wis. B. Bull., Feb. 1956, p. 7; Court Reorganization Plan Details Submitted, Id. at 14 (June 1956).

91. Jones, From the State Capitals 2 (Supp. Rep. July 2, 1957).

92. Mass. Laws Ann. c. 218, §§ 6, 77A (Michie Supp. 1957).

93. Jones, From the State Capitals 1 (Supp. Rep. July 2, 1957).

94. Letter from the Director of Legislative Research, State of Maine, to Mrs. Fannie J. Klein, Dec. 26, 1957, on file in IJA.

one of the recommendations of the Los Angeles metropolitan trial court survey[95] and more recently, a committee of the Los Angeles municipal court judges' association has put forward a plan to consolidate the municipal courts, justice courts, and the existing superior court into one trial court of unlimited jurisdiction.[96]

Court Administration, Congestion, and Statistics.—The state court administrator of New York in January pointed out that "it is imperative that a comprehensive and systematic method of handling business matters of the courts be devised and instituted," and also noted that a recent report on coordination was "a significant admonition to the judges to correct the present inept, inadequate, insufficient, and outmoded system of court business administration."[97] The solution to the problem has been well described by the court administrator of Michigan, chairman of the National Conference of Court Administrators, in an article discussing the purpose and functions of the office of court administrator, and stressing the importance of keeping an accurate current inventory of the condition of the court dockets.[98] To remedy the shortcomings of existing statistical methods in New York, a new system of record-keeping effective July 1, 1957, has been adopted by the state judicial conference.[99]

Meanwhile, state legislatures in California, Connecticut, and Washington have enacted measures to strengthen court administration in whole or in part of their respective judicial systems. The California act establishes an executive officer for the superior court of Los Angeles County, to hold office at the pleasure of the court and to exercise such administrative powers and perform such duties as the court may require.[100] In Connecticut, the chief justice of the supreme court of errors is made "administrative director of the judicial department and responsible for the efficient operation . . . of its constituent courts . . . for the expeditious dispatch of litigation therein and the proper conduct of the business. . . ."[101]

The Washington legislation creates an administrative office

---

95. Holbrook, supra note 9, at 378.

96. L.A. Daily J., December 9, 1957, p. 1, col. 8.

97. Eightieth Annual Meeting, 29 N.Y. State B. Bull. 3, 21-22 (1957).

98. Doyle, The Administrative Officer of the Courts: His Role in Government, 30 State Gov't 262 (1957). See also Chandler, The Director of Administration of Trial Courts, 21 F.R.D. 65, 84-88 (1958).

99. Conway, supra note 87, at 282.

100. Cal. Govt. Code Ann. § 69892.1 (West Supp. 1957). By its terms the act applies to "any county with a population of over 2,000,000," which necessarily limits it, for the present at least, to Los Angeles County.

101. Conn. Pub. Acts Reg. Sess. 1957, No. 651.

under the supervision and direction of the chief justice of the supreme court, with a court administrator to make recommendations for improvement of administrative methods, examine the state of court dockets, and recommend the reassignment of judges to courts where needed. With the chief justice's approval, the administrator may withhold the salary of a superior court judge who refuses to work in another county when assigned to do so. Additional duties of the administrator include the compilation of statistics as to business transacted and the cost of maintaining the judicial system.[102]

Legislative proposals to create administrative offices and administrative officer positions failed of passage in Indiana[103] and Pennsylvania,[104] respectively. In Ohio, the Cleveland Bar Association has recommended that an executive officer be appointed as an interim measure to help the city's court of common pleas to reduce its backlog.[105] And in Massachusetts, the first annual report of the new executive secretary of the supreme judicial court analyzes problems of court congestion in that state and recommends specific solutions.[106]

Despite the forward steps taken in some states, the nation-wide picture of court congestion and delay shows continuing need of improvement in many areas. The Institute of Judicial Administration's annual calendar status study for 1957 indicates there has been little, if any, over-all improvement in reducing the average time interval from "at issue" to trial of personal injury jury cases.[107] The Supreme Court of New York County, however, decreased the interval from "at issue" to trial from 41 months in 1956 to 31.4 months in 1957, and the Superior Court of Worcester County, Massachusetts, in the same period, decreased the interval from 40 months to 11. The court with the longest average interval from "at issue" to trial, as of June 30, was the Superior Court of Cook County, Illinois, with a time lag of 54 months.[108]

Two other reports published by the Institute touch on related aspects of personal injury litigation, one dealing with the subject of contingent fees[109] and the other with the recovery of in-

102. Wash. Laws Reg. Sess. 1957, c. 259.
103. Ind. H.B. 137 (1957).
104. Pa. H.B. 1002 (1957).
105. See The March of Progress, 41 J. Am. Jud. Soc'y 85, 87 (1957).
106. Report to Supreme Judicial Court of Executive Secretary as of June 30, 1957.
107. IJA, State Trial Courts of General Jurisdiction, Calendar Status Study —1957 at 2 (June 30, 1957).
108. Id. at 3-4.
109. IJA, Contingent Fees in Personal Injury and Wrongful Death Actions in the United States (April 22, 1957).

terest as damages.[110]

Recommendations for the immediate initiation of action programs to meet the problems of congestion and delay in state courts were put forward in a report of the executive committee of the United States Attorney General's Conference published in January. They included: the establishment of centralized administrative supervision of all courts in a single head; the maintenance of uniform and up-to-date judicial statistics; the adoption of modernized rules of procedure; the adoption of businesslike methods for supervising court calendars; and the holding of frequent conferences of members of the bar and judges to encourage cooperation in efficient judicial administration.[111]

In the United States courts, the annual report of the director of the administrative office shows an increase in cases filed in the courts of appeals and also in civil cases in the district courts.[112] Of the latter, in districts outside the District of Columbia, the number of private civil actions commenced was more than 10 per cent above the number for the preceding year. Despite this increase, notable improvement was achieved in the Southern District of New York in reducing its pending caseload from 5,600 cases at the end of 1955 to 1,800 ready cases in 1956 and to 821 in 1957.[113] The director's report comments that: "The outstanding accomplishments of this court in a two year period are a tribute to its efficient administration and the effective work of its judges."[114]

In several states, the problems of congestion and delay have become increasingly acute at the appellate court level. Thus, in Colorado the chief justice has warned that the state supreme court's backlog of cases is approaching a crisis,[115] and a judicial conference has been appointed by the governor to study the problem, including the possibility of intermediate appellate

---

110. IJA, Recovery of Interest as Damages in Personal Injury Cases (March 4, 1957).

111. Report of the Initial Meeting of the Executive Committee of the Attorney General's Conference on Court Congestion and Delay in Litigation 2-3 (January 7, 1957).

112. Annual Report of the Director of the Administrative Office of the United States Courts I-1 (September 1957).

113. Id. at I-28.

114. Id. at I-7. The report further notes that "During the past year [the Southern District of New York] has disposed of 301 civil cases per judge, compared with the national average of 230 cases." Ibid. The New York Times reported that the time for a calendared case to reach trial had been cut from 35 months in 1955 to six months in 1957. N.Y. Times, Sept. 23, 1957, p. 16, col. 1.

115. See The March of Progress, 41 J. Am. Jud. Soc'y 85, 87 (1957).

courts as a solution.[116] Similar difficulties are being encountered
by the highest court in Kentucky,[117] and plans are under discussion in Louisiana to increase the number or size of the state's
intermediate appellate courts.[118] The state bar association in
Maryland has adopted a proposal to study congestion in the
court of appeals of that state.[119] A recent article analyzes the
workload of the Oregon supreme court justices, and offers suggested remedies,[120] and the newly-established legislative Interim
Committee on Judicial Administration is charged among other
things with "investigation of the feasibility of instituting a
system of intermediate appellate courts in Oregon."[121] The solution achieved in Florida by the adoption of a constitutional
amendment establishing district courts of appeal was noted in
last year's *Survey*,[122] and its subsequent implementation is discussed in a recent law review comment.[123]

Another approach to the solution of appellate court congestion
is through a study of their internal operating practices and procedures. This has been a subject of intensive consideration in
the annual summer seminars for appellate judges held at New
York University School of Law.[124] A comprehensive report by
the Institute of Judicial Administration, prepared for use in the
1957 seminar, analyzes in detail the comparative internal operating procedures of state and federal appellate courts.[125]

Other solutions to the over-all problem of congestion and delay at the trial court as well as the appellate court level include
the obvious ones of increasing the number of judges,[126] of

---

116. Jones, From the State Capitals 1 (Supp. Rep. Nov. 8, 1957).

117. Legislative Research Commission, Report of the Advisory Committee
on the Judicial System to the Legislative Research Commission and the 1956
General Assembly 1 (Jan. 1956).

118. Tucker, Appellate Jurisdiction of the Supreme Court and Courts of
Appeal in Louisiana, 5 La. B.J. 31 (1957).

119. The March of Progress, 41 J. Am. Jud. Soc'y 85, 87 (1957).

120. Tongue, Delays on Appeals to the Oregon Supreme Court, 36 Ore. L.
Rev. 253 (1957).

121. Ore. Laws 1957, S.J. Res. 24, p. 1350.

122. 1956 Ann. Survey Am. L. 596, 32 N.Y.U.L. Rev. 117 (1957).

123. Note, The Status of Judicial Reform in the State of Florida, 12 U.
Miami L. Rev. 104 (1957). Fla. Laws 1957, c. 57-248, implemented the new
constitutional amendment by establishing three district courts of appeal.

124. Leflar, The Appellate Judges Seminar at New York University, 9 J.
Legal Educ. 359 (1956). See also Vanderbilt, supra note 1, at 274-75.

125. IJA, Apellate Courts. Internal Operating Procedure. Preliminary Report (July 5, 1957).

126. For example, the California legislature authorized an increase in the
number of judges of the superior court in Los Angeles County from 80 to 90.
Cal. Stat. Reg. Sess. 1957, c. 2150.

making retired judges eligible for temporary appointment,[127] or of providing for the assignment of judges from underworked to overworked courts.[128] A still further possibility, noted in previous *Survey* articles, and one that continues to attract considerable attention and interest, is the Pennsylvania plan for the compulsory arbitration of certain controversies of $1,000 or less.[129]

In sum, there is no single panacea for curing court calendar congestion and delay in litigation, nor, as pointed out by Mr. Justice Brennan of the United States Supreme Court, is the absence of calendar congestion necessarily a sign of good judicial administration. Even with the congestion problem cured, there remains "the often hard and arduous job of bringing about fundamental and long overdue changes in our archaic judicial structures."[130]

Pretrial.—Last year's *Survey* noted that California had adopted rules establishing mandatory pretrial conferences in civil actions in the superior court, effective January 1, 1957.[131] In Los Angeles County the superior court created four special departments to handle pretrials exclusively,[132] and a report covering the first six months of operations in 1957 shows not only an increase of 7 per cent over the preceding year in total cases disposed of, but also a saving in the length of time required for trial of pretried cases as compared with those not pretried.[133]

Among articles dealing with the subject of pretrial are those discussing its operation in Texas,[134] and the background of its adoption in Philadelphia,[135] respectively. Mention should be made also of the broadening of the scope of discovery in Cali-

127. Miss. Laws Reg. Sess. 1957, c. 678; Ore. Laws 1957, S.J. Res. 30 (a proposed constitutional amendment to be submitted to the people at the next general election).

128. Ohio Rev. Code Ann. § 2503.04 (Page Supp. 1957).

129. 1955 Ann. Survey Am. L. 682, 31 N.Y.U.L. Rev. 175 (1956); 1956 Ann. Survey Am. L. 606, 32 N.Y.U.L. Rev. 127 (1957); LaBrum, Congested Trial Calendars: It's About Time To Do Something About Them, 43 A.B.A.J. 311 (1957).

130. Brennan, speech originally delivered March 11, 1957 at New York University Law Alumni Ass'n, Inc., reprinted in IJA, Modernizing The Courts 2 (1957).

131. 1956 Ann. Survey Am. L. 607, 32 N.Y.U.L. Rev. 128 (1957). See also Kincaid, Pre-Trial Conference Procedure in California, 4 U.C.L.A.L. Rev. 377 (1957); Nelson, Pre-Trial—An Effective Weapon of Advocacy, Id. at 381.

132. Special Report of the Holbrook Courts Survey, 32 L.A.B. Bull. 207 (1957).

133. L.A. Metropolitan News, Sept. 23, 1957, p. 1. The report gives the following comparative figures for pretried and nonpretried cases: "Jury trials: pre-tried 3.14 days, non pre-tried 4.41. Non-jury pre-tried 1.42, non pre-tried 1.66. Dom. Rel.: pre-tried 1.42, non pre-tried 1.38."

134. Thode, The Case for the Pre-trial Conference in Texas, 35 Texas L. Rev. 372 (1957).

135. Propper, Pre-Trial Comes to Philadelphia, 20 The Shingle 34 (1957).

fornia,[136] the adoption of new discovery rules in Iowa,[137] proposed legislation in Massachusetts for pretrial oral depositions,[138] as well as recent discussions of federal discovery procedure,[139] and of discovery practice in Ohio.[140] A comparative study of pretrial discovery shows that since the adoption of the federal rules in 1938, some 24 states have substantially modified their disclosure rules to facilitate discovery.[141]

A new approach to the subject of the pretrial of protracted federal cases was utilized in August at the New York University School of Law. Through the joint cooperation of the Institute of Judicial Administration, the Committee on Pretrial Procedure of the Judicial Conference of the United States, and the Administrative Office of the United States Courts, a week-long seminar, participated in by 31 federal judges from throughout the United States, was devoted to pretrial procedures and techniques in the handling of anti-trust and other protracted litigation.[142]

Rule-Making and Procedural Rules.— During the summer, both North Dakota[143] and Wyoming[144] were added to the growing list of states that have adopted new rules of civil procedure patterned after the federal rules. In a referendum of the members of the state bar of West Virginia, approval was given, by a vote of nearly four to one, for adoption of proposed rules similar to those used in the federal courts.[145] Consideration is also being given to the adoption of such rules in Idaho[146] and South Caro-

---

136. Cal. Stat. Reg. Sess. 1957, c. 1904. See Selected 1957 Code Legislation, 32 Calif. State B.J. 501, 568 (1957).

137. Vestal, New Iowa Discovery Rules, 43 Iowa L. Rev. 8 (1957).

138. Cross and Cronin, Memorandum in Support of Legislation to Provide for Pre-Trial Oral Depositions of the Parties in Superior Court, Mass. L.Q., July 1957, p. 63; Cross and Cronin, Pre-Trial Oral Depositions, Boston B.J., May 1957, p. 19. On the successful use of pretrial conferences in Middlesex County, Massachusetts, see Cronin, Hon. John V. Sullivan, id., June, 1957, p. 27.

139. Armstrong, The Use of Pre-trial and Discovery Rules: Expedition and Economy in Federal Civil Cases, 43 A.B.A.J. 693 (1957); Orfield, Discovery and Inspection in Federal Criminal Procedure, 59 W. Va. L. Rev. 221 (1957).

140. Woodle, Discovery Practice in Ohio—Pathway to Progress, 8 Western Res. L. Rev. 456 (1957).

141. Weinstein, Gleit, and Kay, Procedures for Obtaining Information Before Trial, 35 Texas L. Rev. 481, 484 (1957).

142. See Seminar On Protracted Cases, Proceedings, New York University Law Center, August 26-30, 1957.

143. N.D. B. News Letter, April, 1957, p. 1.

144. The March of Progress, 41 J. Am. Jud. Soc'y 85 (1957).

145. Bar Approves New Procedural Rules, 1 W. Va. State B. News 389 (1957).

146. See Bar Activities, 43 A.B.A.J. 956, 959 (1957).

lina.[147] In Alabama, meanwhile, legislation designed to modernize and simplify procedure and practice in that state, having passed the lower house, encountered opposition in the senate which has deferred it.[148]

The role of the federal rules in providing leadership for state procedural reform has been reviewed by Judge Alexander Holtzoff,[149] and an article prepared for the Committee on Michigan Procedural Revision extensively surveys the development and scope of judicial rule-making.[150] The need for a continuous study of the federal rules by the Judicial Conference, with a view to making recommendations as to additions and revisions, was discussed at the American Bar Association's regional meeting at Louisville in November under the chairmanship of Mr. Justice Tom C. Clark,[151] and the need for re-establishing on a permanent basis a continuing advisory body on the federal rules has been stressed elsewhere.[152]

Jurors and Jury Selection.—As in past years, legislative concern for jurors was manifested primarily in regard to their compensation, with some consideration given also to the subject of jury exemption. Increased fees for jury service were provided in California,[153] Idaho,[154] Maryland,[155] Missouri,[156] Nebraska,[157] North Dakota,[158] and West Virginia.[159] Exemption from jury service in Florida was extended to certain editorial employees of radio and television stations, practitioners of Christian Science, and members of fire companies;[160] while Rhode Island, in the other direction, eliminated the automatic exemptions previously

---

147. Practice Rules Under Consideration By Judicial Council, S.C.B. Ass'n News Bull., Nov., 1957, p. 1.

148. See Jones, From the State Capitals 1 (Supp. Rep. May 28, 1957); The March of Progress, 41 J. Am. Jud. Soc'y 85 (1957). For discussion of the proposed rules, see Skinner, Alabama's Approach to a Modern System of Pleading and Practice, 20 F.R.D. 119 (1957); A Symposium on the Proposed Alabama Rules of Civil Procedure, 9 Ala. L. Rev. 167 (1957).

149. Holtzoff, Judicial Procedure Reform; The Leadership of the Supreme Court, 43 A.B.A.J. 215 (1957).

150. Joiner and Miller, Rules of Practice and Procedure: A Study of Judicial Rule-Making, 55 Mich. L. Rev. 623 (1957).

151. The proceedings are reported in The Rule-Making Function and the Judicial Conference of the United States, 21 F.R.D. 117 (1958).

152. The Crisis in Federal Rule-Making, 40 J. Am. Jud. Soc'y 99 (1957).

153. Cal. Stat. Reg. Sess. 1957, c. 1406.

154. Idaho Laws Reg. Sess. 1957, c. 144.

155. Md. Laws Reg. Sess. 1957, cc. 276, 425, 451, 474, 527, 809, 820.

156. Mo. Stat. Ann. §§ 494.100, 494.110, 494.120, 494.170 (Vernon Supp. 1957).

157. Neb. Laws Reg. Sess. 1957, c. 134-1.

158. N.D. Laws 1957, c. 280, pertaining to jurors' fees in police magistrate and village justice of the peace courts.

159. W. Va. Acts Reg. Sess. 1957, c. 101.

160. Fla. Laws 1957, c. 57-95.

given to physicians, surgeons, dentists, undertakers, and non-lawyer members of the general assembly when not in session.[161]

Georgia[162] and Misouri[163] enacted measures providing for calling alternate jurors in potentially protracted trials; while a proposal for compulsory reduction in the size of juries from twelve to eight in civil matters in Los Angeles metropolitan courts[164] was disapproved by the governing board of the Los Angeles Bar Association.[165] A legislative council study of the statutes of other states pertaining to jury commissioners, with prospective recommendations as to the need for such an enactment, was authorized in Tennessee.[166]

A California newsman has offered observations and suggestions based on his experiences in jury service,[167] and several articles on the jury system, many of which discuss court congestion, appeared during the year.[168] At long last a break in precedent occurred in Alabama when women were selected for the first time in history to serve on a federal jury,[169] their eligibility having been established by the recently enacted Civil Rights Law.[170]

Traffic Courts and Justices of the Peace.—Articles and surveys continue to stress the need for improvement in the organization and functioning of traffic courts, and the importance of providing fair trials for traffic offenders.[171] Much that has been accomplished in this area can be credited to the active and able efforts of those in charge of the American Bar Association's Traffic Court Program.[172]

---

161. R.I. Acts 1957, c. 124.

162. Ga. Laws Reg. Sess. 1957, No. 394, p. 466.

163. Mo. Stat. Ann. § 494.065 (Vernon Supp. 1957).

164. Holbrook, supra note 9, at 386.

165. Special Report on the Holbrook Courts Survey, 32 L.A.B. Bull. 149, 153 (1957).

166. Tenn. Pub. Acts 1957, H.J. Res. 51.

167. Nichols, Jury Service, 32 L.A.B. Bull. 343 (1957).

168. Ball, Trial by Jury, 32 Calif. State B.J. 313 (1957); Onion, Completing the Jury Panel, 11 Sw. L.J. 158 (1957); Palmer, On Trial: The Jury Trial, 20 F.R.D. 65 (1958); Paul, Jerome Frank's Views on Trial by Jury, 22 Mo. L. Rev. 28 (1957); Slovenko, The Jury System in Louisiana Criminal Law, 17 La. L. Rev. 655 (1957); Tranchitella, The New Jury Look, 20 The Shingle 69 (1957).

169. N.Y. Herald Tribune, Nov. 19, 1957, p. 12, col. 5.

170. Pub. L. No. 315, 85th Cong., 1st Sess. (Sept. 9, 1957).

171. Heffley, Court Responsibility in Traffic, 5 Traffic Dig. & Rev. 11 (1957); Macelwane, The Traffic Court: The Most Important in Our System, 43 A.B.A.J. 322 (1957); Netherton, Fair Trial in Traffic Court, 41 Minn. L. Rev. 577 (1957).

172. See, e.g., A Report to the Mayor, City Council and Judges of The Cleveland Municipal Court on the Study of Traffic Court and Traffic Enforcement Procedures Pertaining to the Cleveland Municipal Court (May 1957); A Report to the City of Madison, Wisconsin on The Superior Court of Dane County (June 1957). The latter study was made jointly by the American Bar Association and the Traffic Institute, Northwestern University.

Movements to abolish and supersede justice of the peace courts are under way in several states. Express provisions to this effect are included in the pending or proposed new judicial articles for Illinois[173] and Kentucky,[174] respectively. New legislation in Ohio replaces justice of the peace courts with a new system of county courts.[175] The New Hampshire legislature abolished the civil and criminal jurisdiction of justices of the peace, leaving them with only ministerial functions.[176] Surveys and studies of justice of the peace courts are in progress or authorized in Colorado,[177] Michigan,[178] and Washington.[179] In Minnesota, a pending general survey of lower trial court systems would include a study of justice of the peace courts.[180]

In some states, notably Michigan,[181] New Mexico,[182] and West Virginia,[183] legislation to secure more accurate financial accounting by justices of the peace has been enacted. While North Dakota increased the fees paid to justices of the peace,[184] and Indiana provided a basic salary for certain justices of the peace and an over-all limitation on fees for others,[185] the Kentucky Court of Appeals in a landmark decision[186] outlawed the fee system in that state under an interpretation and application of *Tumey v. Ohio*.[187]

Conclusion.—On the whole, 1957 gave considerable promise as a year of progress in judicial administration. Major tests of that progress will come in the fall of 1958, when the people of Illinois and Kansas go to the polls to vote on major constitutional changes in their respective judiciary articles.

Meanwhile, 1957 also brought recognition and confirmation of the thesis embraced in Chief Justice Vanderbilt's casebook on modern procedure, published five years ago, that the place to begin imbuing lawyers with the principles of good judicial ad-

---

173. See note 2 supra.
174. See note 6 supra.
175. Ohio Rev. Code Ann. §§ 1907.01.1, 1907.02.1 (Page Supp. 1957).
176. N.H. Laws 1957, c. 244.
177. Colo. Laws Reg. Sess. 1957, H.J. Res. 6.
178. Jones, From the State Capitals 2 (Supp. Rep. May 28, 1957).
179. Justice Court Study, 11 Wash. State B. News 15 (1957).
180. Minn. Laws 1957, c. 951; Minnesota Interim Committee to Study and Investigate Lower Court System, The Bench and Bar of Minn. 9 (Sept. 10, 1957).
181. Mich. Pub. Acts Reg. Sess. 1957, No. 266.
182. N.M. Laws, 1957, c. 130.
183. W. Va. Laws Reg. Sess. 1957, c. 104.
184. N.D. Laws 1957, c. 227.
185. Ind. Acts 1957, c. 322.
186. Roberts v. Noel, 296 S.W.2d 745 (Ky. 1956).
187. 273 U.S. 510 (1927). See Vanlandingham, Pecuniary Interest of Justices of the Peace in Kentucky; The Aftermath of Tumey v. Ohio, 45 Ky. L.J. 607 (1957).

ministration is in the law schools.[188] Both the report of the executive committee of the United States Attorney General's Conference[189] and the report of the Chief Judge of the New York Court of Appeals[190] point to the need of including the subject in the law school curriculum. Perhaps therein lies the ultimate hope for future improvement in this important area of the administration of justice.

188. Vanderbilt, Cases and Materials on Modern Procedure and Judicial Administration (1952) .
189. Report, supra note 111, at 4.
190. Conway, supra note 87, at 285.

JUDICIAL ADMINISTRATION — 1958*

In reporting the salient developments and events of 1958 in the various categories customarily comprising the overall subject, some items of special interest will receive more detailed treatment than the rest. If this makes for a certain unevenness of presentation, it is an inevitable incident, since evaluations as to relative importance necessarily involve subjective predilections of the evaluator.

To some, the demise and resurgence of the court modernization movement in the state of New York should be singled out. To others, the Illinois story of near-success in the hoped-for revision of its court system is the most newsworthy. Alaska's admission to statehood and the promise of an ultramodern judicial structure to implement its constitution are certainly deserving of emphasis. Curiously and coincidentally, each of these three stories was left incomplete, to varying degrees, at the close of the calendar year, as will be noted later.

One event that brought sadness during 1958 was the death on March 17 of Chief Judge John J. Parker of the United States Court of Appeals, Fourth Circuit. His lifetime of interest and leadership in improving federal and state judicial systems received widespread recognition and tribute. At the time of his death he was President of the Institute of Judicial Administration, in which position he had succeeded the late Chief Justice Arthur T. Vanderbilt with whom he had been an active coworker in national programs for court improvement and procedural reform. A great loss also occurred later in the year, in November, with the death of Bolitha J. Laws, Chief Judge of the United States District Court, District of Columbia, also a member of the Institute's governing board, and a leading exponent of modern procedure and pretrial.

General Revisions and Programs.—Perhaps the Illinois story should be told first, with its year-end possibility of reprieve, and the eventual outcome still in doubt. As noted in last year's

---

*Reprinted from 1958 *Annual Survey of American Law,* p. 702. Assistance in the assembling and analysis of materials for this article was furnished by Arthur L. Frank and John D. Kousi, Research Assistants of the Institute.

Survey article, the 1957 Illinois legislature passed (after two prior legislatures had failed to muster the requisite votes) a proposed constitutional amendment substantially revising, simplifying and modernizing the state's judicial system.[1] Hopes ran high that at the November 1958 general election there would be sufficient voter support to achieve the constitutionally-required "majority of the electors voting at said election or two-thirds of the electors voting on any such proposed amendment. . . ."[2] For some time after the election date, so close were the results that the outcome was uncertain. When the final tabulations were announced, the count was 1,589,655 in favor and 893,503 opposed, or less than 3 per cent short of the required two-thirds majority.[3] On the basis of a majority of the total votes cast, the percentage needed was somewhat higher.

However, in tabulating the ballots a number of them, estimated to be in excess of 100,000, were disallowed because the voters had written the word "yes" instead of placing an "x" in the appropriate ballot space, apparently inspired by the campaign exhortation "Vote Yes on the Blue Ballot Judicial Amendment." On December 8, 1958, immediately after the election results were formally determined, an election contest suit was filed in the circut court of Lake County to annul the determination and to declare the amendment adopted, on the basis that the "yes"-marked ballots were impropery rejected.[4] Issue was joined by intervention and answer filed on December 22. On the ultimate decision of the contest proceeding will depend the answer to the question, unresolved at year's end: Will the amendment be declared adopted or will the voters have to wait another four years, as required in Illinois,[5] before a similar constitutional revision can be again submitted to them?

The New York story deserves fuller narration than present space permits. As reported in last year's *Survey,* the plan proposed by the New York Temporary Commission on the Courts, headed by Harrison Tweed, and subsequently modified by the

1. 1957 Ann. Survey Am. L. 593. See also Kohn, Modern Courts for Illinois, 42 J. Am. Jud. Soc'd 42 (1958).

2. Ill. Const. Art. XIV, § 2 (1950).

3. Information supplied by Wayland B. Cedarquist of the Chicago, Illinois, bar. See also N.Y. Times, Nov. 6, 1958, p. 31, col. 2; Illinois Judicial Amendment Apparently Defeated Despite Huge Affirmative Vote, 42 J. Am. Jud. Soc'y 130 (1958).

4. In the Matter of the Contested Election as to the Adoption of the Proposed Amendment to Article VI of the Constitution of Illinois Submitted to the Voters at the November 4, 1958 General Election (Circuit Court of Lake County. Illinois, Gen. No. 69356).

5. See note 2 supra.

legislature, was defeated in the assembly on March 30, 1957.[6] A brief summary of major 1958 developments, in chronological sequence, will serve to telescope the year's highlights into limited compass:

January 1, 1958: New York Times editorial entitled "Court Reform Year" urges that "Thoroughgoing court reorganization is a New Year's resolution that should be solemnly taken by the people of this state. . . . This must be court reform year."[7]

January 6: Tweed Commission issues public statement summarizing its recommendations and plan for 1958.[8]

January 15: New York State Judicial Conference announces endorsement of Tweed Commission plan.[9]

February 3: Concurrent resolution embodying plan introduced in New York senate and thereafter in assembly.[10]

February 19: Joint hearing on concurrent resolution held before judiciary committees of senate and assembly.[11]

March 17: Revised proposal, embodying modifications of earlier plan, introduced in senate by committee on rules;[12] also introduced in assembly.[13]

March 21: Revised proposal passed by senate by vote of 48 to 9.[14]

March 25: Revised proposal defeated in assembly by vote of 94 to 50.[15]

March 26: Assembly refuses passage of bill to continue Temporary Commission on Courts for another year.[16]

April 12: Governor Harriman requests State Judicial Conference to "study and evaluate the court structure of the State and formulate a plan for court reorganization and administration for submission to the 1959 Legislature."[17]

---

6. 1957 Ann. Survey Am. L. 603.

7. N.Y. Times, Jan. 1, 1958, p. 24, col. 1.

8. Id., Jan. 6, 1958, p. 1, col. 2. Detailed recommendations were set forth in the 1958 Report of the Commission to the Governor and the Legislature, filed on February 13, 1958 (N.Y. Leg. Doc. No. 36, 1958).

9. N.Y. Times, Jan. 15, 1958, p. 1, col. 1.

10. N.Y.S. Int. 2174 (1958), N.Y.A. Int. 2710 (1958).

11. Foreword, N.Y. St. Legislative Ann. (1958), xi.

12. N.Y.S. Int. 3705 (1958).

13. N.Y.A. Int. 4321 (1958).

14. See also note 11 supra at xix.

15. Id. at xix.

16. N.Y. Times, Mar. 27, 1958, p. 1, col. 6.

17. See note 11 supra at xvii.

May 14: League of Women Voters announce that they and Citizens Union have requested Institute of Judicial Administration to prepare a complete plan for judicial administration in the state.[18]

May 22: New York Times editorial expresses hope that Institute will undertake task of drafting constitutional amendment for New York based on a model plan.[19]
October 15: League of Women Voters announces its approval of proposed judiciary article prepared by Institute.[20]

October 17: New York Times editorial comments that "the proposed article is certainly a logical embodiment of the basic principles of the kind of state-wide, integrated and simplified judicial structure that the public wants."[21]

November 10: State Judicial Conference presents plan embodying recommendations for modernizing court structure of the state.[22]

December 17: Governor Rockefeller and Republican leaders promise "effective action" on court reform, without committing themselves to any specific program.[23]
December 31: Thus, on the eve of the year ahead, it seemed clear that the subject of court improvement for

---

18. Id. at xvii.

19. N.Y. Times, May 22, 1958, p. 28, col. 2.

20. N.Y. Times, Oct. 15, 1958, p. 36, col. 1. "This draft of a Judiciary Article is confined to fundamentals. It seeks only to establish a simple and unified court system, centralized administration and fiscal control, and minimal basic controls over the qualifications and conduct of judges." We Approve, 35 L.W.V. State News, No. 6 (Oct. 1958), p. 1. For the text of the draft and an explanatory comment, see Inst. Jud. Admin. (hereinafter IJA). Proposed Judiciary Article for the New York Constitution (1958). For analysis and discussion, see Ames, A New Plan for Judicial Reform, 13 Colum. L. Sch. News, No. 3 (Oct. 29, 1958), p. 1.

21. N.Y. Times, Oct. 17, 1958, p. 28, col. 1.

22. N.Y. Times, Nov. 10, 1958, p. 1, col. 4. For the text of the recommendations, and comments, see N.Y. Jud. Conf., Recommendations for Modernization of the Court Structure in the State of New York, Nov. 10, 1958. The Institute plan differs from the Conference plan in several principal respects. The former is a brief but complete draft of a proposed judiciary article; the latter sets forth recommendations for an article to be later drafted. The Institute plan reduces the court structure to a minimum number of tribunals; the Conference plan would retain the surrogate's court, establish a new and separate family court, and provide two lower courts for New York City. The Institute plan provides for strong centralized administration and a consolidated state budget, whereas the Conference plan does not go quite so far toward centralization of administrative and financial controls.

23. N.Y. Times, Dec. 18, 1958, p. 1G, col. 2.

New York was very much alive again, and would be one
of the major issues in the 1959 legislature.[24]

The judiciary article of Alaska's constitution approved in
1956 was described in the *Survey* for that year.[25] When Congress
passed and the President approved the Alaska statehood act
in July 1958,[26] the basis of a modern court structure for the nation's newest state had therefore already been established. Until
the new state's legislature could convene in 1959, however, necessary legislation to implement the organic provisions would not
be effected. Meanwhile, the problem of transition from the existing territorial district courts to the projected new state courts
and a federal district court has presented complications still unresolved at year's end. The statehood act provides for the continuance of the territorial district courts until a federal district
court is established and proclaimed by the President, at some
time within three years after statehood.[27] This interim period
poses a troublesome question of constitutional jurisdiction of
the district courts, harking back to the situation in Florida in
the mid-nineteenth century, when the jurisdiction of territorial
courts, after statehood, to hear federal matters was successfully
challenged.[28]

Other general revision programs of major dimensions include
those of Iowa, Kentucky and North Carolina. The proposed new
judicial article for the Iowa constitution has been readied for
submission to the 1959 legislature and has been approved by the
board of governors of the state bar association.[29] The Kentucky
proposal, described in last year's *Survey*,[30] was withheld from

24. Two Court Plans Will Be Offered to 1959 New York Legislature, 42 J.
Am. Jud. Soc'y 132 (1958).

25. 1956 Ann. Survey Am. L. 116, 118, 32 N.Y.U.L.Rev. 116, 118 (1957). See
also, Egan, The Constitution of the New State of Alaska, 31 State Gov't 209
(1958); Hellenthal, Alaska's Heralded Constitution: The Forty-Ninth State
Sets an Example, 44 A.B.A.J. 1147 (1958); Stewart, A Model Judiciary Article
for the 49th State, 42 J. Am. Jud. Soc'y 52 (1958).

26. Pub. L. 85-508, July 7, 1958, 72 Stat. 339, 48 U.S.C. (1958 Cum. Ann.
Pkt. Pt.), p. 4. The Act was approved by the voters of Alaska on August 26,
1958.

27. Id., § 18.

28. Benner v. Porter, 50 U. S. (9 How.) 246 (1850).

29. Board of Governors Approves Modified Plan of Judicial Reorganization,
18 News Bull. Ia. S.B.A., No. 12 (December 1958), p. 1. The plan was noted
in last year's Survey article, 1957 Ann. Survey Am. L. 593, 595. A second tentative draft, March 15, 1958, is included in a selection of recent and proposed
judicial articles. IJA, Judicial Articles, Selected Recent Proposals, with Explanatory Comments (1958), p. 21. See also Uhlenhopp, Judicial Reorganization in Iowa, 44 Iowa L. Rev. 6 (1958); Progress Report on Iowa Judicial
Reform, 42 J. Am. Jud. Soc'y 62 (1958).

30. 1957 Ann. Survey Am. L. 593, 594, and see, IJA, Judicial Articles, note
29 supra at 58.

introduction in the 1958 legislature, but the latter passed a resolution continuing for another two years the legislative research
commission's study of the court system.[31] In North Carolina, the
bar association committee studying the administration of justice
in that state has published a number of tentative reports and
recommendations looking toward an extensive revision of the
judicial system.[32]

Judicial Selection and Tenure.—Undoubtedly the outstanding event in judicial selection in 1958 was the approval by the
Kansas voters on November 4 of a non-partisan plan for the
nomination and selection of supreme court justices.[33] With
California, Missouri, Alabama, and Alaska having already
adopted somewhat different but comparable versions, the original
American Bar Association plan has thus established at least a
five-state beachhead for the campaigns in progress in other
states.[34] A Nevada plan, approved by the 1957 legislature, is
pending for second consideration by the legislature in 1959.[35]
In Florida, the Missouri Plan has been both supported[36] and opposed[37] in addresses to the Florida bar. Bar association support
for the plan has also been voiced in Rhode Island[38] and Vermont.[39]

In the matter of selection of federal judges, a United States
senator has recommended removal of the Department of Justice
from its role as chief adviser on judicial appointments, the sub-
stitution of "an advisory judicial commission, bipartisan and
objective, who might solicit qualitative recommendations from
local individuals, members of the legal profession and associa-

---

31. Ky. S. Res. 48 (1958). See, IJA, Check-List Summary of 1958 Developments in Judicial Administration (1958), p. 3.

32. Id., at p. 4. See also, Special Issue, 25 Popular Gov't, No. 3 (Nov. 1958);
North Carolina Bar Association Endorses Broad Judicial Reform Program, 42
J. Am. Jud. Soc'y 28 (1958); Convention Report, 9 N.C.B.A. Bar Notes, No. 4
(1958), p. 30; N.C.B.A., Report of the Committee on Improving and Expediting the Administration of Justice in North Carolina (Dec. 1958).

33. Kan. S.C. Res. No. 4 (1957). Kansas Judicial Selection Plan Approved
by Voters on November 4, 42 J. Am. Jud. Soc'y 128 (1958).

34. Judicial Selection is Fundamental, 42 J. Am. Jud. Soc'y 39 (1958).

35. 1957 Ann. Survey Am. L. 593, 597.

36. Gershenson, Missouri Method of Selection of Judges, 32 Fla. B. J. 419
(1958).

37. Moran, Counter "Missouri Plan" for Method of Selecting Judges, 32 id.
471 (1958).

38. Executive Committee Approves Missouri Plan in Principle, 6 R.I.B.J.,
No. 7 (May 1958), p. 1.

39. Vermont Bar Adopts Indemnity Plan, Proposes Judicial Selection
Change, 42 J. Am. Jud. Soc'y 128 (1958).

tions, on a confidential basis," and the setting up of senate standards for the confirmation of judicial nominees.[40]

Judicial Salaries and Retirement.—The progressive upward trend in state judiciary salary levels continues. Thus, in January, the Council of State Governments was able to report that the median salary for justices of courts of last resort advanced from $14,400 in 1955 to $17,000 in 1957, and for trial court judges during the same period there was a 14 per cent increase to $12,500.[41]

During 1958, statutes increasing judicial salaries were enacted which will raise the median figures still higher, and among the states so providing were Colorado,[42] Connecticut,[43] Kentucky,[44] Massachusetts,[45] Mississippi,[46] New York,[47] and Virginia.[48] In New York, it should be noted, statutes are not the only means by which judicial salaries may be raised. This was demonstrated in New York City on December 18, 1958, when salary increases of $2,500 apiece were obtained from the city's board of estimate by 81 justices and judges of the supreme court, general sessions court, county court, and surrogate's court, bringing them to a salary level of $34,500, the highest of any comparable trial courts in the nation.[49]

In the state of Washington, a proposed constitutional amendment to permit raising of salaries so as to eliminate inequities in the salaries of supreme court justices was defeated by the electors at the November general election by a vote of three to one.[50]

Insofar as applicable to judges, there were few changes in existing retirement laws during the year. However, the lack of effective compulsory retirement of federal judges at age 70 has been noted and commented upon in an article by a Los Angeles attorney[51] and in a statement by a retired federal judge.[52]

40. Stennis, Federal Judiciary Selection: The Letter—But the Spirit?, 44 A.B.A.J. 1179, 1181 (1958). See also Cooley, The Department of Justice and Judicial Nominations, 42 J. Am. Jud. Soc'y 86 (1958); American Bar Association Adopts Resolution Calling for a Non-Partisan Federal Judiciary, 42 id. 91 (1958).

41. The Book of the States, 1958-1959 (1958), p. 98.

42. Colo. Laws 2d Reg. Sess., 1958, c. 44.

43. Conn. Pub. Acts 1958, No. 27.

44. Ky. Acts 1958, c. 25.

45. Mass. Acts 1958, c. 675.

46. Miss. Laws 1958, cc. 328, 334.

47. N.Y. Laws 1958, c. 650.

48. Va. Acts 1958, c. 189.

49. N.Y. Times, Dec. 19, 1958, p. 1, col. 1.

50. Wash. Laws Reg. Sess. 1957, Subs. S.J. Res. 9, Pt. 1. See Am. B. Found., Court Congestion, No. 19 (Nov.-Dec. 1958), p. 1.

51. Sheppard, Judicial Retirement: The Age of Judges and the Judge of Ages, 44 A.B.A.J. 145 (1958).

52. Medina, Retirement of Federal Judges, 5 Fed. B. News 200 (1958).

Judicial Conduct, Discipline, and Removal.—The report on Canon 35 of the Canons of Judicial Ethics, proposing retention, with improvements in wording, of present restrictions against broadcasting or televising court proceedings, was debated by the American Bar Association House of Delegates at its midwinter meeting in February 1958, and a motion to defer action was carried.[53] At the August meeting, debate was resumed, and resulted in a vote to refer the whole matter to a special committee "to consider the matter further and make such surveys as seemed necessary to obtain reliable data on the issues involved."[54] Arguments against retention of the ban have been further presented by representatives of the press and news media,[55] and counter-arguments favoring retention have been urged by judges and lawyers.[56] Meanwhile, the Ohio supreme court's ban on photographing or broadcasting state court proceedings has been resisted by the Cleveland common pleas court,[57] and the Oklahoma court of criminal appeals has upheld the televising of courtroom proceedings in a criminal case.[58] With respect to the appearance of judges on television programs, the state bars of California and Michigan have both ruled against such activity.[59]

In the matter of removal of judges, both California[60] and Florida[61] are considering constitutional amendments to improve their removal procedures.

Judicial Councils and Judicial Conferences.—Following an executive order of the governor of November 5, 1957, the 1958 Colorado legislature created a judicial council for that state, to make a continuous study of the organization of courts and their rules and methods of procedure and practice.[62] The council's first report, published in December, contains initial recommendations pertaining to appellate jurisdiction of the courts, judicial review, and various procedural matters.[63] Meanwhile, writers

---

53. Proceedings of the House of Delegates: Midyear Meeting, Atlanta; February 24-25, 44 A.B.A.J. 338, 341, 377-378 (1958).

54. Proceedings of the House of Delegates: Los Angeles, August 25-29, 44 id. 1062, 1063 (1958).

55. Bar Foundation Report Criticized by Newspaper Media Representative, 26 Harv. L. Record, No. 3 (Feb. 20, 1958), p. 3; Daly, Radio, TV News and Canon 35, 26 J.B.A. Kan. 292 (1958).

56. Taylor, Broadcasting in the Courtroom, 60 W. Va. L. Rev. 312 (1958); Bennett, Developments in Courtroom Publicity, 26 J.B.A. Kan. 307 (1958).

57. Courtroom Publicity—Cleveland Paper Defies Photo Ban, 41 J. Am. Jud. Soc'y 188 (1958).

58. Lyles v. State, 330 P. 2d 734 (Okla. Crim. App., 1958).

59. Developments in Other States, 41 J. Am. Jud. Soc'y 189 (1958).

60. Removal of Judges, 33 Cal. S.B.J. 385 (1958).

61. Jones, From the State Capitals 1 (Oct. 9, 1958—CTS).

62. Colo. Laws, 2d Reg. Sess., 1958, c. 33.

63. First Report on Proceedings of the Judicial Council, State of Colorado (1958).

have reviewed the activities and accomplishments of judicial councils in Florida[64] and Texas,[65] and of the judicial conference in Illinois.[66]

In its annual report for 1958, the judicial conference of the United States discusses the expedition of court business, recommendations as to federal rules of practice and procedure, supporting personnel, pretrial procedure, operation of the jury system, and other matters concerning the federal courts.[67]

Court Integration and Unification.—Undiscouraged by last year's failure, nor by the fact that their court reorganization campaign dates back more than 30 years, proponents of the consolidation of local courts in Connecticut are returning to the attack with renewed vigor.[68] California meanwhile is studying the problems of its separate municipal court districts with a view toward possible unification,[69] and a North Carolina bar association committee has recommended a unified judicial organization for that state.[70] Integration of county and superior courts in New Jersey has been recommended by the state bar association.[71] The 1958 Michigan legislature, having failed to pass a measure for consolidated courts in metropolitan areas,[72] approved the continuance of a special committee to study the metropolitan court plan.[73]

Court Administration, Congestion and Statistics.— Growing awareness of the important function to be performed through centralized annd efficient administration of judicial systems, federal and state, is reflected in the programs of interested organizations during the year. Thus the 1958 national conference of the American Society for Public Administration featured a session on court administration, sponsored by the American Judicature Society, and participated in by representatives of the

---

64. O'Connell, Report on Judicial Council of Florida, 32 Fla. B.J. 350 (1958) ; Thomas, The Judicial Council of Florida, 22 F.R.D. 203 (1958).

65. Morehead, Why a Texas Civil Judicial Council?, 21 Tex. B.J. 157 (1958).

66. Kiley, The Judicial Conference: A New "Child" Comes of Age in Illinois, 44 A.B.A.J. 835 (1958).

67. Report of the Proceedings of the Regular Annual Meeting of the Judicial Conference of the United States (1958).

68. New Hope for Connecticut Court Reorganization, 42 J. Am. Jud. Soc'y 126 (1958) ; Clark, Court Reorganization in 1959; A Time for Constructive Action, 32 Conn. B.J. 236 (1958).

69. Farley, Court Survey, 33 Cal. S.B.J. 271, 275 (1958).

70. North Carolina Committee Recommends Unified Court, 41 J. Am. Jud. Soc'y 186 (1958).

71. New Jersey Bar Favors Consolidation of Courts, 42 id. 64 (1958).

72. Mich. S.B. 1141 (1958).

73. Mich. H. Res. 1958, No. 65; IJA, Check-List Summary of 1958 Developments in Judicial Administration (1958), p. 21.

administrative offices of the United States, New Jersey and New York courts, respectively.[74] The annual meeting of the American Judicature Society in August heard an address by the director of the administrative office of the United States courts.[75]

The administrator of the state courts of Washington, in his annual report, describes the effective operation of the visiting judge program by which judges serve outside their own districts to help in other areas where needed.[76] Although the sanction of salary withholding exists in Washington to make such service compulsory, the present program is on an entirely voluntary basis. In Michigan, the refusal of a circuit judge to serve in another circuit, and to be replaced by a judge assigned to preside in the former's court, was the subject of a supreme court contempt proceeding, the first of its kind in the state, upholding the power of the chief justice and the court administrator to make such judicial assignments.[77]

In its 1958 annual calendar status study, the Institute of Judicial Administration notes that the nation-wide average of time elapsed from issue to jury trial of personal injury cases in metropolitan state courts decreased from 10.7 months in 1957 to 9.4 months.[78] The largest average delay for 1958 was in the Cook County superior court of Illinois with 57.2 months, followed by the circuit court of the same county with 38.2 months, the Queens County supreme court in New York with 38 months, the Fairfield County superior court in Connecticut with 31.5 months, the Hartford County superior court in Connecticut with 28.5 months, and the common pleas court of Cuyahoga County, Ohio, with 26.5 months. The greatest improvement in decreasing delays was in Massachuetts where Suffolk County dropped from 30 months in 1957 to 11.2 months in 1958, and Hampden County from 21 months to 8.2 months.

Congestion and delay in the federal courts provided the theme for addresses by Chief Justice Earl Warren to the American Law

74. Batson, Administering the Courts—Federal, State and Local, 42 J. Am. Jud. Soc'y 13 (1958). Mrs. Fannie J. Klein, research coordinator of the Institute of Judicial Administration, served as chairman of the session.

75. Olney, The Administrative Office of the United States Courts, 42 J. Am. Jud. Soc'y 78 (1958).

76. Second Annual Report of the Administrator for the Courts, State of Washington (1958), p. 19. For recent developments in Oregon authorizing the assignment of judges, see The 5th Annual Administrative Report relating to the Circuit Courts of the State of Oregon (1958), p. 22.

77. In re Assignment of Huff, 322 Mich. 402, 91 N.W. 2d 613 (1958).

78. IJA, State Trial Courts of General Jurisdiction, Calendar Status Study —1958 at 1 (June 30, 1958).

Institute in May[79] and the American Bar Association in August.[80] It was also the subject of a two-day conference of 150 representatives of state and national bar and other organizations called by the United States Attorney-General in June, where among other things the need for additional federal judges was stressed.[81] The Chief Justice has pointed out that United States district judges dispose of an average of 232 cases apiece a year as compared with 169 cases in 1941, and yet during the same period, the backlog of civil cases alone has increased from 137 to 243 cases per judge.[82] The 1958 report of the administrative office of the United States courts shows that the median interval from issue to trial of civil jury cases in the 86 federal districts is 9 months, with the highest median interval being 34 months in the eastern district of New York, and the next highest in the western district of Pennsylvania with 33.8 months.[83] Clearly, congestion and delay remain one of the major problems in the field of judicial administration.[84]

Pretrial.—Further information from California, which has now completed its second year under the mandatory pretrial rule for civil cases in the superior court, confirms the encouraging initial results reported in last year's *Survey*.[85] In San Francisco, for example, pretrial during 1957 is credited with reducing the waiting time from 21 to 13½ months in jury litigation and a comparable acceleration of nonjury cases.[86] A Michigan supreme court rule making pretrial conferences mandatory in all

---

79. Warren, Delay and Congestion in the Federal Courts, 42 J. Am. Jud. Soc'y 6 (1958).

80. Warren, The Problem of Delay: A Task for Bench and Bar Alike, 44 A.B.A.J. 1043 (1958).

81. Shortage of Federal Judges is Stressed at Court Congestion Conference, 42 J. Am. Jud. Soc'y 20 (1958). See also Recommendations of Conference on Court Congestion and Delay, 42 id. 60 (1958); Proceedings of the Attorney General's Conference on Court Congestion and Delay in Litigation, June 16 and 17, 1958.

82. Note 80 supra at 1044. See also Shafroth, Report of Administrative Office Shows Federal Court Dockets Still Congested, 44 A.B.A.J. 551 (1958).

83. Annual Report of the Director of Administrative Office of the United States Courts (Sept. 1958), Table C6.

84. Burger, The Courts on Trial, 22 F.R.D. 71 (1958); Nims, The Law's Delay: The Bar's Most Urgent Problem, 44 A.B.A.J. 27 (1958); Court Congestion and Delay—What's Being Done to Speed up Justice, 41 J. Am. Jud. Soc'y 182 (1958); Jacobson, Court Calendar Congestion Causes and Cures, 7 Clev.-Mar. L. Rev. 125 (1958).

85. 1957 Ann. Surv. Am. L. 593, 608.

86. Kincaid, A Report on Pre-Trial Procedure, 33 L.A.B. Bull. 339 (1958). See, King, Judicial Administration: California Adopts the Pretrial Conference, 44 A.B.A.J. 962, 965 (1958).

civil cases in the circuit courts became effective July 1.[87]

The late Judge Laws, in an introductory article to a symposium on the subject, summarized the basic procedure, requirements, and benefits of successful pretrial.[88] Other articles presented the topic from the viewpoint of plaintiff's counsel,[89] and from that of the defense,[90] and also a review of questions and answers,[91] followed by the script of a motion picture demonstration of a pretrial conference.[92] Elsewhere, another authority on pretrial in the federal courts has reviewed the factors and elements required for successful functioning of the pretrial conference, has stressed the importance of the judge's role therein.[93] The role of attorneys in the pre-pretrial stage, in advance of the pretrial hearing before the judge, has also been reviewed and evaluated.[94]

Rule-Making and Procedural Rules.—Although no state adopted complete new rules of procedure during the year, 1958 nevertheless witnessed several significant developments in the rule-making field. Perhaps the most noteworthy was the enactment by Congress of the recommendation of the judicial conference of the United States that they be authorized to study the rules of practice in the federal courts and submit any necessary changes to the Supreme Court.[95]

A proposal to vest power to promulgate rules of pleading, practice and procedure in the supreme court of Mississippi failed of enactment,[96] and in South Carolina a bill to adopt a new set of rules for civil actions,[97] based on the federal rules, was de-

---

87. Mandaotry Pre-Trial Conferences to be Held in All Michigan Courts, 42 J. Am. Jud. Soc'y 64 (1958). For an excellent report on the successful operation of pretrial in Utah, see Fox, Pre-Trial Conferences in the District Court for Salt Lake County, 6 Utah L. Rev. 259 (1958).

88. Laws, A Trial Judge Looks at Pre-Trial Procedure, 4 Practical Lawyer 17 (1958).

89. Lorry, Pre-Trial—As Viewed by Plaintiff's Counsel, 4 id. 23 (1958).

90. Connolly, Pre-Trial—As Seen by the Defense, 4 id. 30 (1958.

91. McNeal, Pre-Trial—Some Questions and Answers, 4 id. 37 (1958).

92. Pre-Trial—A Conference, 4 id. 46 (1958).

93. Murrah, The Pretrial Conference: Conceptions and Misconceptions, 44 A.B.A.J. 39 (1958). For a discussion of the functions of pretrial, see Yankwich, Crystallization of Issues by Pretrial: A Judge's View, 58 Colum. L. Rev. 470 (1958).

94. Winters, The Pre-Pre-Trial Conference Without the Judge in Federal District Courts, 37 Neb. L. Rev. 449 (1958).

95. Pub. L. 85-513, July 11, 1958, 72 Stat. 356, 28 U.S.C. § 331. For a panel discussion of this proposal, conducted by the Section of Judicial Administration of the American Bar Association, see The Rule-Making Function and the Judicial Conference of the United States, 21 F.R.D. 117 (1958).

96. Miss H.C. Res. 53 (1958).

97. S.C.H. 2352 (1958).

feated by the state senate after passing the house.[98] It is expected
that the 1959 legislature will consider the subject.[99]

In their tentative report, the subcommittee on practice and
procedure of the North Carolina bar association committee
studying the state's judicial system, recommended that the supreme court be empowered to promulgate rules of civil and
criminal procedure and practice in all the courts of the state,
with the judicial conference as an advisory body.[100] It is to be
noted that this proposed advisory function resembles the present
federal system. It was announced, after the endorsement by the
West Virginia state bar of proposed rules of civil procedure patterned after the federal rules,[101] that the judicial conference
would present the new rules to the supreme court of appeals for
adoption.[102] In Vermont the rules revision commission submitted
the preliminary report to the state bar association.[103] The recommendations were designed to bring Vermont's practice more into
line with the federal rules, and after the bar's comments are received, final recommendations will be drafted for submission to
the 1959 legislature.[104]

To familiarize Wyoming's lawyers with the operation of their
new rules of civil procedure, the university of Wyoming college
of law held an Institute on the new rules.[105]

Jurors and Jury Selection.—The need for improving the
quality of juries continues to receive attention. In rejecting a
defendant's contention that the distribution of jury handbooks
infringed on the statutory methods of instructing the jury, the
Florida supreme court approved of and complimented the use of
such handbooks.[106] The court of appeals for the seventh circuit
on a rehearing of a reversed conviction, withdraw from its first
opinion that the contents of jury handbooks were prejudicial,[107]

---

98. South Carolina Bar Association Annual Meeting, 10 So. Car. L.Q. 531,
559 (1958).
99. Id. at 560.
100. A Tentative Report of the Subcommittee on Practice and Procedure
for the Committee on Improving and Expediting the Administration of Justice
in North Carolina of the North Carolina Bar Association (May 1958).
101. See 1957 Ann. Survey Am. L. 609.
102. The March of Progress, 41 J. Am. Jud. Soc'y 155, 156 (1958).
103. Rules Revision Commission, Redraft of Proposed Rules, August, 1958;
see Jones, From the State Capitals 2 (Supp. Rep. Aug. 14, 1958—CTS).
104. Ibid.
105. Proceedings, Institute on Wyoming Rules of Civil Procedure, 12 Wyo.
L.J. 175 (1958).
106. Ferrara v. State, 101 So. 2d 797 (Fla. 1958). For a sample of jury handbooks see The Institute of Judicial Administration, Handbook on Jury Service
(1958).
107. United States v. Gordon, 253 F. 2d 177 (7th Cir. 1958).
108. Horton v. United States, 256.F. 2d 138 (6th Cir. 1958). See United
States v. Mathison, 256 F. 2d 803 (7th Cir. 1958).

and a subsequent sixth circuit case upheld the use of a juror's handbook. In Massachusetts a bill requiring each prospective juror to be furnished with a juror's handbook was proposed,[109] and a resolution providing for the study of the subject was adopted.[110] In two articles of significance, one proposed methods of improving jury selection,[111] and the other defended the jury system against attacks by those who advocate its abolition in personal injury cases.[112]

As above noted, methods for decreasing court congestion and delay in jury trials are an omnipresent problem. The adoption of standard jury charges as a possible time-saving device is being urged in Ohio,[113] and the successful use of tape recordings in Indiana in instructing the jury has aroused interest and favorable comment from both bench and bar.[114] Kentucky rejected a bill that would have abrogated a defendant's right to trial by jury in cases in inferior courts where the fine is fifty dollars or less.[115]

Increased compensation for jurors was a matter of bar association concern in North Carolina[116] and of judicial council or conference discussion in Florida[117] and Nevada.[118] However, legislative attempts to provide for increases failed in Kentucky[119] and New York.[120] A constitutional amendment in Louisiana allowing women to serve on juries was withdrawn,[121] while in Mississippi a similar attempt by statute failed.[122] North Carolina[123] and Florida[124] have recommended the establishment of a jury commission to facilitate the selection of jurors. An interesting article, by one who had just completed jury service, explains the personal benefit and satisfaction derived from serving on a jury.[125]

---

109. Mass. H.B. 1292 (1958).

110. Mass. Res. 1958, c. 77 (1958).

111. Comment, Jury—Pre-Trial Selection—Suggested Improvements, 56 Mich. L. Rev. 954 (1958).

112. McKenzie, What is Truth? A Defense of the Jury System, 44 A.B.A.J. 51 (1958).

113. Jones, From the State Capitals 2 (Oct. 3, 1958—CTS).

114. Katz, Reinstructing the Jury by Tape Recording, 41 J. Am. Jud. Soc'y 148 (1958).

115. Ky H.B. 429 (1958).

116. A Tentative Report of the Subcommittee on the Jury System to the Committee on Improving and Expediting the Administration of Justice in North Carolina of the North Carolina Bar Association (April 1958).

117. Meeting of Judicial Council of Florida, 32 Fla. B.J. 198 (1958).

118. Jones, From the State Capitals 3 (Oct. 9, 1958—CTS).

119. Ky. S.B. 25 (1958).

120. N.Y.S. Int. 2636 (1958).

121. La. S.B. 342 (1958).

122. Miss. S.B. 1515 (1958).

123. See note 116 supra.

124. Meeting of Judicial Council of Florida, 32 Fla. B.J. 138 (1958).

125. Streit, Serving on the Jury, 41 J. Am. Jud. Soc'y 151 (1958).

Traffic Courts and Justices of the Peace.—Dissatisfaction with the existing methods of traffic law administration and with the functioning of justices of the peace in relation thereto has produced·further critical studies and articles during the year. A comprehensive pilot study in Arizona points up the need of, among other things, integrating courts of limited jurisdiction into the state court system and improving their procedures.[126] An equally detailed survey of traffic courts in Illinois, prepared for the state's traffic study commission by the American Bar Association's committee on traffic court program, includes recommendations for continuing supervision through the appointment of a state traffic court administrator.[127] Importance of the traffic courts in relation to traffic safety was stressed at a traffic court conference in Texas[128] and in a Wisconsin law review symposium.[129] Meanwhile, a California judge has proposed a reappraisal of the present approach to traffic law enforcement and has cricticized the use of criminal law methods to enforce traffic laws not generally viewed by the public as criminal in nature.[130]

In Colorado, a report of the legislative council for submission to the legislature on the subject of justice courts reviews the recommendations of various organizations, and proposes, in addition to specific immediate changes, a long-range overhaul of the justice court system by constitutional amendment to be worked out in conjunction with the judicial council.[131]

Conclusion.—A former presiding justice of the appellate division of New York's supreme court has ably stated today's—and tomorrow's—challenge as follows:

> Court organization and procedures to meet the needs modern society are the concern of judges, practicing lawyers, law teachers and law students. The courts as an institution, the processes of litigation from beginning to end, the total administration of justice, call for our urgent attention, and deserve the most thoughtful and constructive action of which a great profession is capable.[132]

126. Research Staff, Ariz. Legis. Council, Report on Justice of the Peace Courts in Arizona (Oct. 1958).
127. A.B.A., The Changing State and the Unchanging Courts, A Report on Courts Trying Traffic Cases in Illinois (1958).
128. Traffic Court Conference, 21 Tex. B.J. 89 (1958); Traffic Courts, 21 id. 216 (1958).
129. Selected Problems in the Administration of Traffic Law, 1958 Wis. L. Rev. 171 (1958). See Houghton, Introduction: Wisconsin's Traffic Problem, ibid.
130. St. Clair, The Traffic Problem: The Lawyers' Responsibilities, 44 A.B. A.J. 633 (1958).
131. Colo. Legis. Council, Justice Courts in Colorado (Dec. 1958), p. xvii.
132. Peck, Court Organization and Procedures to Meet the Needs of Modern Society, 33 Ind. L.J. 182, 197 (1958).

"OUR FAITH IN JUSTICE":

Puerto Rico Shows the Way to Better Courts

(From American Bar Association Journal, Vol. 42, p. 24, January 1956).

On the fourth day of next month, the new, modern home of the Supreme Court of Puerto Rico will be dedicated at San Juan, with Chief Justice Earl Warren participating in the ceremonies. The new Supreme Court building is a striking example of modern architecture; it is also a symbol of justice—modern justice, with an efficient court system, court-made rules of procedure and an Office of Court Administration. Mr. Elliott describes the workings of Puerto Rico's new judicial system in this article.

The Constitution of the Commonwealth of Puerto Rico is a noteworthy document, and among its significant provisions is the creed that comprises the last paragraph of its preamble:

> We consider as determining factors in our life our citizenship of the United States of America and our aspiration continually to enrich our democratic heritage in the individual and collective enjoyment of its rights and privileges; our loyalty to the principles of the Federal Constitution; the coexistence in Puerto Rico of the two great cultures of the Amercan Hemisphere; our fervor for education; *our faith in justice;* our devotion to the courageous, industrious, and peaceful way of life; our fidelity to individual human values above and beyond social position, racial differences, and economic interests; and our hope for a better world based on these principles [Italics supplied.]

Puerto Rico's Constitution, with its advanced provisions for a unified and efficient judicial system, is but one feature of the dramatic dynamism that has characterized the island's rapid development in recent years. On the economic side, "Operation Bootstrap" is proving that a paucity of natural resources need not doom an area to lasting industrial poverty or dependence on outside aid. And on the political side, Puerto Rico has forged ahead with a succession of gains that might well be the envy of other less enterprising jurisdictions.

Bear in mind that the first free and popular election for the position of Governor, in lieu of presidential appointment, was not authorized until 1947, and that Luis Muñoz Marin took office in January, 1949, as the Island's first elected chief executive. Bear in mind, too, that it wasn't until Public Law 600 was enacted and approved in 1950 that the people of Puerto Rico received a substantial measure of autonomy to "organize a government pursuant to a constitution of their own adoption". In implementation thereof, and with a "deliberate speed" that might well set a precedent for democratic entities everywhere, a representative constitutional convention was elected, drafts were proposed, debated and voted upon, a final draft agreed to, approved by the people on referendum, and ratified by the United States Congress and the President substantially as proposed—all in the span of two years. In its final form, the Constitution of the Commonwealth of Puerto Rico became effective on July 25, 1952.

To take effect simultaneously on "Constitution Day", the Legislature of Puerto Rico, with the advice and assistance of a committee of leading lawyers and government officials, with the consultative guidance of Judge Charles E. Clark and William D. Rogers, and with the active co-operation of the Puerto Rican Supreme Court, formulated and enacted the Judiciary Act of July 24, 1952. This statute not only implements the organic provisions of the new Constitution's Judicial Article. It accomplishes a number of landmark achievements in the field of judicial administration.

But neither constitution nor statute—forward-looking though both might be as documentary promises of hoped-for ideals—would alone suffice to mark Puerto Rico as a pace-setter in the competition for actual progress in improving court organization and administration. It is what has been accomplished under and because of them in the three and a half years since their adoption that merits the attention and admiration of the American Bench and Bar. It is in this respect that the dedication of the new Supreme Court building in San Juan offers a striking symbol of modern progress a well as a striking example of modern architecture. The dedication ceremony, with Chief Justice Earl Warren participating, is scheduled to take place on February 4, 1956.

A New Building . . . A New Judiciary Act. No less striking than the architecture of the new Supreme Court building are the structure and design of the new Puerto Rican court system itself. A transition blueprint was provided in 1950 when Puerto Rico adopted an Organic Act of the Judiciary, by which the existing heterogeneous judicial structure was consolidated and stratified into four levels, with justice of the peace courts at the base, then

Municipal Courts with limited civil and criminal jurisdiction, then the District Courts with jurisdiction over felonies, civil matters above $1,000, and appeals from Municipal Courts, and finally at the top the Supreme Court of Puerto Rico with typical appellate jurisdiction. For special purposes, district judges still sometimes sat on a minors' guardianship court or, on other occasions, as a supplies appeals court. Also retained were two separate courts at the district level: a court of eminent domain and a tax court. Appeal lay from the district courts to the Supreme Court as a matter of right, and from the justice of the peace and municipal courts to the district courts on trial *de novo* in the latter, with a further discretionary review on certiorari in the Supreme Court.

It remained for the new Constitution and the Judiciary Act of 1952 to achieve further simplification and complete the integration of the judicial system. Section 1 of the Judiciary Act succinctly describes the new structure as follows:

> The judicial power of the Commonwealth of Puerto Rico shall be vested in a single unified judicial system for purposes of jurisdiction, operation and administration, consisting of the Supreme Court as the court of last resort, and the Court of First Instance, which together shall constitute the General Court of Justice.
>
> The Commonwealth of Puerto Rico is hereby constituted a single judicial district, over all of which the General Court of Justice shall exercise its power of authority.

The Supreme Court, as the apex of the new structure, continues with substantially the same appellate and limited original jurisdiction as before, but with the Chief Justice clearly designated as the responsible administrative head of the entire system. The trial courts comprising the Court of First Instance are organized in two divisions, the upper of which, the Superior Court, with thirty judges, corresponds generally to the former District Court and the basic or new District Court of fifty-five judges succeeding to the same general judicial functions as those previously exercised by the old Municipal Courts and the Justices of the Peace.

One striking feature of the integrated trial court is the complete flexibility it provides for the trial of cases and the disposition of judicial business. Jurisdiction and venue questions no longer interpose obstacles. Instead, it is specified in Section 10 of the Judiciary Act that " . . . no cause shall fail on the ground that it has been submitted to a division without jurisdiction or authority or to a part of the court with improper venue. Every case may be heard in the division or part where it is brought by agreement of the parties and consent of the judge presiding at the time in such part or, if not so heard, shall be transferred by order of the judge to the appropriate division or part in accordance with such rules as may be adopted by the Supreme Court." And a succession of decisions by that Court has confirmed the spirit of the Act by recognizing both the flexible and the nontechnical nature of its provisions.

Judicial Qualifications . . . Selection and Tenure. Puerto Rico already had, at base, an appointive method of judicial selection. As before, so under the new provisions, judges are appointed by the Governor with the advice and consent of the Senate. Supreme Court justices hold office during good behavior and the number of justices may be changed only by law upon request of the Supreme Court. By virtue of the Judiciary Act, judges of the Superior Court are appointed for twelve-year terms and District Court judges for eight-year terms. Justices of the Peace, whose functions now are primarily of an investigative and preliminary nature in criminal matters instead of adjudicatory, are appointed for four-year terms.

The Constitution prescribes, as qualifications for appointment to the Supreme Court, admission to practice for at least ten years in Puerto Rico and also five years of residence. The Judiciary Act specifies that Superior Court judges, to be eligible for appointment as such, must be 25 years of age, members of the Bar, and of "good repute"; District Court judges must be 21 years of age, and similarly qualified; and a person to be appointed Justice of the Peace must be at least 21 years of age and must be of good repute.

One feature of the new legislation is an improved scale of judicial salaries including not only higher minima for all courts but also a progressive scale of automatic increases for trial court judges and Justices of the Peace after fixed intervals of service within the over-all term of appointment. Under the Constitution retirement is mandatory at age 70, and a retirement and pension system has been established by the Legislature for Supreme and Superior Court judges with retirement optional at 60. District Court judges are under the retirement and pension system for employees of the Commonwealth Government.

While Supreme Court justices are removable by traditional impeachment proceedings, the Judiciary Act establishes for the judges of other courts a special procedure under which charges may be filed with the Administrative Director and reported by him to the Chief Justice. If subsequent investigation discloses cause, the matter is prosecuted before the Supreme Court by the Secretary of Justice or other officer designated by the Court, which may, after hearing, impose a penalty of censure, suspension or removal.

As already noted, certain judicial functions of Justices of the Peace have been transferred to the new District Courts, leaving the former with the authority to fix and accept bail and "to issue warrants for arrest and for search and seizure in appropriate cases as established by law". Since the District Courts are courts of record and their determinations not subject to trial *de novo* on appeal as was formerly the procedure for review of municipal court decisions, a unique feature of the new Judiciary Act directs the Office of Court Administration to provide the District Courts "with adequate equipment for recording mechanically the incidents of each case". Under Rule 2 of the Rules for Appeals from the District Court to the Superior Court (1952), "Unless at the commencement of or during the trial the parties waive their right to have the proceedings recorded mechanically, the district judge shall order the entire proceeding recorded mechanically." Although the judge's notes are primarily the record on appeal, when such a recording is prepared it becomes part of the record to be forwarded with the judgment roll to the Superior Court whenever requested by a party. Puerto Rico thus became one of the first jurisdictions to incorporate this technological device in its judicial machinery.

Pursuant to the provisions of the Judiciary Act, the Supreme Court promptly established rules for procedure on appeal from the District Court to the Superior Court, and upheld its authority to do so in one of its early decisions thereafter. *Gonzalez* v. *Superior Court,* 75 D.P.R. 585 (1953). Other decisions have clarified the procedures and time limits for such appeals. See, for example, *Cintron* v. *Superior Court,* 76 D.P.R. 191 (1954). One immediate consequence of the new appellate procedure, supplanting the former trials *de novo,* was a decrease in the number of appeals to about 40 per cent of the former figure.

Further review by the Supreme Court in cases so appealed is obtainable only on certiorari in that Court's discretion. As for review by the Supreme Court of Superior Court decisions generally, the pre-existing scope of and grounds for appellate review have been carried forward, but with procedures established by Supreme Court rule.

Rule-Making . . . Lodged in the Courts. The Judiciary Article of the new Constitution states in Section 6: "The Supreme Court shall adopt for the courts rules of evidence and of civil and criminal procedure which shall not abridge, enlarge or modify the substantive rights of the parties." Such rules are submitted to the Legislature, which has power to disapprove as well as to amend, repeal or supplement. Section 7 of the same article directs the Supreme Court to adopt "rules for the administration of the courts". Both of these grants of rule-making power are reaffirmed in Section 2 of the Judiciary Act of 1952.

Implementing its new authority, the Supreme Court in December, 1952, adopted Rules of Administration for the Court of First Instance, effective February 1, 1953, prescribing such matters as the days and hours for court sessions, the appointment and functions of the Administrative Judge for each of the court's several parts, and matters relative to pre-trial conferences and court calendars. Rule 9 imposes restrictions on continuances, and Rule 11 require the dismissal of all pending civil causes which have been inactive for more than six months unless good cause is shown, and the rule further warns that motions for continuance or extension of time are not sufficient "activity" to prevent dismissal. Another important rule requiring weekly reports by judges on their judicial activities will be noted later.

Proposed Rules of Civil Procedure have been prepared in draft form by a Committee with Judge Charles E. Clark as Consultant, and have been submitted to the Bar and others for study and suggestions. The Rules are expected to be ready for presentation to the Puerto Rico Legislature in January, 1956. Similarly, a Committee on Rules of Evidence, headed by former Supreme Court Justice Ortiz and assisted by Professor E. M. Morgan, has completed its draft which after study by the Bar is also expected to be submitted to the Legislature in January.

In the preliminary preparation or study phase are proposed Rules of Criminal Procedure, Rules on Preservation and Destruction of Records, and Rules on Small Claims—all pursuant to authority granted or confirmed in the new Judiciary Act.

Essential to the efficient functioning of any judicial system, and more especially to one as solidly integrated and articulated as Puerto Rico's, is a single, responsible individual or agency at the top with full authority, adequate information, and competent assistance to keep the machinery of justice operating smoothly. Puerto Rico's Constitution provides this by making its Chief Justice the top manager, with power to assign judges and other personnel from part to part in either division of the Court of First Instance, as well as from one division to another. It also provides him with what is the vital heart of a modern judicial system, namely, an Office of Court Administration under an Administrative Director. While a somewhat similar office had existed in the Department of Justice since 1945, it remained for the new Constitution to give it vitality by integrating it closely with the supervisory powers of the Chief Justice. Thus the Constitution specifies that "The Chief Justice shall direct the administration of the courts and shall appoint an administrative director who shall hold office at the will of the Chief Justice."

The Judiciary Act of 1952, in turn, delineates the principal duties of the Administrative Office as follows:

> The function of the Office of Court Administration shall be to assist the Chief Justice in the administration of the General Court of Justice of Puerto Rico by examining the administrative methods and efficiency of the court personnel, and the state of the dockets and the pending case loads of the courts, collecting statistical and other data as to the court operation, preparing and keeping proper books of accounting, submitting estimates and drawing the necessary requisitions for public funds appropriated for operation of the judicial system, making recommendations to the Chief Justice for the improvement of court operation and the assignment and transfer of judges, and generally performing such tasks and taking such steps as the Chief Justice shall direct for the better administration of the Court. [Section 26.]

The Chief Justice appoints virtually the entire personnel of the court system, including clerks of court, probation officers and public defenders. The Administrative Director appoints his own staff, with the approval of the Chief Justice, and his office is organized into three main divisions: Statistics and Procedure, Personnel, and Administrative Services. To enable it to perform its extensive housekeeping functions for the entire judicial system, the Office of Court Adminisration is granted, by legislative appropriation, an annual budget in excess of $150,000 per year. It should be noted that the 1954-1955 budget for the entire Judicial Branch of Puerto Rico, comprising seven Supreme Court justices, thirty Superior Court judges, fifty-three District Court judges, forty-two Justices of the Peace, and 634 supporting personnel, was $2,528,356.

One of the key functions of the Administrative Office as strengthened and supplemented by the Supreme Court Rules of Court Administration is the compilation of current statistics on judicial business. Section 28 of the Judiciary Act directs the judges, secretaries and other personnel of the General Court to furnish information and statistical data bearing on the state of dockets and reflecting other judicial business transacted by them. Rule 12 of the Rules of Court Administration calls for a weekly report to be rendered by each judge of the Court of First Instance, such report to contain information as to days and hours spent on the bench, reasons for not having decided any pending case tried on the merits within forty-five days after submision and other pending judicial matters within fifteen days after submission, and such other information as the report form shall require. In addition, the secretaries or clerks of the court are required to send monthly statistical reports on civil and criminal cases and such other reports as the Administrative Director may request.

The information thus supplied by the judges and clerks provides complete and up-to-date data to enable the Administrative Director to advise the Chief Justice on the need for assignment of judges and redistribution of work to equalize the caseloads among the several courts and to keep the judicial machinery functioning smoothly. The data are published in the Administrative Director's annual and semi-annual reports which set forth in complete tabular form the statistics compiled. To assist in such compilation, the office has installed electric tabulating equipment which makes it possible to compute a wealth of statistical information promptly and accurately.

Mention has already been made of Rule 11 of the Rules of Court Administration, requiring the dismissal of civil cases which have been inactive for six months. During the first five months of the rule's operation nearly 5,000 cases were dismissed in the Superior Court and approximately 4,000 in the District Court, thereby substantially reducing the backlog of pending civil cases. It should perhaps be noted that the delays incident to civil jury trials in metropolitan courts of states such as in New York, Connecticut and Massachusetts are not a factor in Puerto Rico because of the non-availability of jury trial in civil matters under Puerto Rican law. Nevertheless, a indicated in the Administrative Director's reports, disposition of civil business by the Court of First Instance has shown steady improvement under the new administrative provisions.

Among other activities of the Administrative Office has been the preparation of a probation manual. It has also prepared, with the assistance of the Institute of Judicial Administration, an Administrative Manual for clerks and marshals of the Court of First Instance. The Administrative Office has undertaken an ex-

tensive program for improving the physical facilities and location
of the courts, including the planning of a building program for
the Superior and District Courts. To these essential housekeeping
functions should be added the responsibility of the Administrative Director, at the direction of the Chief Justice, of appearing
before the Legislative Assembly and its committees in connection
with matters affecting judicial administration.

Puerto Rico has been aided in the achievement of the objectives expressed in the new Constitution by the calibre of its
leaders in all branches of the government. The energy and
ability of Chief Justice A. Cecil Snyder and of his Associate Justices are significant factors in the progress achieved. The Island
has been extremely fortunate, too, to have had as its Administrative Directors in the new reorganization such highly capable
men as Judge Federico Tilén and his successor, Lucas F. Sérbia
Cordova. It is in large measure due to such leadership, and to
the vigor and understanding of the members of the Legislative
Assembly and of Puerto Rico's Governor Luis Muñoz Marin,
that Puerto Rico has accomplished the objectives sought.

Mention should be made of other important developments
recently completed or now in process. For example, in March,
1955, there was adopted throughout Puerto Rico, pursuant to
1954 legislation, a system for using a non-fixable traffic ticket.
One significant feature and incidental enforcement device is a
provision whereby an offending driver's license is withheld in
lieu of bond for his court appearance.

Section 30 of the Judiciary Act directs the General Court of
Justice and the Office of Court Administration to encourage the
promotion of legal aid. Pursuant to this mandate a Legal Aid
Society has been organized with the assistance of the National
Legal Aid Association and a plan is now well advanced whereby,
with the co-operation of the Bar Association and the Law School
of the University of Puerto Rico, and supported by legislative
appropriations and public contributions, legal aid will soon be
available on a broad and systematic basis throughout the Island.
Also, a Division of Social Services has been established in the
Office of Court Administration which will handle juvenile probation, adult probation, domestic relations and support.

Other pending developments include the steps now being
taken to establish simplified procedures for the handling of small
claims. This is in accordance with Section 2 of the Judiciary
Act which authorizes the Supreme Court to adopt "Rules for
the informal adjudication of claims of one hundred dollars
($100) or less."

Both Puerto Rico and the United States as a whole can well be proud of the Island's achievements during the past several years. With a population of nearly 2,300,000, with a geographical area approximately three fourths that of the State of Connecticut, with a metropolitan area of over 592,600 population in 1955, and with an increasingly diversified industry, Puerto Rico presents problems not vastly different from those confronting many states. It has made such significant headway toward achievement of the goals set as Minimum Standards of Judicial Administration by the American Bar Association in 1937 and 1938 that other jurisdictions may well take heed of how these results were accomplished. The dedication of Puerto Rico's new Supreme Court building, therefore, is a fitting occasion to focus national attention on the subject of judicial administration as exemplified by the Commonwealth of Puerto Rico.

SAFEGUARDS OF JUDICIAL INDEPENDENCE*

In order to understand the concept of judicial independence in the United States, and the several safeguards by which it is or might be assured, it is necessary to adopt a multi-dimensional approach. The complex of governmental structures, the variety in norms and customs, their evolution in historical perspective, and the cross-currents of political and social demography, all contribute to a non-uniform, and at times a conflicting, congeries of factors. Nonetheless, both the ultimate objective and the starting-point are clearly discernible. It is the means of achievement and the measurement of progress toward that end that provide the problem of analysis.

The objective is not hard to define. If justice means, as is for present purposes subsumed, the impartial and wise assessment of rights and duties as between man and individual man, or as between man and the collective man denominated "the state", the task of administering it in this humanistic age devolves on man himself. Divine guidance as a spiritual force is a support, but not a substitute, for human perception. To insure that quality of human perception that is requisite for the task is far more difficult than to state the *desiderata* that comprise it. The latter have been briefly and ably summarized by an American writer as follows:

> All agree that we want good judges. All agree, surely, on the primary qualities that a good judge must have: honesty and courage, wisdom and learning; the kind of humility that enables a man to rise above the faults and prejudices of his own inner self, and to see and think and decide on higher ground.[1]

The starting-point, for the United States, inheres in its organic charters. The Declaration of Independence, for example, is spe-

---

1. Haynes, The Selection and Tenure of Judges 8 (1944).

* Paper prepared for presentation at the Fourth International Congress of Comparative Law, Paris, France, 1954.

(Revised, February 1, 1958).

cific in its indictment of the existing royal abuses against which its framers were incensed:

> He has obstructed the Administration of Justice, by refusing his Assent to Laws for establishing Judiciary Powers.

> He has made Judges dependent on his Will alone, for the Tenure of their Offices, and the Amount and Payment of their Salaries.

Judicial independence, as envisioned by these hardy sponsors, had tangible causative attributes. It was to be attained by a departure from something then known, disliked, and inveighed against. But the direction of that departure was not clearly or unanimously perceived then, nor is it so perceived now. Experience with a variety of developments in the intervening century and nearly four score more of years has aided but not completed the crystallizing process. The most that can be attempted is to sketch the outlines as they have emerged in their present heterogeneous form and to offer such subjective appraisals as the viewer deems himself competent to suggest.

To appreciate the difficulties of simplifying the picture it is necessary to postulate the special characteristics of the judicial and governmental systems in the United States that distinguish them, individually or collectively, from systems elsewhere. It is not proposed to enter into extended analysis and comparison. Rather, what is here offered is a brief and necessarily imperfect outline of those features that shape the American development, and the factors that emerge against that background.

To begin with, the diversity of governmental structure between the federal and the state organizational patterns, and among the forty-eight states themselves, makes for a diversity, sometimes marked and sometimes slight, among the various judicial systems.

Characteristic also is the lack of a career judiciary, by either tradition or training, in the sense in which the term is understood in the systems of many other countries. American judges are not predestined to their tasks nor do they have the assurance, at the outset of their respective professional instruction stages, that by special courses of study, special examinations, and supplemental or incidental apprenticeship service, they will become novitiate jurists with the prospects of ascending by orderly progress to higher levels in the judicial hierarchy. Rather, they are chosen from among, and possess in general the same qualifications as, other members of the bar.

1. *Judicial Independence in the American Polity.*

Here, also, lies a feature of the American system, but a feature that is fortunately becoming less significant. The differences in requirements for admission to the bar among the several states are gradually disappearing, as minimal specifications of educational standards, both quantitative and qualitative, achieve increasing acceptance. Nevertheless, the basic matrix of the bar from which the judges are chosen is of sufficiently uneven quality to preclude assaurance that any and all lawyers, although eligible, are competent to become judges.

A further factor which identifies the American polity, at least by contrast to authoritarian regimes, is the basic bi-partisan nature of the political system. In many localities, but in by no means all, the selection of American judges is an essentially partisan matter and the choice is therefore susceptible of dictation by other considerations than those of inherent ability and experience.

Finally, the position of the judge in the American community, whether the level be local, state or federal, is almost generally regarded as one of greater prestige and importance than that of public servants generally, with the possible exception of top governmental executives.

With the foregoing factors to serve as a background, the principal safeguards to insure judicial independence in the United States can be grouped under five headings as follows: (1) Methods of selection, (2) tenure, (3) compensation, (4) retirement benefits, and (5) methods of removal. While there are possibly other safeguards of equivalent significance, these five can be generally regarded as receiving wide recognition and concern among the continuing programs for improvement of the American judicial system.

It is proposed to examine, first, the status of these five factors as they obtain in the federal judicial system, and, second, the much more complex picture presented in the state systems. The latter will require both historical and comparative analysis in order to arrive at a tentative evaluation of achievements and progress.

2. Safeguards in the Federal Judicial System

a. Methods of Selection

The Constitution of the United States specifies that "The judicial Power of the United States, shall be vested in one supreme Court, and in such inferior Courts as the Congress may

from time to time ordain and establish."[2] The Constitution
further prescribes that:

> The President . . . shall nominate, and by and with
> the Advice and Consent of the Senate, shall appoint . . .
> Judges of the supreme Court, and all other Officers of
> the United States, whose appointments are not herein
> otherwise provided for, . . . but the Congress may by
> Law vest the Appointment of such Inferior Officers, as
> they think proper, in the President alone, in the Courts
> of Law, or in the Heads of Departments.[3]

With respect to the Chief Justice and Associate Justices of the
Supreme Court, the method of judicial selection is clear and
explicit: nomination and appointment by the President with
the advice and consent of the Senate. Equally clear, in the interpretation and application of these provisions, is the intention
that the initial choice of all other federal court judges, presently
comprising the United States Courts of Appeal and the United
States District Courts, rests with the President subject to similar
senatorial confirmation.

In practice, the power of the Senate and of Congress to control judicial appointments is greater than the language of the
organic provisions indicates. Through an unwritten rule of
senatorial courtesy, if a Senator who is of the same political
party as the President expresses personal objection to a judicial
nominee, the colleagues of the objecting Senator uniformly join
in refusing to give the required confirmation. The assertion of
such Senatorial prerogative has been relatively infrequent in
appointments to the United States Supreme Court and the
Courts of Appeals, but it gives the Senators considerable authority in the selection of judges of the Federal District Courts.

There is also a practice followed by a number of Presidents
in the appointment of District Court Judges, that where the
state from which the judge is chosen does not have a Senator or
Senators of the same political party as the President, he will consult with the local member of the House of Representatives who
is of such party, or with the party leaders in the state.

The method of appointment by the President "with the advice
and consent of the Senate" also applies in the selection of judges
for certain specialized United States courts, such as the Court of
Claims and the Court of Customs and Patent Appeals, as well

---

2. U.S. Const. Art. 1, § 3.
3. U.S. Const . Art. 2, § 2.

as in the principal courts of certain territories and insular possessions of the United States, such as Alaska and Hawaii.

b. *Tenure of Judges.*

The Constitution provides expressly that: "The Judges,
both of the supreme and inferior Courts, shall hold their Offices
during good Behavior . . ."[4] Such provision is a recognition and
codification of the English principle of appointing judges to hold
office *"quamdiu se bene gesserint"* and constitutes a primary bul-
wark and safeguard of judicial independence.

The provision of tenure for life during good behavior applies
to appointments to all of the principal United States courts and
to most courts of specialized jurisdiction. In the territories of
Alaska and Hawaii, however, judicial appointments are for
limited terms. Thus, the members of the Supreme Court and
the Circuit Courts of Hawaii and of the District Court of Alaska
hold office for four years "unless sooner removed by the President", and those of the District Court of Hawaii hold office for
six-year terms, unless so removed.[5] Also, the judges of recently-
established Court of Military Appeals, on expiration of the initial staggered terms, are now appointed to hold office for 15
years.

c. *Compensation of Judges.*

The same provision of the Constitution that specifies the
tenure of federal judges also guarantees that they "shall, at
stated Times, receive for their Services, a Compensation, which
shall not be diminished during their Continuance in Office."
By legislation in 1955,[5a] their compensation was provided as follows: for Justices of the Supreme Court, $35,000 per year; for
Judges of the Courts of Appeal, $25,500; and for District Court
Judges, $22,500. The Chief Justice or presiding judge of each
of the several courts receives $500 more than the associate jus-
tices or judges. The judges of the Court of Claims, the Court of
Customs and Patent Appeals and the Court of Military Appeals,
receive salaries of $25,500 per year. The compensation of judges
of the Tax Court and the Customs Court is $22,500 per year.
It should be noted that the salaries of all federal judges are
subject to both federal and state income taxes, so that the actual
net compensation is lower than the amounts given.

---

4. U.S. Const. Art. 3, § 1.

5. Pub. L. No. 294, 83d Cong., 2d Sess. (Feb. 10, 1954), § 3 (a), amends 28
U.S.C. § 134, to provide that the term of the District Court for the Virgin
Islands shall be eight, rather than the four years previously provided, making
"that term of office consistent with that of both Puerto Rico and the Canal
Zone."

5a. Pub. L. No. 9, 84th Cong., 1st Sess. (Mar. 2, 1955).

By way of comparison with the foregoing figures, the salary of the President of the United States is $100,000 per year, plus an annual expense allowance of $50,000. Members of the Senate and the House of Representatives receive salaries of $22,500 per year.

d. *Retirement and Pension Provisions.*

A significant factor in the security of judicial office, and hence a contributory safeguard of judicial independence, is the sufficiency of provision for continued compensation on retirement from active service. In the federal system the provisions are relatively liberal, guaranteeing to all judges holding office during good behavior the benefit of retiring at age 70, after 10 years' service, on full pay for life.[6]

In 1956, the United States Congress adopted meaures to supplement the retirement provisions by providing for annuities for the widows and dependents of deceased federal judges.[6a] Similar provisions have been enacted in several of the states, and have contributed greatly to the attractions and security of the judicial office. Under the new federal law, the widow and dependents would receive an amount equal to 37½ percent of the deceased judge's average salary.

A federal judge who becomes permanently disabled during his term of office, may retire from active service, on furnishing the President a certificate of disability signed by the appropriate presiding judicial officer. If such disabled judge has served continuously for 10 years, he receives full salary; if less than 10 years, he receives one-half salary on retirement.

e. *Removal of Judges*

The procedures for removal of federal judges from office come within the general constitutional provisions relating to impeachment. They are as follows:

> The President, Vice President and all civil Officers of the United States, shall be removed from Office on Impeachment for, and conviction of, Treason, Bribery, or other high Crimes and Misdemeanors.[7]

> The Senate shall have the sole Power to try all Impeachments. When sitting for that Purpose, they shall be on Oath or affirmation. . . . And no Person shall be

---

6. These benefits have recently been extended to judges "attaining the age of sixty-five years and after serving at least fifteen years continuously or otherwise" by Pub. L. No. 294, 83d Cong., 2d Sess., § 3 (Feb. 10, 1954).

6a. Pub. L. No. 973, 84th Cong., 2d Sess. (Aug. 3, 1956).

7. U.S. Const. Art. 3, § 4.

convicted without the Concurrence of two thirds of the Members present.[8]

Judgment in Cases of Impeachment shall not exceed further than to removal from Office, and disqualification to hold and enjoy any Office of honor, Trust or Profit under the United States; but the Party convicted shall nevertheless be liable, and subject to Indictment, Trial, Judgment and Punishment, according to Law.[9]

The bringing of impeachment proceedings against federal officers, including judges, is so rare that very few precedents have been established under these provisions during the many years that they have been in existence.

3. *The Contest for Safeguards in the State Systems.*
   a. *Early Colonial Problems.*

In the original American colonies prior to the Revolution, it was customary for the courts to be created by the colonial governors with the consent of their respective councils. The appointing power was generally in the governors, although the king reserved the power to appoint chief justices by direct royal order. In the colonies of Connecticut and Rhode Island, judges were elected by the legislative body, but in the others the principle of appointment by the executive prevailed.

Until the middle of the eighteenth century, it was not unusual to appoint judges to hold office during good behavior, their salaries being provided by the local legislatures. But thereafter, and to prevent the appointees from becoming too independent of British authority, the crown limited the tenure of colonial judges to the pleasure of the appointing power, and this principle continued in most of the colonies until the time of the Revolution.

In New York, the legislative assembly, through its control over the expenditure of public funds, was able to gain a substantial measure of appointing power through the device of naming in appropriation bills the persons to be paid therefrom. In this manner the authority previously conferred by the king or the governor and his council was substantially circumvented. Moreover, in spite of the general requirement that judges be appointed to hold office only at the pleasure of the appointing power, the New York legislature asserted its insistence that judicial appointments be with tenure during good behavior. In

---

8. U.S. Const. Art. 1, § 3, Cl. 6.
9. U.S. Const. Art. 1, § 3, Cl. 7.

Massachusetts, popular feeling was deeply stirred by the action of the king in 1772 forbidding judges of the superior court from receiving their grants of salary from the local government, and substituting therefor a grant from the crown.

b. *Judicial Selection in the Original States.*

The status of judicial selection in the period immediately following the Revolution can be summarized as follows: In seven of the original states—Connecticut, Georgia, New Jersey, North Carolina, Rhode Island, South Carolina, and Virginia—the selection of judges was vested in the legislature. In Delaware and Pennsylvania, it was vested in the governor and the legislature jointly. In Maryland, Massachusetts and New Hampshire, appointment was by the governor subject to confirmation by his council, and in New York the power was vested in a special "council of appointment" comprising the governor and certain members of the legislature.

The concern of the colonists in the matter of judicial tenure has been described by a writer as follows:

> In theory it was universally agreed that the judges must be independent, and to this end the usual tenure in the early constitutions was during good behavior. This was the tenure provided in the constitutions of Massachusetts, Delaware, Maryland, Virginia, North Carolina, South Carolina, and in those drawn up in New Hampshire and Vermont. New York had the same tenure, except that there the judges retired at the age of sixty years. In Pennsylvania and New Jersey the appointments were for seven years. In Connecticut and Rhode Island, where they did not frame constitutions but continued their charter governments, the judges were still appointed annually by the legislature. . . .[10]

c. *The Jacksonian Era and Popular Election.*

It is apparent from the background data that the method of choosing judges by popular election was not generally accepted, nor possibly even seriously considered, by the constitution-framers in the early states. Also, the principle of life tenure during good behavior prevailed in a majority of the constitutions. The election of President Andrew Jackson, however, was accompanied and followed by a strong movement in favor of "the common man" and inaugurated the era of "Jacksonian democracy" in the 1820s. The effects of this movement survive to the

10. Carpenter, Judicial Tenure in the United States 4 (1918).

present time and contribute a strong factor in the American conceptualism of desirable safeguards of judicial independence. It gained impetus with the westward expansion and the addition of new population areas unsteeped in the aristocratic traditions of the eastern seaboard. The growth of judicial power and the assertion of its supremacy in determining the constitutionality of legislation, also contributed to judicial unpopularity.

Georgia and Mississippi were two of the early states to provide for the popular election of judges, and were among the first to combine such election with short terms of judicial office. In 1846, New York adopted similar measures and thereafter many states rapidly followed suit. In consequence, by 1860 some 22 of the 34 states then comprising the Union had provided for popular election of judges, and 21 of the states had adopted short-term judicial tenure.

C. *Current Status and Proposals for Reform.*

The publication in 1949 of a comprehensive survey, "Minimum Standards of Judicial Administration", edited by Chief Justice Arthur T. Vanderbilt of the New Jersey Supreme Court, provided one of the first authoritative studies of the extent of progress in the growing movement for reform in judicial administration. That movement had already focused attention on the problems of judicial selection and tenure and the necessity of safeguards to strengthen the assurance of a qualified, competent and independent judiciary. Some steps had already been taken in several of the states by providing that in the election of judges a non-partisan ballot would be used, so that, in theory at least, political qualifications would not be a factor of primary significance in guiding the voters' choice.

In California, by constitutional amendment adopted in 1934, the initial appointment of appellate court judges by the governor was made subject to approval by a special commission on qualifications, and the appointee's subsequent re-election is on the basis of his record alone rather than in contest with an opposing candidate.

The American Bar Association in 1937 endorsed a plan set forth in the following resolution:

> *Whereas,* the importance of establishing methods of judicial selection that will be most conducive to the maintenance of a thoroughly qualified and independent judiciary that will take the state judges out of politics as nearly as may be, is generally recognized; and
>
> *Whereas,* in many states movements are under way to

find acceptable substitutes for direct election of judges;

Now therefore be it resolved, by the House of Delegates of the American Bar Association that in its judgment the following plan offers the most acceptable substitute available for direct election of judges:

(a) The filling of vacancies by appointment by the executive or other elective official or officials, but from a list named by another agency, composed in part of high judicial officers and in part of other citizens, selected for the purpose, who hold no other public office.

(b) If further check upon appointment be desired, such check may be supplied by the requirement of confirmation by the state senate or other legislative body, of appointments made through the dual agency suggested.

(c) The appointee after a period of service should be eligible for reappointment periodically, or periodically go before the people upon his record with no opposing candidate, the people voting upon the question, "Shall Judge Blank be retained in office?"

A modified version of this plan was adopted in Missouri in 1940 and has come to be widely known as the "Missouri Plan."

Of the states in which methods other than popular election obtain, Delaware, Maine, Massachusetts, New Hampshire and New Jersey provide for appointment by the governor, subject to confirmation by the state senate or governor's council. In other states, certain classes of judges are so appointed. In Connecticut, Rhode Island, South Carolina, Vermont and Virginia, some or all of the judges are elected by the legislature.

In two of the states with appointive systems, Massachusetts and New Hampshire, the judges hold office for life during good behavior. In New Jersey, judges of the supreme court and of the superior courts are appointed initially for a term of seven years, and on reappointment have life tenure during good behavior. In Rhode Island, superior court judges hold office for life.

In all other states, the judges hold office for stated terms only, varying from 2 years to 21 years for appellate judges, and from 2 years to 14 years for trial court judges. The median term for both groups is 6 years.

Special mention should be made of judicial selection and tenure in Puerto Rico which, by virtue of its new constitution adopted and approved in 1952, became a commonwealth with a republican form of government. Judges are appointed by the governor with the advice and consent of the Senate, and the justices of the supreme court hold office during good behavior.

The matter of judicial salaries is a subject of concern in most of the states, and efforts to raise compensation to a level commensurate with the dignity of the office are making gradual but perceptible headway. The present median salary for appellate court judges is approximately $16,000 per year, and for trial court judges approximately $13,000. The largest salaries are those in New York, where the judges of the highest appellate court receive $37,500 per year, the chief judge, an additional $2,500, and judges of the general trial courts receive from $26,000 to $32,000 annually.

Substantially all of the 48 states have provisions for retirement benefits or pensions for some or all of their judges. Typical plans provide for retirement compensation in the amount of from ½ to ¾ of annual salary after periods of service of from 10 to 20 years, and permit or require retirement at ages ranging from 60 to 70.

Removal of judges from office, as in the case of the federal constitution, is provided for in most state constitutions through the device of impeachment proceedings. The cumbersomeness of these procedures is an effective deterrent to their hasty or ill-advised use, and they are very rarely invoked. They have been supplemented in some state constitutions by other provisions for removal, for example, automatic forfeiture of judicial office on conviction of certain crimes. In Massachusetts and New Hampshire, removal may be effected by address of the governor to both houses of the legislature; and in California, Utah, Washington and Wisconsin, by joint resolution of both houses. In Louisiana, Michigan and New York, special courts are provided to hear removal charges, and in several of the western states, judges may be recalled from office by vote of the people.

4. *Evaluation of American Safeguards of Judicial Independence.*

The foregoing review indicates the range and variety of standards in the selection, tenure, compensation, retirement and removal of judges in the United States. Substantial unanimity of viewpoint as to the most desirable features of an adequate system of safeguards to insure judicial independence, competence and integrity, can be achieved only by stating it in terms of general objectives. Thus, the method of selection should be the one that will best insure the choice of the most competent persons to serve as judges. The term of office should be such as to leave the judicial incumbent free of subservience to the necessity of securing re-appointment or re-election at frequent intervals. Compensation and retirement provisions should be such as to attract and retain the best qualified members of the bar to serve in judicial positions. Given these safeguards, the need of provisions for removal would assume secondary importance, but whatever removal procedures are provided should be such as to prevent precipitate action and to guarantee fair and impartial deliberation by those charged with deciding the issue of removal.

The elective system of judicial selection is still deeply-rooted in the political structure and popular sentiment of many of the states. So also is the custom of relatively short terms of judicial tenure. In practice, it is pointed out, these are not always the deterrents they would seem to be in theory. In a great percentage of instances vacancies in elective judicial offices are filled initially by appointment, and the appointee in a subsequent election has the advantage of incumbency which is frequently tantamount to his retention in office by the voters.

Nevertheless, the trend of considered thought in the United States is in the direction of an appointive judiciary, with tenure for life during good behavior. The federal system, whatever its shortcomings, is widely viewed as producing a higher norm of judicial ability than does, by and large, the popular election of judges for short terms. To eliminate the impact of political considerations on the choice of appointees to judicial office, further safeguards have been advocated, such as non-partisan nominating commissions to screen or designate the proposed list of candidates, or the advance submission of the names of proposed appointees to the members of the bar, or a governing group thereof, for approval as to judicial qualifications. Another alternative is the frank recognition of political partisanship and the assurance of balance through a requirement that, in multi-judge courts, no more than a certain number of the judges shall be of the same political party.

It is reasonably safe to assert that no single, uniform, nation-wide plan will eventually emerge from the variety of present prototypes and proposals above reviewed. But whatever the ultimate solution or solutions may be, the safeguards of judicial independence in the United States will be one of the principal bulwarks of a republican form of government whose history and traditions demonstrate a constant strving to guarantee to the people a fair, fearless, and independent judiciary.

JUDICIAL SELECTION AND TENURE *

(From *Wayne Law Review*, Vol. 3, p. 175, Summer 1957).

Concern for the independence and integrity of our judiciary is deep-rooted in American tradition. Our sturdy colonial ancestors were forthright in asserting, among the royal abuses by the British sovereign denounced in the Declaration of Independence, the charge that "He has made Judges dependent on his Will alone, for the Tenure of their Offices, and the Amount and Payment of their Salaries." Their concern is manifested in the safeguards of the federal Constitution: Presidential appointment of judges with the advice and consent of the Senate, coupled with the provision for tenure during good behavior. It was manifested also in the early state constitutions or charters vesting authority for judicial selection in the legislatures either alone or jointly with the governor, or in the latter with provision for confirmation. Direct popular election of judges was nowhere accepted, and in only a few of the original states were the terms of judicial office limited to periodic reappointments. The usual tenure, as in the federal system, was during good behavior.

It remained for the era of Jacksonian democracy and its aftermath to sweep aside these early methods and substitute, as a concomitant of the movement in favor of the common man, the concept of popular election of judges for relatively short terms. Thus, by 1860 some 22 of the 34 states that then comprised the Union had provided for popular election of judges, and 21 of the states had adopted short-term judicial tenure. But not all states followed the popular trend. Delaware, Maine, Massachusetts, New Hampshire and New Jersey still retain the appointive system, and in several other states, namely, Connecticut, Rhode Island, South Carolina, Vermont, and Virginia, some or all of the judges are elected by the legislature.

In two of the states with appointive systems, Massachusetts and New Hampshire, the judges hold office for life during good behavior. In New Jersey, judges of the supreme court and of the superior courts are appointed for an initial term of seven years, and on reappointment have life tenure during good behavior. In Rhode Island, superior court judges hold office for life.

---

* This paper was delivered on May 10, 1957 as the Franklin D. Hepburn Memorial Lecture for 1956-57 at Wayne State University Law School.

In all other states, the judges hold office for stated terms only, varying from 2 years to 21 years for appellate judges, and from 2 years to 14 years for trial court judges. The median term for both groups is 6 years.

The foregoing brief summary will serve as an introduction to the current picture and present problems. Much more could be said by way of historical elaboration and detail, and much has in fact been said by leading writers such as Haynes, Carpenter, Winters, and others on the subject of judicial selection and tenure. For my purposes, however, the modern era begins in the 1930s—1934, to be exact, because it was in that year that California took a significant step away from the popular election concept. The voters there adopted a constitutional amendment providing for the initial appointment of appellate court judges by the governor, subject to approval by a three-member ex-officio commission on qualifications. Each such appointee comes before the voters at periodic intervals without an opposition candidate and solely on the question "Shall.. be elected to the office for the term expiring ....? Yes.......................... No................."

This method, it should be noted, combines the appointive method with restrictions on the initial choice and with the opportunity for periodic popular vote on the question of the appointee's retention. Since judicial offices in California are not identified by political party labels, the voter's approval is necessarily based on considerations of judicial merit only, and the incumbent judge is not beholden to partisan political leaders for his appearance on the ballot. The plan has worked well—so much so that its extension downward to include trial court judges, with selection from a panel of three qualified persons nominated by an enlarged qualifications commission, is now being strongly advocated.

Actually, such a change would not be a radical departure from the existing theoretically elective system. A recently-completed survey of the metropolitan trial courts of the Los Angeles area notes that approximately 74% of Los Angeles County's trial judges in office in February, 1955, had been initially appointed by the governor to fill judicial vacancies, and that it is extremely rare that an incumbent judge is defeated in subsequent elections. The author of the survey observes:[1]

> Faced with the fact that our elective system for judges
> in this county has in reality become for the most part an

1. Holbrook, A Survey of Metropolitan Trial Courts, Los Angeles Area 48 (1956).

appointive system with life tenure, inquiry was made
among lawyers and judges as to the success of the
system.

Of the judges answering, thirty-eight out of fifty-two
suggested that there should be some preliminary screen-
ing of the list of nominees from which the governor
might make his appointment, and this suggestion also
came from many of the lawyers interviewd.

The California Plan of 1934 was a forerunner to the proposal
put forward by the American Bar Association in 1937, the essential features of which, as embodied in the resolution of the
Association's House of Delegates, were:[2]

(a)   The filling of vacancies by appointment by the
executive or other elective official or officials, but from
a list named by another agency, composed in part of
high judicial officers and in part of other citizens,
selected for the purpose, who hold no other public
office.

(b)   If further check upon appointment be desired,
such check may be supplied by the requirement of confirmation by the State Senate or other legislative body
of appointments made through the dual agency suggested.

(c)   The appointee after a period of service should
be eligible for reappointment periodically or periodically go before the people upon his record, with no opposing candidate, the people voting upon the question,
'Shall Judge Blank be retained in office?'

A variant of this plan was adopted by Missouri in 1940, applicable to the state supreme court, the intermediate courts of
appeals, the circuit and probate courts of Jackson County and
the City of St. Louis. Nominating commissions are composed of
equal numbers of lawyers elected by the bar and laymen appointed by the governor, for six-year staggered terms, and with
a judicial officer serving as *ex officio* chairman. The commission
selects three qualified persons for each vacancy and submits
their names to the governor, who must appoint from among the
three thus submitted. The Missouri Plan has been widely discussed. It has served as a guide or model for similar movements
in a score of other states where, despite determined opposition
by defenders of the status quo, there is gradually increasing sup-

2. 62 A.B.A. Rep. 893 (1937).

port for its adoption. In the past few years, for example, comparable plans have been formulated in Arizona, Arkansas, Colorado, Florida, Georgia, Kansas, Illinois, Iowa, Michigan, Nebraska, Nevada, New Mexico, New York, Ohio, Oklahoma, Pennsylvania, Washington, West Virginia, Wisconsin and Wyoming. Is there a likelihood that any of these will be adopted in the near future? I think there is. But not until the legislatures and the voting public are persuaded that the merits of such plans outweigh the arguments in opposition.

Defenders of the present methods of popular election of judges put forth a variety of stalwart contentions. An able justice of the New York Supreme Court's Appellate Division has urged the bar of that state to cooperate with political leaders in securing qualified judicial candidates. He asserts that:[3]

> If the bar will recognize, as I think it should recognize, that political considerations are fair considerations in the nomination and election of judges, and that political leaders have a legitimate interest and responsibility in the matter, the bar can by an equally fair and firm stand gain recognition of its legitimate interest in securing candidates possessing the requisite personal and professional qualifications.

An upstate New York attorney, strongly opposed to the Missouri Plan, expressed his views as follows:[4]

> The quality of judicial fitness of upstate Supreme Court justices, all of whom have been nominated and elected in accordance with the system proposed to be changed, is not exceeded by that of judges of comparative jurisdiction in any other state.
>
> Adoption of the Missouri Plan would not remove the selection of judicial candidates from politics. Under the Plan the Governor would appoint two members of the Commission, and then the Governor, not the Commission, would nominate candidates for judicial office. He would select one candidate from a list of three persons recommended by the Commission . . . .
>
> To vest in the Governor the power to nominate candidates for judicial office in the manner proposed in the Missouri Plan would grant him power which would be

---

3. Peck, *The Bar, Politics, and Judicial Selection*, 24 N.Y.S.B. Bull. 32, 38 (1952).

4. Runals, *Selection of Judges—an Upstate View*, 25 N.Y.S.B. Bull. 90, 96, 99 (1953).

subject to abuse. The fact that it would not be abused by the present Governor is no answer. The system of selection would be frozen in our Constitution. The people can rid themselves of party leaders more readily than they can amend the Constitution.

But whether party leadership can give adequate assurance of the selection of competent and qualified judges, and whether the bar's voice in the matter can be effective in a politically-elective system, have been questioned. The dangers that inhere in such a system are pointedly illustrated by a New York lawyer as follows:[5]

> For example, in 1932, there was a bi-partisan deal to create two vacancies in the Supreme Court of the first district and to fill them with one Democrat and one Republican nominally selected at judicial conventions held simultaneously by both parties. A vigorous campaign by the local bar associations produced 300,000 votes for each of two independent candidates, but failed to upset the deal.
>
> In 1943, a bi-partisan nominee for the Supreme Court of the first district was discovered before election day to have promised Frank Costello his "undying loyalty" for Mr. Costello's assurance that the nomination was "in the bag." When the matter was examined into publicly, the nominee denied knowing of Costello's underworld history and explained his motives by saying "in furtherance of my candidacy for the office of judge of the Supreme Court I enlisted the aid and cooperation of friends and acquaintances, to whom I am deeply grateful." An attempt by the political parties to cancel their nominations after these facts became known, and an effort by independents to defeat the nominee, were unsuccessful.

The New York lawyer continues:

> Political leaders, an alarming number of whom have been close associates of Frank Costello et al. generally control appointment of personnel to exempt positions in the courts. These are allocated with due regard to "party loyalty" and, even in the many positions which call for a legal background, without necessarily requir-

5. Gallantz, *Judicial Selection—A Metropolitan Proposal,* 25 N.Y.S.B. Bull. 101, 102, 103 (1953).

ing that the appointee be a lawyer. Out of 76 political district leaders who themselves had been employed in the courts of the first district on or before January 1, 1952, '50 or 72% were non-lawyers in positions, such as secretaries and clerks to justices, calling for a legal background,'

If the evil flowing from this situation needs elaboration, it may be illustrated by the fact that one non-lawyer district leader who was a close associate of Costello, and who held the position of chief confidential attendant to the Board of Justices of the Supreme Court, first district, was accused under oath of having demanded $25,000 for a nomination to a minor judicial post. Although he swore that the charge was false, an analysis of his finances by the [New York State] Crime Commission "revealed that in the significant years of 1947, 1948 and 1949, he spent $10,000 more than his ascertained receipts, the source of which he was unable to explain."

In December, 1953, the New York Citizens Union "Searchlight" gave the following summary:

1. Judges are awarded party nominations by district or county leaders whose selections are final despite the folderol of subsequent party primaries, judicial conventions and November elections.

2. Judges, thus chosen, often turn around and reward district leaders or their relatives and political cronies with sinecure jobs as clerks and secretaries exempt from civil service tests.

3. Some of these district leaders associate with criminals and are tough characters themselves; they ought not be the persons who award to judicial aspirants party nominations which are frequently equivalent to election!

New York City is not the only metropolitan area faced with these problems, nor are they exclusively a feature of partisan methods of judicial selection. A former chief justice of Pennsylvania is quoted as stating:[6]

We had a non-partisan act for the selection of judges, and when that act was in force the first Municipal Court

---

6. Fox, *Judges and Politics*, 27 Temp. L. Q. 1, 3 (1953).

in Philadelphia had to be selected, and I came into the hotel two or three nights before the primary, and a then very potent figure in Philadelphia politics was sitting alone in the dining room. This was the Bellevue-Strat-ford Hotel in Philadelphia. I knew him well. He called me over and said, "I am selecting here in this room the entire Municipal Court in Philadelphia, because the names that I mark on this long list of candidates (and I think there were from 50 to 60 on that) . . . will be the men who are selected."

Another Pennsylvania lawyer, writing for the American Bar Association Journal in February, 1955, summarized his findings and conclusions as follows:[7]

(1) That political leaders are the main influence in the selection of judges;

(2) That they are so recognized by the chief magistrate of the state;

(3) That a group within the political class have a tie-in with the rackets. In Philadelphia, the Kefauver Committee found it to be the numbers game; and

(4) That some leaders attempt to exercise their influence on some judges.

Do such actions generate or destroy confidence in our courts? Of course there can be only one conclusion—THEY DESTROY.

The political selection of judges has its impact not only on the choice of candidates but also on the economic life and pocket-book of the judge after he has been elected. The following extract of a letter from a chief justice of the New York City Court, published on the editorial page of the New York Times of March 17, 1956, and asking that his salary and that of his fellow justices be substantially increased, is singularly frank in its open admissions:[8]

In order for any candidate to elective office to win in a county-wide contest it is necessary for him to have solicited and used active aid and cooperation of many organizations and individuals; political, civic, religious, labor, fraternal, social welfare and many others. This means that after ascending the bench and as long as he

---

7. Harris, *The Selection of Judges The Virtues of the Pennsylvania Plan,* 41 A.B.A.J. 142, 143 (1955).

8. P. 18, Col. 3.

remains on it the City Court justice, like any other justice elected on a county-wide basis, is met with demands for contributions and subscriptions to various worthy causes in which his former helpers are active participants. Frequently these are demands which he cannot refuse and where pleading lack of money is not accepted as a satisfactory excuse.

One of the most conspicuous examples of this is the well-known hundred-dollar-a-plate dinner, many of which occur in each year.

To this letter, the Times editorial pointedly appended the following comment:

This candid description of the burdens borne by any man grateful for the support that made him a judge, or seeking re-election to the bench, or elevation to a higher court, moves us in sympathy to suggest a possible remedy: appointment of judges, rather than election of them.

An argument often heard in defense of the elective method is that the voting public is perfectly competent and qualified to select its judges. But how much does the average voter really know about the judicial candidates for whom he casts his ballot? In an address to the New York State Bar Association in 1955 the then president of the Association of the Bar of the City of New York summarized the results of a poll conducted by a well-known organization immediately after the November 1954 election. Only 1% of the voters polled in New York City could remember the name of the Chief Judge of the Court of Appeals whom they had elected with the endorsement of both major political parties. The same was true of the voters in the semi-rural areas of up-state Cayuga County. Two-thirds or more of the voters in each locality polled were unable to name a single judicial candidate for whom they had voted, and 80 per cent or more could not name any court being contested. Commenting on these results, President Klots stated:[9]

The method of electing judges directly by popular vote is, of course, one that has great superficial appeal. It is subject to all the familiar arguments which arouse popular emotions: Should not the people be the choosers of those by whom they are to be judged? Are

9. *The Selection of Judges and the Short Ballot*, 27 N.Y.S.B. Bull. 38, 40 (1955).

not the people the best qualified to select the best candidates? These and others like them are arguments which demagogic leaders always find ready at hand. The fact is, however, that, certainly in the more populated districts in the state, it is based on an entirely false premise. The premise on which the successful operation of the democratic process must always rest is that the people shall know something about the candidates for whom they are voting. Unless this is so, democracy becomes a pure mockery. Any impression that the people in such communities choose their own judges is pure delusion and any assertion to that effect is pure gibberish. The act of choosing implies a conscious act of the will. The voter does not exercise any real act of choice when he pulls down the lever over the name of a man whom he has never even heard of before he entered the polling booth and whose name he cannot remember the day after he has voted for him.

Arguments for and against the Missouri Plan have been summarized in a student Comment:[10]

> Louis Tendler, staff correspondent for the Detroit News, who has made an extensive study of the system, feels that it has three principal benefits:
> 1. It would remove the courts from politics by relieving judges of the necessity of campaigning for reelections.
> 2. It would attract the best qualified men to the bench by offering them greater security than now.
> 3. It would transfer the nominating process from the voters, who don't know the judicial qualifications of a candidate, to informed non-partisan nominating commissions.

The Plan has its critics also and they feel that:

> 1. It would tend to limit arbitrarily the number of candidates who might wish to seek judicial office.
> 2. It would tend to freeze mediocre or poor judges on the bench.
> 3. It would not satisfy the democratic elective process to have judges run on their record alone, unopposed by other candidates.

In light of the contentions pro and con, it might be well to

---

10. 16 U. Det. L. J. 180, 184 (1953).

take a look at the actual operation of the plan in Missouri in the seventeen years it has been in effect. Has it achieved the re-sults predicted for it? Has it produced the evils presaged by its critics?

The background of judicial selection in Missouri prior to 1940 was described by Jacob M. Lashly, former President of the American Bar Association, in an address at the regional meeting of the Association held in Baltimore last October:[11]

> Before the adoption of the new plan, the state opera-ted under a partisan political election system for the selection of judges as well as all other political officers. Judicial positions were party posts of political impor-tance. In the two large cities of the state political com-mittees took over and selected the nominees. This is known as practical politics. Either those running on the Democratic ticket were elected or those whose names appeared upon the Republican ballot were chosen. Culture and training had little relevancy if the candi-date was a good campaigner.

The constitutional amendment embodying the Missouri Plan was adopted by a majority of over 90,000 voters. Opposition political groups succeeded in obtaining a resubmission to the people in 1942, and this time the Plan was reaffirmed by a ma-jority of over 180,000 votes. In 1955 an effort in the Missouri legislature to repeal parts of the Plan was defeated in the House of Representatives by a vote of 2 to 1 and was not even brought to a vote in the Senate. Clearly, the voters and legislators of Mis-souri have not manifested any strong discontent with their new system of judicial selection.

But has it succeeded in divorcing judges from politics? Lashly offers the following proof:[12]

> Since the adoption of the plan in 1940, 40 non-parti-san selections have been made. Three times in that interval the governor was Democratic and once Repub-lican. In the beginning the governors were disposed to select for appointment from the proffered panel a mem-ber of . . . [their] own political party, but eventually a more objective approach on the part of the governors has become evident and the plan now is working so as

---

11. Missouri Plan for Selection of Judges, Baltimore Daily Record, Oct. 13, 1956, p. 5, col. 1.

12. *Ibid.*

to produce bi-partisan results. Notwithstanding the preponderance of three Democratic to one Republican term in the governor's office, out of the 40 appointed under the plan in the 16 years of its operation, 26 have been Democrats and 14 Republicans.

At the general elections between the years 1942 and 1954, inclusive, the election results alternated. The state went Republican twice, Democratic three times, and one time (1952) Republican in the Presidential election and Democratic as to state offices. During that period 53 judges came up for retention upon their respective records. In not a single instance did the voters discriminate as to party politics in their votes upon the judicial ticket. The uniformity with which the election results reveal an utter indifference to the political complexion of the judges whose records were on trial leaves no doubt at all of the complete and practical divorcement of those judicial offices from political considerations.

Has the Plan succeeded in securing good judges? Probably the best source of such appraisal is the lawyers themselves. Missouri like Michigan has an integrated all-inclusive bar and for the past several election years its members have been polled as to their approval or disapproval of incumbent judges on the ballot for retention in office. In the 1956 state bar canvass there were three judges of the Missouri Supreme Court, one Republican and two Democratic. The bar vote for each was an overwhelming 94% or better for approval.

Has the relative security of judicial tenure under the Plan resulted in lazy judges? Undoubtedly, under any plan a lazy man will still be lazy, but the Missouri Plan has strengthened rather than lessened the incentives of a judges to devote his full time to judicial business by relieving him of the burdens of campaigning for party nomination and election. An indication of improved judicial efficiency is the fact that the Supreme Court of Missouri has brought its docket to a current basis, whereas under the old system it had been from two to three years behind for more than half a century.

If the Plan is as good as its proponents claim, why has it not been adopted elsewhere? In December, 1955, there was put before the Alaska Constitutional Convention, assembled at the University of Alaska and composed of elected delegates chosen from throughout the territory and representing a cross-section of its population and economic life, a proposed Judiciary Article embodying the principles of the Missouri and American Bar Association plans. A motion to delete the plan and to substitute for it a system of popular election of judges was made and seconded. During the several hours of debate that followed, every argument in support of or opposition to the judicial selection plan was listened to attentively by the delegates. Contentions were made that the plan was undemocratic, that it would take from the people their inherent right to choose their judges, and that control over the bench would be vested in the hands of the select few comprising the nominating council. At the close of debate the matter was put to a vote, and the plan carried by a vote of 51 delegates in favor to two opposed. In April 1956 the proposed Constitution for the State of Alaska, to become effective upon admission to statehood, was put before the voters of the territory and was approved by a vote of better than two to one.

This is not to say that "As Alaska goes, so goes the nation." But the legislature of Kansas has just passed a constitutional amendment for submission to the people in 1958, embodying the principles of the Missouri Plan for the selection of its state supreme court justices. There is some likelihood that the Colorado Plan will be given legislative approval either in this session of the Colorado legislature or in an early future one. In a number of other states, headway for similar plans is gathering support and momentum. The time may not be too far away when the present majority of states now retaining the elective system will become a substantially decreasing majority if not an actual minority. When that era arrives we shall be well on the way to regaining the strength and esteem for our judiciary the loss of which was deplored more than fifty years ago by Roscoe Pound when he stated in his famous St. Paul speech of 1906:[13]

> Putting courts into politics, and compelling judges
> to become politicians, in many jurisdictions has almost
> destroyed the traditional respect for the Bench.

That such respect can be regained and that it must be maintained should be the faith and hope of every American citizen,

---

13. *The Causes of Popular Dissatisfaction with the Administration of Justice*, 29 A.B.A. Rep. 395, 415 (1906).

CITIZEN SUPPORT FOR COURT REFORM*

The decade following World War II is one of notable progress by bar associations in the area of public relations and recognition of the layman's interest in improving the administration of justice. Public doubts and public criticism, however, will continue to be voiced,—as indeed they should be—until certain long-needed reforms are fully achieved.

The basic causes of discontent are many and varied. As Chief Justice Stern pointed out a year ago, popular doubt stems from such factors as "the law's delays, its complicated techniques, its uncertainties and its somewhat unworldly and mystic atmosphere." I should like to support that observation by quoting from a layman, Dean Elmer L. Kayser of George Washington University, who spoke at the American Bar Association meeting in Atlantic City, in 1946. Here is his statement:

The layman in a courtroom feels that he is an alien. The stuffy rooms in which witnesses wait their turn to testify, the notorious lack of accommodation for jurors give added emphasis to the Ellis Island impression. Velvet draperies, gilt eagles and silken robes, the elevated bench and, I am afraid at times, a tone of voice that matches, may easily suggest to the modest citizen an Olympian race of beings before whose awful majesty he can only cringe. He notes the members of the bar moving about with freedom and easy aplomb while he, the witness or juror, is herded about.

He hears cases postponed or continued to meet the convenience of the bench and bar. The woman juror is thinking of that sugar stamp just running out. The business man there as a witness is wondering why that subpoena did not come during the slack season, instead of on a rush day.

He finds himself set down in Babel, amidst a new confusion of tongues. The stentorian tones of criers specializing more on volume than clarity, lengthy compound sentences of interminable length, a technical

*Address to Pennsylvania Bar Association, Spring Lake, New Jersey, June 22, 1954.
(Also printed in Report of the Fifty-Ninth Annual Meeting of the Pennsylvania Bar Association, Vol. LX, p. 96.)

nomenclature, spiked with polysyllables and Latin terms, pronounced as no Cicero or prep sophomore was ever taught. Truly the poor layman feels like an alien. It is true I have painted with raw colors on my palette. All of these observations would probably apply to no single court. To many courts, none at all would apply. The picture, though perhaps overdrawn, is suggestive.[1]

This discontent of the layman stems in many instances from direct and distasteful personal experience of the citizen as juror, as witness, or as litigant. It also stems from public reports of corruption and incompetence in government, including the agencies of law enforcement. The other day I noted this headline in a midwestern paper reporting the results of a questionaire sent to policemen throughout the State: "Get Rid of Politics." As one of the items included in the report, there is a paragraph headed: "Judges Accused of Interference", and I quote it:

> Another often-made suggestion by policemen who answered the questionnaire was, "Clean up the courts."

> In 38 specific cases they cited instances where judges had interfered with performance of duty.

> They accused the judges of taking part in "fixes", of being lenient with friends of friends, and of reducing the charges against a defendant for political reasons.

Citizen discontent stems in part, at least, from a lack of adequate public information on what has been done, is being done, or must be done to correct existing evils. Let us examine a few of these specific causes and the means to remedy them. For example, the importance of jury service as a basic public obligation is not fundamentally disputed by the average citizen. In fact the creed set forth in a prize-winning essay in the contest sponsored by the American Bar Association will be accepted by laymen generally:

> I am a JUROR.
> I am a seeker after truth.
> I must listen carefully and with concentration to all the evidence.
> I must heed and follow the instructions of the court.
> I must respectfully and attentively follow the arguments of the lawyers, dispassionately seeking to find and follow

---

1. Kayser, Justice and the Layman, 14 J. Bar Ass'n of D.C. 6 (1947).

the silver thread of truth through their conflicting
assertions.
I must lay aside all bias and prejudice.
I must be led by my intelligence and not by my emotions.

This is the concluding statement of the "creed":

My verdict must do justice, for what is just is "true and
righteous altogether"; and when my term of jury service
is ended, I must leave it my with citizenship unsullied,
and my conscience clear.

This is undoubtedly what the citizen likes to think of the
obligations of jury service, but along with it, what he does
demand, and rightly so, is that methods of jury selection be
impartial, and designed to assure that all qualified perons will
be called upon to share the responsibility. He objects to lack of
adequate jury facilities, to needless waste of time in standing by
for his services to be used, and to failure to instruct him in advance as to what his responsibilities are.

Let me give you here the evidence from a second layman.
This time, it is a newspaperman, Jack Foster, the Editor of the
Rocky Mountain News. He feels that a humane court is the
strongest protection a layman has against that exercise of ar-
bitrary power. He proceeds to point out some weaknesses of
courts in general, in an article entitled "The Layman and the
Courts."[2] He states that in theory the American Jury is the
truest symbol of democracy at work—a mingling of people from
all walks of life to deliberate upon a matter concerning some-
one like themselves. But is our jury system functioning up to
its best abilities? Following are criticisms from some jurors:

1. Sitting around for long periods, without being called
   upon for service irks an individual who has left a
   busy job.
   (a) Jurors should be allowed to make necessary
       business calls when not serving.
   (b) Jurors should not be called to court unless
       there is some certainty that they will be called
       upon to serve, if qualified.

2. The aloof, disinterested attitude of the judge toward
   the juror, and the proceedings in general are criticized.

2. 32 A.B.A.J. 621 (1946).

3. Pressure upon the jury to decide quickly or pressure at all may bring about unfortunate results.

4. Judges do not speak to the jurors about the importance and seriousness of their role, the need for sensible and human justice.

5. The judge should be closer to the layman, and the layman to the judge—it is only through a humane interpretation of the law by the judge that its "dignity" and "splendor" will be brought home to the layman.

As a footnote from overseas, I should like to add a comment from the message of Lord Cooper, Lord Chief Justice of Scotland, to the Society of Public Teachers of Law in England. He pointed out that the true definition of a judicial function would be one "which every *human* community craves, without which no *human* community can hold together, and on the well or ill performance of which the well-being of every *human* community depends."[3] You will notice I stress the word "human."

These objections of laymen are being recognized, and met, by improvements such as those accomplished in the District of Columbia and elsewhere, through the joint efforts of citizen leaders comprising representatives of bench, bar and public. I should advise you, if you have the opportunity, to spend a day in the new United States Court House in the District of Columbia, to see what thought and care and planning have been there given to the interests of jurors and witnesses. Also, I commend to you the report of the American Bar Association's Committee on Cooperation with Laymen. It is particularly relevant to the topic I am discussing with you tonight.

The plight of the citizen as a witness is not new. It was portrayed more than a century ago by Charles Dickens in the historic lawsuit of *Bardell v. Pickwick*. You will remember that the trial took place in 1828, before Mr. Justice Stareleigh of the Court of Common Pleas. Somewhere in the courtroom is the redoubtable Samuel Weller, but his turn as a witness is not yet. Mr. Winkle is on the stand. But let Mr. Dickens tell the story in his own words:

> Mr. Winkle was then examined by Mr. Skimpin, who, being a promising young man of two or three and forty, was of course anxious to confuse a witness who was notoriously predisposed in favor of the other side as much as he could.

---

3. [1953] J. Soc'y Pub. Teach. Law 91 (emphases supplied).

"Now, sir," said Mr. Skimpin, "have the goodness to
let his Lordship and the jury know what your name is,
will you?" and Mr. Skimpin inclined his head on one
side to listen with great sharpness to the answer, and
glanced at the jury meanwhile, as if to imply that he
rather expected Mr. Winkle's natural taste for perjury
would induce him to give some name which did not belong to him.

"Winkle," replied the witness.

"What's your Christian name, sir?" angrily inquired
the little judge.

"Nathaniel, sir."

"Daniel—any other name?"

"Nathaniel, sir—my Lord, I mean."

"Nathaniel Daniel or Daniel Nathaniel?"

"No, my Lord, only Nathaniel; not Daniel at all."

"What did you tell me it was Daniel for, then, sir?"
inquired the judge.

"I didn't, my Lord," replied Mr. Winkle.

"You did, sir," replied the judge, with a severe frown.
"How could I have got Daniel on my notes, unless you
told me so, sir?"

This argument was, of course, unanswerable.

I suppose we have all known judges like that. And we have
all heard, at times, and even observed recently on television,
the examination of witnesses conducted along the following lines:

"Now, Mr. Winkle," said Mr. Skimpin, "attend to
me, if you please, sir; and let me recommend you, for
your own sake, to bear in mind his Lordship's injunc-
tion to be careful. I believe you are a particular friend
of Pickwick, the defendant, are you not?"

"I have known Mr. Pickwick now, as well as I can
recollect at this moment, nearly—"

"Pray, Mr. Winkle, do not evade the question. Are
you, or are you not, a particular friend of the defendant's?"

"I was just about to say that—"

"Will you, or will you not, answer my question, sir?"

"If you don't answer the question you'll be commit-
ted, sir," interposed the little judge, looking over his
note-book.

"Come sir," said Mr. Skimpin, "yes or no, if you
please."

"Yes, I am," replied Mr. Winkle.

"Yes, you are. And why couldn't you say that at once, sir?"

Finally, an abjectly humiliated Mr. Winkle escaped from the witness stand in this closing paragraph:

"You may leave the box, sir," said Sergeant Snubbin. Mr. Winkle *did* leave the box, and rushed with delirious haste to the George and Vulture, where he was discovered some hours after by the waiter, groaning in a hollow and dismal manner, with his head buried beneath the sofa cushions.

Today, times are changing. Judicial bad manners, the confusing technicalities of court room procedure, and the inconsiderate treatment of witnesses, are all targets of proposed reform and improvement. Again, the advice and cooperation of laymen provide a vital factor in securing needed change. Philip L. Graham, publisher of the Washington Post, has made that clear in an article entitled "Treatment of Witnesses",[4] in which he says:

Those individuals among the public who may be called as witnesses need to be assured of fair treatment— assured that they will not be tricked or duped and harassed in examination and cross-examination; that they will only be called on to give as painlessly and as easily as possible their contribution to getting at the truth in the case at bar.

The public taken as a whole needs to be convinced that the judiciary and the Bar are constantly striving not merely to play an adversary game, but to establish truth, and thereby direct justice as near as may be possible.

Mr. Graham goes on to describe what is being done:

Some schools are already holding model trials to educate our children regarding the principles of our judicial system. The Bar Associations can help in developing and extending this method of education.

In regard to individual witnesses some lawyers have urged that they be given instructions of their rights and duties, either through written instruction sheets or through talks by the judge. Other lawyers think you can develop more pre-trial activity in criminal cases, in

---

4. 34 A.B.A.J. 23 (1948).

order to save witnesses from delays and confusions over the admissibility of documents and the like.

It seems to me that you have need of using these devices, along with the whole armory of public relations techniques, to get across better understanding—better public relations—on the administration of justice.

Although seldom a litigant in civil matters, the average citizen today does at some time or other become involved with traffic laws and traffic court administration. Here is where American justice in operation is most widely encountered, and where public impressions of our court system are most often formed. If discrimination, unfairness, incivility or outright corruption occur at this level, then popular respect for the whole judicial structure is shattered. Improvement in traffic laws and in the conduct of our traffic courts is so fundamental both to public safety and to law enforcement generally, that militant nationwide support is gaining daily. Judge Bolitha Laws, reporting on "Laymen's Accomplishments in Washington, D. C.", was able to point out in 1951:

> Through a laymen's committee on traffic courts, we have accomplished in the District of Columbia one of the most effective traffic safety programs which has brought to the District of Columbia twenty-seven awards in ten years as the city outstanding in the nation, in traffic matters.

Among other factors of citizen concern are the reports of outright political partisanship in the selection of judges and court officials, the congestion and delay of civil cases in the trial courts, the mounting costs of litigation, and need for overhauling and simplification of an inefficiently cumbersome court structure. Toward correction of these defects, the American Bar Association's "Minimum Standards of Judicial Administration" are being constantly implemented by state and local bar associations throughout the country.

That reforms are being achieved, gradually but perceptibly, is due in large measure to the recognition by bar associations that an informed and enlightened citizenry is an essential starting-point. The enlistment of laymen in the membership of bench and bar groups, the advice and counsel of businessmen and civic leaders, and the development of bar association public relations programs, have been a significant development of the past ten years. In 1945, the Section of Judicial Administration of the American Bar Association took the important step of bringing laymen into conferences with judges and lawyers to help in the solution of the problems of court administration. In New Jersey, the now almost legendary success under Chief Justice Vanderbilt's leadership in achieving effective citizen support for comprehensive reform is known everywhere. Current campaigns for court revision in Illinois and elsewhere are based on a broad groundwork of making the public fully aware of the need for their help. Past experience in other states has shown that without such help, a program, no matter how obviously meritorious, is almost foredoomed to failure.

How can the goal of citizen support for court reform be obtained? The ways and means are well pointed by the report of the Pennsylvania Bar Association's Committee on Public Relations, wherein recent and new developments in the overall area of informing the public on bar association activities and programs are summarized. Also, the American Bar Association's manual entitled "Public Relations for Bar Associations", published last year, gives ample and detailed suggestions in methods of effectively utilizing media of communication, including the press, speakers' bureaus, radio, television, motion pictures, pamphlets, and institutional advertising. Successful campaigns in various areas are outlined, together with illustrative materials, dealing with such matters as jury service, court organization, legal aid, and many others. To these references I would also add the American Judicature Society's "Handbook for Bar Association Officers" by Glenn Winters published this year. It contains a great deal of valuable material which can be useful.

My last layman witness is Winston Paul, Chairman of the New Jersey Committee for Constitutional Revision, and Member of the 1947 New Jersey Constitutional Convention. In a recent article[5] he suggested:

> The campaign for public support will require the enlisting of speakers for whom a handbook, printed or mimeographed, should be prepared; the arranging for numerous public and group meetings of service clubs, churches and schools; and the distribution of literature, embellished, if possible, with cartoons.

Many citizens are unfamiliar with the present court system of their state and with the reasons for improving it. It is therefore of primary importance that information on these points be widely disseminated. Newspapers can be induced to run series of articles. Leading editors

---

5. 42 Nat. Munic. Rev. 280 (1953).

can be persuaded to write editorials. Just as the evan-
gelist is psychologically sound in seeking first to con-
vince the individual of his sinfulness, so the average
citizen must first be convinced of the need for improvement in the judicial system. Charts can be prepared
showing the present court setup and comparing it with
the simpler and improved proposed plan. Comparisons
can be made with the systems of other states. Articles
can be written for state law journals and for the week-
lies and Sunday papers which circulate in the State.

In summary and conclusion, the present challenge was ably
stated by Chief Justice Earl Warren when, as Governor of
California, he addressed the American Bar Association's Section
of Judicial Administration at the Atlantic City meeting in 1946.
Speaking on the subject "Cooperation with Laymen: A Practical Program Needed by the Profession", he emphasized the
legal profession's obligation to work closely with the public,
for whose protection our system of justice was established. America's strength as a democracy, he stated—and I quote his remarks
in closing as fundamental principles to which all of us subscribe
—"depends upon the willingness of people to live and work together in a spirit of unity. Recognizing this, we of the legal
profession, the craftsmen of the administration of justice, will
derive our greatest satisfaction from working in this spirit of
unity with those for whom we build; and what is more, we will
build more usefully and enduringly—not for ourselves alone,
but for our country—the hope of the world."

INDEX

189